Dostoyevsky
His Life and Work

Dostoyevsky at the age of fifty-eight

Ronald Hingley

Dostoyevsky

His Life and Work

Charles Scribner's Sons

NEW YORK

Contents

1

Illustrations

Pages 177–180

Oil portrait of Dostoyevsky by V. Perov, in Tretyakov Gallery, *Moscow—SCR*

Dostoyevsky's residence at Staraya Russa (photograph, 1880)— *Novosti Press Agency*

House at Optina Pustyn where Dostoyevsky stayed in 1878 (photograph)—*from 'Fyodor Mikhaylovich Dostoyevsky . . .'*

Russian monks, c. 1880 (engraving)—*from Victor Tissot, 'La Russie et Les Russes', Paris, 1884; courtesy of the Librarian, School of Slavonic and East European Studies*

Members of the terrorist group 'Narodnaya Volya' (photographs)— *Mansell Collection*

Execution of political conspirators, November 1880 (engraving)— *Mansell Collection*

Pages 199–202

The unveiling of the Pushkin monument in Moscow, June 1880 (drawing by A. Bauman after N. Chekhov)

Dostoyevsky in 1880 (photograph)—*Novosti Press Agency*

Desk at which Dostoyevsky wrote *The Brothers Karamazov* (photograph, 1881)—*Novosti Press Agency*

Dostoyevsky's funeral (engraving)—*SCR*

The Emperor Alexander II (photograph)—*Mansell Collection*

Assassination of Alexander II (lithograph)—*Novosti Press Agency*

Preface

'My task has been to present a modest and sublime figure. But life is such a ridiculous business—sublime only in its inner significance. And so I have been forced . . . to invoke its most trivial aspects, reluctantly and for the sake of . . . truth, in my sage's biography. Then again, some of his teachings are expressed with such excess of vehemence that they will be scouted as downright preposterous. Preposterous they of course are, on a mundane level. But on a different and deeper level they are, I think, valid.'

The passage comes from a letter of 24 August 1879 where Dostoyevsky explains the difficulties that he has encountered in creating 'Father Zosima', the saintly figure who was intended to dominate his last novel, *The Brothers Karamazov*. It is while analysing this crux that he also chances to define, so delightfully and helpfully, the task facing his numerous biographers during the last hundred years.

As the beginning to my book I have preferred this quotation (also discussed on pages 194–5) over a host of rival candidates. They include the magnificent piece of unconscious self-analysis by Dostoyevsky that is cited on page 143 and contains an especially telling observation: 'He belonged to the category of unquestionably intelligent persons who spend all their lives behaving idiotically.' Not that all Dostoyevsky's self-criticism is unconscious, for he was well aware of his own faults, and could be unfair to himself. 'My nature is base . . .' he once wrote (see page 130). But he went on to add what is certainly true: '. . . and excessively impetuous. Everywhere and in all things I go to the limit. All my life I've overstepped the mark.'

My interest in Dostoyevsky goes back to before the Second World War. As a schoolboy I chanced to pick up *The Brothers Karamazov* in Constance Garnett's translation; and became, as it were, a permanent casualty. No other author contributed more to my decision, taken many years ago, to specialize in Russian language and literature. Since then I have lectured on Dostoyevsky as part of my teaching duties at Oxford, and have also published a critical work, *The Undiscovered Dostoyevsky* (1962), which is still in print (reprinted 1975). So far as I know, this remains the only book in which Dostoyevsky's humour has been analysed in detail, and in which his technique of deploying spectacular *skandaly* ('scandalous scenes') is examined. Stress is also laid on his skill as a craftsman; on the kinds of strain to which he exposes himself and his characters; on the oscillations to which he and they are especially prone in the context of humiliation and status-seeking.

There is surprisingly little that I would now unsay in this critical assessment of fifteen years ago. Philosophically, however, I have come closer to accepting at least one of Dostoyevsky's main doctrines: the most significant, I believe (in the form in which he expresses it) of all his basic obsessions. I refer to his rejection of humanity's attempts to construct an ideal society based on reason. That there is no surer road to hell than the mission to impose universal social justice is more obvious to me in 1978 than it was in 1962, and I am less disinclined than I then was to attribute to the missionaries concerned the moral depravity with which Dostoyevsky tends to invest them. To the more positive elements in his creed—his fierce nationalism and religious fanaticism—I remain as immune as ever, but have become less intolerant and (I hope) more understanding of them in the interim.

To attempt a new, compendious biography of so baffling a man and so complex an artist is to face a challenge. It was this stimulus, combined with the fascination of the subject, that made me eager to attempt the present biography. It has required efforts no less intense than those demanded by my two previous biographies, of Stalin and Chekhov: both, as it happens, much longer works. But it is no accident that the References at the end of the present volume contain a comparably full account of the sources.

So extensive is the published material on Dostoyevsky that there could be no question of supplying a comprehensive bibliography. I have therefore restricted myself to an Index of Sources that simply lists the works quoted or invoked in the text, these being only a small fraction of the authorities who have been consulted over the years. The titles speak for themselves, but it may be worth singling out from them a few recent contributions containing evidence previously unavailable or difficult of access.

The new thirty-volume Moscow-published edition of Dostoyevsky's complete works in Russian, *Polnoye sobraniye sochineniy v tridtsati tomakh*, began to appear in 1972, and is cited in the Index of Sources as '*Works* (1972)'. Here is a distinguished scholarly publication which, when completed, will supplant the admirable previous thirteen-volume edition of Dostoyevsky in Russian, cited as '*Works* (1926)', and the ten-volume '*Works* (1956)'. At the time of writing the first seventeen volumes of *Works* (1972) are to hand, containing all the belles-lettres with all surviving variants to and drafts of the same, together with extensive commentaries. In the commentaries we find the history of the texts and of their reception in fuller detail than had previously been available, together with meticulous accounts of their numerous biographical links. I must be the first biographer who has been privileged to use this material in full, and its value has been more than can be easily expressed. To it must be added the recent, Moscow-published *Literaturnoye nasledstvo: F. M. Dostoyevsky* (1973; 'Ln' in the Index of Sources). It contains, among many other stimulating, previously unpublished items, an important newly deciphered section from the diary of Dostoyevsky's second wife. Worth mentioning too among recent contributions is the short newspaper article of 1975 by G. Fyodorov in which he seeks to cast doubt on the generally accepted thesis that Dostoyevsky's father met his end by murder. But that is a mere gloss, of course. The main source of the present biography, outweighing all others, is inevitably A. S. Dolinin's excellent four-volume edition of Dostoyevsky's letters in Russian (Moscow–Leningrad 1929–59).

Turning from this important Soviet-published material to western-published authorities who have also been found useful, and who also figure in the Index of Sources, I especially welcome Joseph Frank's recent detailed study *Dostoyevsky: the Seeds of Revolt: 1821–1849.* It covers the same period as my first four chapters, and at nearly ten times the length; but is only the first book in a projected series of four wherein the whole of Dostoyevsky's life and work is eventually to be treated. *Seeds of Revolt* is an important contribution; it has caused me to modify not a few of my own views, and I look forward to its sequels. But, as those who consult my Reference Notes will discover, I differ fundamentally from Professor Frank on certain pivotal aspects of interpretation. I disagree too on many issues of substance with the earlier critical and biographical study by Konstantin Mochulsky, as I also do with the still earlier biography by E. H. Carr. Nevertheless I greatly admire both these works, together with Joseph Frank's. 'One may respect a man greatly while differing radically from his views' (Dostoyevsky on Chernyshevsky). And so I unhesitatingly commend all three studies to any readers of my book who may not know them, and who may wish to consider a Dostoyevsky approached from angles that diverge from mine. Other useful biographies in English or in English translation are those of Grossman and Yarmolinsky.

Except where otherwise indicated the translations in this volume are my own, including all those from Dostoyevsky himself. My rendering of *inok* ('monk') as 'sage', in the first paragraph of this Preface and on page 194 below, is a deliberate liberty. What may, in quotations from Dostoyevsky's letters, appear as eccentric italicization is due to my decision to retain the emphasis expressed in the original; emphasis added by myself is as indicated in the Reference Notes. All nineteenth-century dates are 'old style', which means that they lag behind those used in western Europe by twelve days. To indicate the length of certain works by Dostoyevsky, and sometimes also the rates of remuneration that he received, the word 'signature' is used to translate the Russian *pechatny list* (literally 'printer's sheet'). The signature represents roughly 6,400 words of print, or sixteen pages of a book of normal format. When the length of Dostoyevsky's work is measured in 'pages', units of normal page length (about four hundred words) are meant. Wherever, in quotations from Dostoyevsky or other authors, I employ a sequence of three or four dots, this indicates an omission made by myself, and is not a feature in the punctuation of the original.

I am most grateful to my wife for expert and detailed editorial advice; to Jeremy Newton, who has kindly read the manuscript and advised on the editing; to Harry Willetts for much valuable informal advice based on a rare insight into the subject.

Frilford, Abingdon   Ronald Hingley
1978

I

Boy and Youth

Early in the morning of 22 December 1849 Fyodor Mikhaylovich Dostoyevsky, officially described as 'Lieutenant of Engineers, retired', was ordered out of his cell in the Petropavlovsky Fortress in the Imperial Russian capital, St Petersburg. He was then taken across the River Neva, by carriage in a convoy flanked by mounted Cossacks, to the Semyonovsky Square in the south of the city. Blinking in the wintry sunshine, the twenty-eight-year-old former army officer—and, it seemed, unsuccessful novelist—was paraded on the snow with twenty friends and former associates. They were surrounded on all four sides of the huge square by troops.

Dostoyevsky and his friends had been arrested several months earlier for treason. Their conspiracy against the Russian state had consisted of little more than debating judicial reform, serf emancipation, socialism and revolution in informal discussion circles. But to discuss these subjects at all, however privately, in the Tsar-Emperor Nicholas I's later reign had been to take a grave risk. Perhaps the spice of danger had been the chief attraction to the young author, gambler and hypochondriac who now waited, shivering on the snow after embracing the other accused. Dostoyevsky was fair-haired, freckled, with small, deep-sunk eyes under a high-domed forehead; shortish of stature, but broad-shouldered and of fairly strong build. He wore the rumpled civilian clothes in which the police had arrested him in the previous April. Paler even than usual after eight months in the dungeons, he formed with his friends a sharp contrast to the glittering battalions and squadrons massed on all sides. Orders cracked, drums rumbled ominously.

The presiding General stepped forward and began reading from a document. Only now did the twenty-one young men learn that they had been tried and condemned in their absence—to immediate death by firing squad! 'Criminal conversations ... reading a felonious missive ... full of impudent expressions directed against Supreme Authority and the Orthodox Church ... plotting to write anti-government articles and to disseminate them by means of a home lithographic press': these were the main charges for which Dostoyevsky personally had to pay the penalty.[1]

That the young men were to be executed three at a time, with Dostoyevsky himself in the second batch, soon became evident after they had been arrayed in the prescribed white 'shrouds' with long, trailing sleeves and hoods. The first victims were each secured to a post, their arms were bound behind their backs by the sleeves, and the hoods were pulled over their faces. At the word of command, three guards detachments took aim at almost point blank range and the order to fire was instantly expected. But then an aide-de-camp galloped across the square bearing a sealed packet. A drum roll halted the proceedings, and the condemned men heard the presiding General laboriously intone the last-minute commutation of their sentences: most to periods of *katorga* (Siberian hard labour and exile). Two days later the political criminal and future great novelist, his ankles secured by the customary fetters, had begun his two-thousand-mile journey to a new life as a convict at Omsk in Siberia.

The mock execution had been a cruel farce, deliberately staged to teach the culprits a lesson on the detailed instructions of the Emperor; he had, perhaps, even maliciously chosen the General, a notorious stutterer, who haltingly read out the sentences. Thus, at the whim of this crowned martinet, specialist in gallows humour and hounder of imaginative writers, did the young Dostoyevsky spend several minutes in full expectation of imminent death. During that time, as he later indicated, all his previous life passed in review through his mind.[2]

From the St Petersburg square Dostoyevsky's thoughts must have gone back to his native Moscow, where he had been born as a hospital doctor's second son and had lived until his sixteenth year.

By contrast with the regimented, tense and artificial St Petersburg, 'Mother' Moscow casually sprawled like a huge, haphazard village. Meandering lanes and broad untended avenues aimlessly led to waste plots or stagnant ponds. The gleaming white walls and gilded domes of many churches, by tradition numbering forty times forty, were glimpsed through the green foliage of lime trees, or melted into the monochrome background in winter. Alongside colonnaded official buildings, near the mansions of rich merchants, slumped the log cabins of the poor.

Of this mixture of pomp and squalor Dostoyevsky's own birthplace provided an example. The area was a slum in the north of the city. It had its foundling home, its mad-house, its cemetery for suicides and unidentified corpses as well as the Maryinsky Hospital for the Poor where the future chronicler of orphans, lunatics, suicides and murderers first saw the light of day on 30 October 1821. The hospital's imposing central block had a pediment and Doric colonnade. It was flanked by two substantial detached three-storeyed wings, and it was in one of these, in a modest ground-floor apartment, that Dostoyevsky lived from early infancy until the age of fifteen. The flat was a perquisite to which his father, Dr Mikhail Andreyevich Dostoyevsky, was entitled as a state-employed senior resident physician. Here he and his wife Mariya Fyodorovna reared four sons and three daughters born to them between 1820 and 1835.

The premises still stand, and the former family flat is now preserved as a museum. Here Dostoyevsky's modern admirers may brood on the sinister vaulted staircase that confronts them as they enter the building: did it inspire the many crimes and other eccentric happenings so persistently located on stairways in the novels? Or the visitor may contemplate the large hall where, in a dark corner behind a screen, Fedya (as Fyodor was called) and his brother Mikhail, older by one year and the only intimate of his childhood, would read Walter Scott or recite Pushkin to each other by the light of a tallow candle. There is the kitchen where some of the family's servants would spend the night on the traditional sleeping shelves; the dining-room where the doctor and his wife entertained their few guests, mostly the wife's relatives; the living-room in which the master of the house would take his after-lunch nap while his terrified third son Andrey kept watch for two hours with a freshly picked lime switch, charged to prevent a single fly from alighting on the sleeper.[3] Here too the eldest boys were taught Bible stories by a visiting deacon and elementary French by a Monsieur Souchard. Here Latin was instilled into them by their stern and unrelenting father.

We shall not delve far back into the genealogy of the Dostoyevskys. The family name occurs fairly frequently from the sixteenth century onwards, and Tatar, Lithuanian, Belorussian and Polish connections have been established or suspected. For all that, Dostoyevsky himself was 'in every ordinary sense of the word . . . as he always believed himself to be, a Russian of the Russians.'[4] It is with slightly more interest that we note among his forbears or presumed forbears on both sides of the family a fair number of assassins, bandits, drunkards, lunatics and men of God. To this last category the novelist's paternal grandfather belonged as a humble parish priest in Podolia on the south-western marches of the Russian Empire. Here Fedya's father had learnt his Latin at the local seminary before running away from home at the age of fifteen to study medicine at Moscow.

The young doctor had served as military medical officer throughout the Napoleonic invasion of Russia in 1812. Whether dour by nature, or rendered so by amputating hundreds of limbs without anaesthetics, he was rarely known to smile. He closely supervised his children and taught them to study from an early age. 'At the age of four he [Fyodor] was set in front of a book and insistently told: "Study!" '[5] When the father drilled his two elder boys in Latin declensions they were not permitted to sit down, but stood trembling with apprehension. At the slightest mistake their father would abuse them as blockheads and idlers, or throw down Bantyshev's primer in disgust. But though he was strict his nature was not cruel. His worst punishment was to lose his temper entirely and cut short the lesson. He never beat his children, never even made them kneel in penance or stood them in the corner. Nor would he send them to one of the state high schools, where corporal punishment was customary; but enrolled his two eldest sons, when Fedya was twelve years old, at one of Moscow's best and most expensive private preparatory schools, Chermak's.[6] Here they boarded five days a week for three years, were never beaten, and received a liberal education from some of the city's most respected teachers.

Humane and enlightened in his way, Fyodor's father yet involuntarily oppressed his beloved wife and children because he easily lost his temper and because he imposed, from the best of motives, an excessively rigorous regimen. He was generous in paying school bills, but obsessively mean in other matters. For ever counting and recounting spoons, he suspected his coachman of drinking his vodka and accused his laundry maid of stealing his shirts. He often told his sons that he was a poor man, that they would be beggars when he died, that they must make their own way in the world.[7] This was not idle talk. The doctor was indeed poor, and all the more so because he insisted on keeping up an establishment beyond his means: seven servants, a carriage, four horses and eventually a country estate.

Mikhail Andreyevich laid down many domestic restrictions. His children might sedately parade the hospital's well-tended lime avenues under their nurse's supervision. But they might not play ball games or converse with the patients who shuffled about in striped night-shirts, striped caps and buff dressing-gowns—a rule that Fedya was quick to break when his father's back was turned. During family walks in the near-by Maryinsky Coppice the doctor himself would turn the conversation to such edifying subjects as the principles of mathematics. And when Mikhail and Fyodor went out of the house they must be escorted, usually by the family coachman who drove them in the doctor's carriage. In this they proceeded to and from Chermak's boarding school, returning home each week-end. No less restrictive was their father's ban on handling money, even in the smallest amounts.

Did this provision help to create in his second son the extreme perversity in matters financial that he was to develop as soon as he left home?

Rarely did the parents go out together in the evening. When they did the mother would whisper instructions before leaving to the children's nurse, who was also the unofficial housekeeper, the grossly overweight, snuff-taking Alyona Frolovna: would she see that her charges enjoyed themselves as much as possible?[6] Only in the doctor's absence might his boys and girls laugh and play in this home where there were perhaps no toys; at any rate none are mentioned in the sources.

The mother, Mariya Fyodorovna, was devoted to her husband. As a good wife of the period she obediently submitted to him, but without allowing herself to be trampled on. It was fortunate that she had strength of character, for her husband had taken it into his head that she was unfaithful to him, and his unjust accusations sometimes led to painful scenes, as when he once reduced her to hysterical sobbing on being informed of one of her later pregnancies. His obsession can be followed in their correspondence between Moscow and the country estate that they acquired in the early 1830s. 'I swear to you . . .' she wrote to him on 31 May 1835, 'that my present pregnancy is the seventh and firmest bond in our love for each other. My love for you is pure, holy, chaste and passionate, and has never swerved since the day of our marriage. But will this oath satisfy you? Never have I taken such an oath before: firstly because I feared to lower myself by swearing to my fidelity in the sixteenth year of our union; and secondly because your prejudices have disinclined you to listen to my assurances, let alone to believe them.' In this and other touching appeals we sense the wife's loving understanding of the husband whose fears were real, however fanciful the wounding suppositions on which they were based.[9]

So moving is the old-fashioned Russian in which the accused mother defends her honour that we sense in her, rather than in the harassed Mikhail Andreyevich, the parent from whom Dostoyevsky inherited his literary talent. But man and wife must also have unintentionally combined to provide a rich stock of literary copy as the growing boy watched and sought to understand the somewhat unbalanced father who, though profoundly attached to the mother, was yet impelled to torment her on occasion. Their son's works abound in characters who cannot stop themselves persecuting those whom they most love.

Dostoyevsky's mother was a cheerful spirit who made the best of life despite her husband's occasional unkindness. She was an educated woman: well read, with a taste for poetry and novels. She sang, too, and played the guitar; as did her light-hearted and dissolute brother, Fyodor's Uncle Mikhail. But the uncle's visits ended abruptly when Dr Dostoyevsky slapped his face after the visitor had been detected 'carrying on' with one of the maids.[10]

The cultural tastes and skills of Dostoyevsky's mother are unusual in one who sprang from a Moscow trading family of the humbler sort. Her father was a cloth dealer in a small way. But her mother's father had literary and ecclesiastical connections, having been a proof-reader with the Moscow Church Press, while one of Dostoyevsky's great uncles on the same side of the family was a professor of pharmacology and Dean of Moscow's medical faculty. But Fyodor's most important maternal relatives were the Kumanins, his mother's sister and her husband; rich merchants who lived in great style in their own ornate Moscow mansion. Good-hearted, somewhat condescending, themselves childless, they were a valuable support in times of need. Yet neither Dr Dostoyevsky nor his famous son ever liked them. To the son they represented material success and bourgeois complacency, qualities that he detested.

For many of the above details of Dostoyevsky's childhood, as for many which will follow, we are indebted to a single source—the memoirs of his brother Andrey, who was three and a half years his junior. Andrey Mikhaylovich's memoirs were published remarkably late (in 1930), and long after the death of both brothers. But they have the ring of authenticity, they have been generally accepted as reliable, and they do indeed appear to be so to the extent that they can be checked from other sources. But it is unfortunate that we should be so heavily dependent on a single witness, and more unfortunate still that Fyodor Mikhaylovich himself should have left comments so few and so late on these early years. Still, brief and unsatisfactory as they are, his own recollections are obviously of the greatest importance, and it is time that we invoked them.

Most of Dostoyevsky's references to his own childhood are more favourable and decorous than the conditions recorded by Andrey might seem to warrant. 'As far back as my memory goes, I recall my parents' love for me', Fyodor wrote in his *Diary of a Writer* of 1873. His mother and father had both been 'progressive people', he reflected when writing to Andrey at the end of the 1870s. And he added, with reference to his male parent alone, that 'you and I could never be such good family men and fathers, old boy.' Again, when writing to Andrey in March 1876, Dostoyevsky claimed that both their parents had been inspired by a 'drive to become *better people* in the literal and *highest* sense of the words. Such was the basic idea of both Father and Mother.'

But Dostoyevsky also makes this significant reservation: 'despite all their deviations.'[11]

'Deviations? How considerable these perhaps were, on his father's part, Dostoyevsky had already indicated nearly twenty years earlier, when writing to his young friend Vrangel on 9 March 1857. Vrangel had recently become involved in a quarrel with his own father, and the following are the terms in which Dostoyevsky attempts to console him. 'What most worries me on your behalf, dear boy, is your relationship with your father. That such unpleasantnesses are unbearable I realize, having an exceptionally close knowledge of the matter based on experience. And they are all the more disagreeable because, I know, you love each other.' Dostoyevsky goes on to speak of 'infinite mutual misunderstanding that only grows more and more involved. You can't get rid of it by hook or by crook. . . . Characters like your father are a strange mixture of the most gloomy suspiciousness, pathological sensitivity and generosity. That's what I conclude about him, though I don't know him, for I have *twice in my life* experienced precisely the same relations as yours with him.'[12] That Dostoyevsky had himself and his late father in mind when offering these comments is obvious. They are unique in reflecting the son's inability to get on with his father, nowhere else directly testified by himself. But it is tantalizing that we are given as little detailed insight into the 'mutual misunderstanding' as into the 'deviations'.'

Another notable direct reference by Dostoyevsky to his father occurs in a letter to his second wife of April 1871. From this we learn that the deceased Mikhail Andreyevich had manifested himself to his son in a nightmare, and 'in a dread aspect that he had *only twice* presented to me in life.' Such an impact did the baleful phantom have on the dreamer that, as we shall relate in due course, it cured him once and for all of his ten-year-old addiction to gambling.[13] I have italicized the words 'only twice' and 'twice in my life' in the above and the preceding quotation, since it seems likely that Dostoyevsky on each occasion had in mind two specific, especially horrifying clashes with his father, of which we otherwise know nothing.

Turning back through the decades to comments made by the adolescent Fyodor before his father's death in June 1839, we find no suggestion of the hostility which it may seem tempting to detect as smouldering beneath the surface. The most revealing passage from this early period is contained in Fyodor's letter to Mikhail written in May 1839, only a month before their father's sudden death. 'I'm so sorry for poor Father', the boy wrote. 'What a peculiar character! And, dear me, how he has suffered! I could weep with frustration at having no means of comforting him. And Father is so unworldly, you know. He has been in this world for fifty years, but he still judges people as he did thirty years ago. Where ignorance is bliss!'[14]

The passage reveals a considerable tenderness for the father together with a capacity for objective judgement remarkable in a youth whose own knowledge of the world was evidently greater than his limited experience of it might seem to warrant. That the passage is hard to square with any overt resentment of the father need hardly be stated. From this comment, and from the whole tenor of Dostoyevsky's somewhat sparse observations on his father, we must conclude that any serious hostility, if such existed on the son's part, was latent rather than conscious.

The boy's attitude to his mother is even more elusive. Four of his letters to her survive—all from the summer of 1835, all short and un-informative. To them we can only add the brief, pious references quoted above, in which the middle-aged novelist brackets his mother and father together as laudably 'progressive' parents. That the boy adored so lively and sympathetic a mother is an attractive and plausible inference, but we cannot actually document it from his own statements.

We are similarly ill-informed on the young Dostoyevsky's childhood relations with his siblings other than the soul-mate Mikhail and the eventual memoirist Andrey. There was another younger brother, Nikolay, and there were the three sisters Varvara, Vera and Aleksandra. Endowed with strong family feeling, Dostoyevsky was to maintain contact, however sporadic, with all six throughout life: most especially, after Mikhail, with his favourite sister Vera.

Life

However oppressed Fyodor may have felt by occasional clashes with his father, much of his early family life was enthralling and ex-citing. Referring to his temperament and spirit, his mother called him a 'flame', and spoke of his irrepressible pranks, for he was livelier, more highly-strung than her placid eldest son. Even in his infancy the main object of his passions was literature. He would listen enchanted as unlettered story-tellers—the enserfed wet-nurses or maids of the household, or the nanny-housekeeper, Alyona Frolovna—recited traditional Russian folk tales in the vivid language of the common people, so different from educated speech. Fedya's mother began teaching him to read at the age of four from an antique volume con-taining a hundred and four Bible tales. The boy also conceived a passion for the Book of Job; it no doubt helped to fuel the obsession with suffering that was to haunt him all his life. Then there was the pleasant family habit of reading aloud in the evenings. The mother might offer one of Mrs Ann Radcliffe's 'Gothic' novels in Russian translation, while the doctor's taste ran to the monumental *History of the Russian State* by Karamzin. All this material Fedya and Mikhail soaked up so readily that it at once became part of them. Russia's poets fired the boys' imagination: Zhukovsky, Lermontov, and above all Pushkin. They eagerly monitored these authors' current output as it appeared in a magazine to which the doctor subscribed: *Biblioteka dlya chteniya* ('The Reading Library'). It published in Russian translation, or at least reviewed, leading French novelists of the day—Balzac, Hugo, George Sand, with whose works the boys first made their acquaintance on its pages. The twelve-year-old Fedya further performed the remarkable feat, or so he later claimed, of reading 'the whole of Walter Scott' during his summer holidays: in Russian, inevitably, since he never knew English. Another enthusiasm was for Schiller, first encountered during a rare visit to the theatre where he saw *The Robbers* at the age of ten.[15]

Such were some of the many works which the doctor's two eldest sons pored over in their screened-off bedroom by candlelight. The addiction lost nothing from exposure to Chermak's boarding school, where arts subjects were well taught. Here Fedya impressed one fellow-pupil as a serious, pensive, pale boy who disliked games, spent playtime reading and preferred the company of older pupils.[16] But Mikhail Dostoyevsky remained his only true intimate. Already Fedya, aloof and distant throughout life except with the few soul-mates who fully engaged his sympathies, found it hard to recognize a lesser tie than that of brother.

Cooped in their flat or boarding-school during most of their childhood, the Dostoyevsky boys enjoyed the occasional outing all the more. So devout a family was naturally regular in its attendance at the hospital chapel. Visits were occasionally paid to the city's Kremlin: to its clutch of cathedrals and other antiquities fascinating to Fedya with his deep and growing feeling for ancient Russia. Annual pilgrimages were also made by carriage to another leading centre of the Orthodox faith: the Monastery of the Trinity and St Sergius, forty miles northeast of Moscow. On a more secular level the boys could also attend the street fairs in Smolensk Square; here, chaperoned by their medical great-uncle who lived near by, they could admire waxworks, monkeys, performing dogs, clowns and buskers.

The most important of all reliefs from Muscovite claustrophobia came through the opportunity, which Fedya had from the age of ten, to spend three-month family summer holidays enjoying country air and country pastimes. In 1831–2 their father bought adjoining estates at Darovoye and Cheremoshna about a hundred miles south of

Moscow. At Darovoye the family lived in a small thatched shack, being free to roam the local ravines, woods and fields. Fedya organized a band of 'savages'; acted Crusoe to his brother Andrey's Man Friday; staged a mock procession with icons naughtily purloined from a near-by chapel. His mother had a local stream dammed, which offered bathing and fishing facilities, with worms specially dug for the young masters by serf children of their own age. These were also organized as 'horses' to pull the infant squires in a game of troikas. And the serf boys were sometimes 'sold' at an imaginary horse fair, with much comic inspection of their teeth and hooves. All this Fedya and his brothers much enjoyed: the serf boys' reactions are not recorded.[17]

Here too Fedya had a memorable encounter with an adult serf, Marey, whom he was to incorporate over thirty years later in a famous passage of his published *Diary of a Writer*. Frightened by an imagined wolf, the small boy had been comforted by this grizzled, muddy-fingered ploughman in a particularly tender manner beyond the capacity of anyone other than a Russian and a muzhik; or so the peasant-fancying Dostoyevsky implied when he came to write up the incident in later life. Dostoyevsky also encountered a certain Agrafena, village idiot, rape victim and model for Stinking Lizaveta in *The Brothers Karamazov*.[18]

The Dostoyevsky children loved Darovoye and Cheremoshna, but these settlements presented a very different spectacle to the adult eye. Dr Dostoyevsky must indeed have been eager to become a landed gentleman at all costs if he was prepared to saddle himself with such dismal properties: infertile, criss-crossed by ravines, the haunt of rustlers and of peasants so poor that they were frequently forced to strip the very thatch from their miserable shacks to feed their beasts at times of fodder shortage. Nor is it clear how a doctor earning a mere six hundred roubles a year, supplemented by erratic private practice, raised even with the help of mortgages or loans from relatives the twelve-thousand-rouble purchase price for estates running to over a thousand acres. Whatever his means and motives, he had suddenly become, in effect, a small-scale slave-master, for with the land he had also taken on the personal ownership of serfs. At little over a hundred head, this was too small a unit to be profitable. Moreover, the doctor and his wife had as little experience of handling the Russian muzhik, that most recalcitrant of farm beasts, as they had of tilling the soil themselves. Shouting at the peasants, sending a serf to the stables for a flogging after he had failed to bow to his master: such methods were to prove fatally counter-productive in the end.

To reflect on the doctor's predicament is to be reminded of some of

Above and right Dr Mikhail Andreyevich
Dostoyevsky and Mariya Fyodorovna
Below Dostoyevsky's birthplace, the
Maryinsky Hospital for the Poor,
Moscow

Left The Emperor Nicholas I
Below The coronation of Nicholas I in the Kremlin, Moscow
Opposite above The Moscow River and the Kremlin in the 1830s
Opposite below Monastery of the Trinity and St Sergius, near Moscow, visited annually by the Dostoyevsky family

Below A Moscow boulevard in the second
quarter of the nineteenth century
Bottom Street market in the Red Square,
at about the time when Dostoyevsky left
Moscow for St Petersburg

Russia's broadest social problems. The far-flung Empire with its rapidly increasing multi-racial population was a predominantly peasant community. In the middle 1830s peasants numbered some forty million souls in a population of about forty-five million, being mostly bonded, either as serfs to individual owners, or else to the state. The average villager, who could be bought and sold like a cow or a plough, was illiterate; he was poorly fed, poorly clothed, poorly housed; he had a short expectation of life. That serfdom was a shameful and wasteful institution, that it should be abolished, had long been agreed by most educated Russians. Even the Emperors Alexander I and Nicholas I, whose reigns spanned the years 1801–55, wished to emancipate the peasants, but were defeated by the technicalities of the problem. In any case these monarchs were themselves the incarnation of the second Russian institution which, after serfdom, most seemed to disgrace the Empire: that of absolute monarchy. Ruling without constitutional restraint over a largely enslaved community, the Tsar-Emperors presided over a system ripe for radical reform or (the view was increasingly taken later in the century) for bloody revolution.

As for social categories intermediate between peasantry and Emperor, we have noted the Dostoyevskys' link with the clergy and their closer links with the merchant class. With the highest class of all, the *dvoryanstvo* (gentry), their contacts were at first minimal. This social élite comprised only about one per cent of the population, but was culturally and administratively influential far beyond its size. It formed the main bulwark of the throne, while also supplying a high proportion of the revolutionaries who eventually sought to destroy that institution. Early nineteenth-century Russian literature was very largely written by, for and about landed gentlemen. Another monopoly of the gentry was the right, denied in law to other classes, of owning serfs.

In 1828 Dostoyevsky's father, hitherto a lowly medical official, had received a promotion, to the grade of 'Collegiate Assessor', entitling him to claim the dignity of a *dvoryanin* (gentleman). Being hereditary, this same dignity was simultaneously conferred on his sons, with the result that Fyodor formally belonged throughout most of his life to the highest stratum of Russian society. But this was not how he saw himself. There was a vast difference between the lower gentry, to which he belonged, and its upper reaches, the milieu of such rich contemporaries and professional rivals as Ivan Turgenev and Lyov Tolstoy. Envying their wealth and position, the status-obsessed Dostoyevsky often called himself a 'proletarian'.

The year 1837 was a time of upheavals for the Dostoyevskys. In February, Fyodor's mother took to her bed and died of tuberculosis after calling for an icon and blessing her grief-stricken family. Another death occurring at about the same time, that of Russia's national poet Pushkin, seems to have affected the two eldest sons almost as much as their mother's. Fyodor said that, had he not already been in mourning, he would have asked his father's permission to wear mourning for Pushkin.[19] Shortly after this double shock the boy contracted a severe throat infection that left the lifelong legacy of a hoarse and chesty voice.

The next disaster was the implementation of a harsh and regrettable decision by Dr Dostoyevsky, that his two eldest sons should go to St Petersburg and enter the army's Chief Engineering Academy: the basis, he hoped, for lucrative civil or military careers in an age of intensive fortification-building. Here was the negative side of the father's concern for the sons whose education he had so far promoted in accordance with their natural bent. The wise course would have been to let them study literature at Moscow or St Petersburg University. Neither had the slightest leaning towards the military life or applied technology; and Fyodor was later to describe the decision as a mistake which 'ruined our futures.'[20] One wonders, though, when considering so creatively perverse a talent as his, whether bouts of intense frustration may not have been essential to its evolution. In any case his father's decision was final, and in May 1837 he and his two sons set out by carriage on the week-long four-hundred-and-fifty-mile journey to the capital.

At a post-station on the way occurred an ugly incident that left a lifelong impression on Fyodor. One of the Tsar's all-powerful couriers was seen to drive off at high speed while viciously punching his peasant coachman again and again on the neck. This scene, typical of imperial Russian *mœurs*, utterly horrified Dostoyevsky, and may have inspired the painful scene in *Crime and Punishment* where Raskolnikov dreams of a horse battered to death by a frenzied peasant.[21]

In St Petersburg Dr Dostoyevsky found lodgings for his sons and arranged for them to attend a crammer's where they would be prepared for the Chief Engineering Academy's entrance examination later in the year. The widower then returned to Moscow to arrange his affairs.

Though Fyodor did not know it, he was never to set eyes on his father again.

2

Cadet and Officer

Entering the Chief Engineering Academy in January 1838, the sixteen-year-old Dostoyevsky felt lonely and abandoned, especially as he found himself unexpectedly separated from his brother. Mikhail had been rejected on medical grounds, but obtained a place in a similar establishment at the Baltic port of Reval two hundred miles to the west.

The Academy, at which Fyodor was to board during his four cadet years, was an impressive, solidly built fortress adorned with Ionic columns, surmounted by a gilded spire and flanked by canals. It stood near the centre of the Empire's capital city, which soon took so powerful a hold of his imagination that it almost drove Moscow from his head. St Petersburg breathed a magic air of disturbing unreality with its many canals, its mists, the pale northern light, the 'white nights' of summer. There were the many uniforms; the air of tension and bustle; the majestic public buildings and palaces, the broad boulevards; and also, for even this imposing museum of a metropolis had its squalid side, the slums. The eerie capital was to become the favourite setting for Dostoyevsky's fiction as well as his most favoured place of residence.

At first his life was largely confined to the closed world of the Academy. This was a small, select school catering for a hundred and twenty pupils; of whom, as may seem surprising, two-thirds consisted of German and Polish citizens of the multi-national Russian Empire. It was probably here that Dostoyevsky began to conceive the extreme contempt in which he was later to hold members of these two nationalities. In any case the youth envied many of his new associates for being better off than he was. Among these uncongenial brothers-in-arms he was subjected to frequent drill parades, to the bellowings of non-commissioned officers, to occasional manœuvres under the eye of the Emperor Nicholas, to summer camps at near-by Peterhof, to winter guard duties. Somehow he shambled through it all in a uniform that always looked wrong. His shako, his pack, his musket hung on him like the fetters worn by hermit ascetics to mortify the flesh.[1] The most 'unregimental' figure in the whole establishment, he also had the unfortunate knack of irritating highest authority? Once, when reporting for orderly duty to the Grand Duke Mikhail, the Emperor's younger brother and an even more notorious martinet, Cadet Dostoyevsky addressed this potentate as 'Your Excellency' instead of 'Your Imperial Highness'. It was an appalling gaffe in the military context. Then, when already a young officer, Dostoyevsky executed a piece of inept draftsmanship that chanced to be submitted to the Emperor himself, prompting the sovereign to enquire 'what imbecile' had been responsible.[2] How fortunate that the boy had never conceived any high, or even low, military ambitions.

Dostoyevsky's incompetent drill, aggravated by impertinence to his instructor in algebra, led to the only major hitch in his military career: he was kept back at the end of his first year to go through the same course again. When writing to his brother Mikhail about this disaster, he hit on a pregnant phrase: 'Hitherto I had never known the meaning of injured self-esteem.'[3] For this gap in his education he was soon compensating in full. It is at the Engineering Academy that we first trace the hypersensitive obsession with status which helped to inspire some of his early works.

The Academy might have been expressly designed for the bruising of young Dostoyevsky's self-esteem, especially through the vicious bullying that was its most lamentable tradition. New recruits were regularly tormented by seniors. Water was poured down their necks and into their beds; they were forced to lick up pools of ink spilled over their exercise-books; or they might be trapped under a table and kicked when they tried to crawl out. Any attempt to defend oneself, any reporting of these doings to authority, which turned a blind eye, led to vicious retaliation and even to serious injury.[4]

Cadet Dostoyevsky must have suffered abominably from such outrages, in so far as he did not perversely enjoy them. In some ways he was ideally suited to become the butt of his coarser fellows. There was his psychological insecurity, his air of looking and being different, and his superior intelligence that naturally antagonized mediocrities, while his lack of physical aggressiveness made the baiting tolerably safe. We also know beyond doubt, as will be later recounted, that Dostoyevsky became an object of general mockery in the literary circles of St Petersburg a few years after resigning his commission. Yet eye-witnesses at the Engineering Academy have him less as the victim that we might expect than as the protector of other victims: again and again he would successfully intervene to protect younger boys from bullying.[5]

A less admirable side to his character may be traced in letters to his father. Here are professions of filial devotion that sound sycophantic to a modern ear. One also notes that they inevitably precede demands for cash remittances. Money is needed for postal expenses; to pay the priest's fee for administering communion; to buy a new shako because the drab army-issue variety might attract the Tsar's disapproval; to purchase extra tea, extra boots, a trunk for storing books. Some of these were genuine needs, but it becomes clear as one reads between the lines that the lust for tea, boots, special shakos and so on had little to do with practicalities. They were status symbols required to demonstrate to his fellow-recruits that he was not a poor boy, and that his position in life was no lower than theirs. A contemporary at the Academy, Pyotr Semyonov, plausibly if somewhat priggishly writes that *he* managed easily on less money than Dostoyevsky simply because he did not suffer from the kind of insecurity that has to be compensated for by conspicuous consumption.[6]

So far as we can tell Dostoyevsky's father usually sent him the money that he asked for, not being as mean in every respect as posterity has sometimes portrayed him.

To paint Dostoyevsky's military life as pure gloom would be misleading. Even the syllabus had its attractions: it was not all hated mathematics and boring military technology, but also included history and architecture, together with French and Russian literature. By cramming in extra-curricular reading in these last two subjects, the cadet and junior officer robustly defended a vocation for letters that no regimentation and bullying could destroy. Busy with classes, parades and prescribed study all day, he would sit reading by candlelight far into the night at a window overlooking the Fontanka Canal, crouched over a small table in his second-floor dormitory, wearing a blanket over his underwear, unmindful of draughts.[7] His letters reflect the exalted spirit in which he assaulted the treasury of global belles-lettres. 'Balzac is immense! His characters are the product of the Mind of the Universe! ... Whole millennia struggled to create this crux inside the Soul of Man.' Thus Dostoyevsky wrote to his brother Mikhail, that fellow-addict of literature. Similar effusions embraced 'the fiery, passionate Racine besotted with his own ideals' and the author of *Le Cid*: 'Read it, O pitiable one, read it and prostrate thyself in the dust before Corneille', he orders Mikhail. And in answer to his brother's boast that he too has been reading a great deal, Fyodor catalogues his own extensive conquests in French, German, English and Russian literature.[8] Much of this material must have been read in Russian translation, for though he was soon to know French well enough to translate an entire novel creditably, he was never to become equally fluent in German, and was to remain ignorant of English.

No author captivated Cadet Dostoyevsky more than 'Schiller, whom

I learnt by heart, whom I raved about. Never, I think, did fate intervene so happily in my life as when it introduced me to this great poet at this epoch.' He speaks of devouring Schiller jointly with an unnamed soul-mate, 'a creature whom I adored. ... Reading Schiller *with him* I could measure *against him* the noble, fiery Don Carlos, the Marquis of Posa.' This unnamed 'adored' friend was probably Ivan Berezhetsky, a fellow-cadet known to have been Dostoyevsky's closest associate at the Academy.[9] Previously he had contracted a similar ecstatic friendship with a poet, Ivan Shidlovsky, six years older than himself. Shidlovsky was the picturesque victim of an unhappy love affair, and a future dipsomaniac monk, with whom the young Fyodor indulged in similar exchanges of enthusiasm over his literary interests. Such were the few male intimates of this young man who knew no women at this stage of his life and remained aloof except with a few fellow-spirits.

Attribute

Cadet Dostoyevsky impressed several observers as a calm, imperturbable, even phlegmatic youth. He was modest in behaviour; he conscientiously and effectively discharged his military and academic duties after the initial setback when he was kept down for an extra year; he seemed older than he was; he disliked social occasions and cultivated solitude; he was so devout in his religious observances that he received the nickname 'Photius' after a recently deceased archimandrite of saintly character. Of the emotions that blazed behind this decorous façade only his brother and a few close intimates could guess. Nor could his military associates divine that this uncommunicative youth was secretly imagining himself as 'a Pericles, a Marius, a Christian at the time of Nero, a medieval knight at a tourney, an Edward Glendenning in Walter Scott's novel *The Monastery*.' Referring to this period in an article of 1861, he speaks of himself as 'so deeply sunk in reveries that my youth passed by without my even noticing.'[10] But in summer 1839 he received news that could not fail to shatter his dreams. He was informed that his father had suddenly died on his country estate.

Dr Dostoyevsky had been sadly demoralized by the death of his wife. Though only in his late forties, he had resigned his hospital post on grounds of ill health, including failing eyesight, in July 1837; had arranged for his undisposed children to be looked after by their aunt and uncle Kumanin; and had retired to Darovoye. Here he would prowl about, pathetically haranguing the deceased Mariya Fyodorovna. He also took a serf girl, Katya, as his mistress; and in 1838 Katya bore a child, possibly his. His son Andrey claims that his father's 'addiction to strong drink had evidently increased, and he was rarely in full command of his faculties.'[11]

The manner of the doctor's death remains a mystery. For eighty years after the event the world at large had no reason to suspect that he might have perished from causes other than natural. But then, in 1920, the novelist's surviving daughter Lyubov (Aimée) revealed for the first time, in a book published in Munich, that her grandfather had been murdered by his own serfs, who had (she said) smothered him with the cushions of his carriage somewhere between Darovoye and Cheremoshna.[12]

Lyubov Dostoyevskaya could have had no first-hand knowledge of the matter, having been born thirty years after her grandfather's death, besides which her biography of her father bears many obvious signs of unreliability. But her claim that Mikhail Andreyevich was murdered received confirmation when the memoirs of his third son Andrey were posthumously and belatedly published in 1930. Andrey had been fourteen years old when his father died, but he was nowhere near Darovoye at the time. Nor does he make it clear where he obtained his information, except that some of it came from the former children's nurse Alyona Frolovna, who had accompanied Dr Dostoyevsky to his country estate as his housekeeper. Andrey's version of the murder differs from Lyubov's: he has his father suddenly lynched, in a manner unspecified, by a dozen peasants whom he was abusing in a fit of rage.[13] That Mikhail Andreyevich was slain without any shedding of blood was the testimony, received at second-hand, of Fyodor Mikhaylovich's niece Mariya Ivanova, who herself lived in Darovoye in extreme old age: on into 1926, when that estate was converted into the Dostoyevsky Collective Farm.

By now literary historians were touring the locality collating old wives' tales for all they were worth. One tradition had Dostoyevsky *père* forcibly choked with vodka; another had him smothered while his sexual organs were crushed between stones. This last frightful detail could be linked with other significant pointers: one of the ring-leaders was identified as the uncle of the squire's serf-mistress Katya; a second was the father of another serf girl, Akulina, whom Dr Dostoyevsky has also been inferred as promoting to concubine at a tender age. The suggestion is that the murder was the muzhiks' revenge for the violation of their juvenile womenfolk by the doctor-ogre. But the main motive may have been his alleged drunken rages and habit of ordering floggings in his fiefdom. Even in the 1920s he was still remembered in the locality as a 'wild beast', being contrasted with his kindly wife.[14] So at least one aged peasant chose to portray him, citing the stories told by his own father; but one suspects that this witness, and perhaps others among the new collective farmers, may have taken the invitation to dilate on events eighty years old as a challenge to their inventive powers.

Though one or other of these blood-curdling versions may be true, an entirely different possibility exists—that Dr Dostoyevsky has been unjustly maligned to posterity, and even that he may not have been murdered at all.

Much of the above material—the indecorous details of the retired doctor's purportedly drunken and lecherous last years, the reputed circumstances of his alleged murder—seems to rest on dubious hearsay information: contradictory, late and at several stages removed from first-hand evidence. This point is made in a recent (1975) Moscow-published article by G. Fyodorov, based on an examination of the relevant local-government archives, and the first scholarly scrutiny of the case to invoke that documentary evidence. Fyodorov concludes that Dostoyevsky's father did after all die a natural death. He points out that two local doctors independently and at different times certified the cause as apoplexy, and that the sole reason to suspect violence was the assertion of a Major Khotyaintsev, a neighbouring landowner. The Major was involved in a long and (according to Fyodorov) acrimonious legal dispute with the Dostoyevskys over boundaries, and must be presumed to have invented the story of the murder in order to inculpate their serfs. And his motive in doing so? Revenge against the whole hated Dostoyevsky clan by ruining the estate for the doctor's heirs; for it would become valueless should its peasants be collectively exiled to Siberia, the normal punishment for a landowner's murder.[15]

At this point Fyodorov's reconstruction begins to sound as fanciful as some of the more exotic murder details, a reminder that Kremlin-dominated literary authority has a strong interest in demonstrating after all these years that the death of Dostoyevsky's father was from natural causes. To prove this would be to render the biography of a major cult figure more decorous, in accordance with the basic hagiographic bias of Kremlin-directed criticism, while simultaneously discrediting a wide range of hate-objects: wicked pre-revolutionary landowners; 'bourgeois' critics and biographers; and above all Freud, whose interpretation of the novelist (to be mentioned below) might seem to collapse if the father should turn out not to have been the victim of homicide after all.

Though Fyodorov, or at least his sponsors, may indeed have a vested interest in proving this case, it does not necessarily follow that he is wrong. He points out that Khotyaintsev's allegations led to an eighteen-month official enquiry into Dr Dostoyevsky's death, and that the investigation failed to substantiate murder. All this, most especially the contemporary medical evidence, casts a measure of doubt on the imputation of homicide. But it is far indeed from dismissing the possibility entirely, given the venality of Imperial Russia's local government officials—who might, for instance, have been bribed by the rich Kumanins—and the low level of competence of her rural doctors. It must also be remembered that the country's most highly developed folk craft was that of passively resisting, deviously defying and generally bamboozling non-peasants.

There is hardly any chance that we shall ever know for certain just how Dr Dostoyevsky met his end. Even the date, believed to be 8 June, is not certain. What is more important, in any case, is that his son Fyodor must have believed his father to have been murdered; it seems an inescapable inference from the fact that his brother Andrey and his daughter Lyubov both thought so. But nowhere, in the length and breadth of the source material, is Dostoyevsky himself recorded as referring to the manner in which his father died. Nor do we know how, when or in what form the news reached him. It is likely that he learnt of it by letter from the Kumanins, as we must presume that his brother Mikhail did from a surviving letter from him to them of 30 June.[16] Perhaps Fyodor received the bad tidings while engaged on the usual summer military manœuvres. In any case slowness of communication and transport made it impossible for either brother, or for any other close relative, to attend a funeral that must have been hurried through in the end: the peasants had left the corpse outside *in situ* in a heat-wave for at least two days.

Since news of his father's allegedly violent death must have been profoundly disturbing to so highly-strung a youth as Dostoyevsky, we can only marvel at the extent to which he put it out of his mind once and for all, at least so far as the record is concerned. His letters of 1839 contain two perfunctory references to the matter. He has 'wept many tears over Father's passing', he informs his brother Mikhail on 16 August; and 'Father's sad death' figures briefly in a long, self-abasing missive to the Kumanins written four months later. Never again was he to allude to his father's end, and (as is indicated above) he is only rarely recorded as mentioning Mikhaïl Andreyevich at all. That he 'positively disliked speaking of his father, and asked not to be questioned about him', is the testimony of a doctor-friend of the late 1840s, and it is confirmed by the other sources.[17]

For this reticence Dostoyevsky was one day to compensate with a work that must be examined in greater detail in due course, his last and most famous novel *The Brothers Karamazov*. Here, in nearly a thousand pages of print, he studies the murder of a fictional father, Fyodor Pavlovich Karamazov. All four sons of that miserly, drunken, lecherous parent are presented as in some degree implicated in his murder. From this a crucial question arises: did the young Dostoyevsky himself at some level of his mind desire the death of his own allegedly miserly, drunken, lecherous father: desire it and therefore, in his own mind and according to his own perverse sense of logic, in some mysterious and wholly impossible sense accomplish it? If there is any simple explanation for the persistent need to punish himself which so harassed him throughout his life, may it not conceivably lie in a neurotic, unreasoning, unconscious feeling that it was he, not the serfs of Darovoye and Cheremoshna, who had somehow struck down the father? Was it to atone for this imaginary crime that Dostoyevsky spent so much of his life 'seeking suffering'?

Such, considerably paraphrased, is Freud's interpretation of Dostoyevsky—widely accepted in the 1920s but now sometimes claimed to be devoid of substance.[18] Since it neither has been nor, presumably, ever can be proved we cannot accept it. Nor, however, can we refute it. And so I do not apologize for invoking it occasionally as a possible source of illumination. To do so is by no means to commit oneself in any degree whatever to the central hypothesis of 'Freudian' guilt, not to mention other details of Freud's interpretation involving Dostoyevsky's supposed castration complex and latent homosexuality.

Another, recently propounded explanation of Dostoyevsky's guilt feelings, as allegedly provoked by news of his father's murder, comes from a recent biographer who takes a firm anti-Freudian stance. This interpretation has Dostoyevsky overwhelmed with remorse on behalf of the ill-treated peasants of Darovoye and Cheremoshna; and so he should have been, for was not the money that paid for his tea and boots wrung metaphorically from the sweat of their brows? 'If his father had been mistreating the peasants abominably, was not he [Dostoyevsky] really to blame? Was it not to satisfy his purely fanciful "needs" that his father had come to his horrible end?'[19] Here, then, we have a Dostoyevsky who 'murdered' his father not through some subconscious urge, but in the more direct sense of having provoked the father to intensify his exploitation of his serfs, and hence to arouse their murderous instincts, in the son's selfish interests. This theory is almost as ingenious as Freud's, and must be welcomed as contributing yet another dimension to a baffling, fascinating and ultimately unresolvable problem. But it makes far more of the young Dostoyevsky's supposed social conscience than my own reading of the evidence permits. Of his concern for persons with whom he was not in direct contact I find little trace in the relevant memoir material and still less in his correspondence of the period.

Opposite above St Isaac's Bridge, St
Petersburg, in the 1840s, showing St
Isaac's Cathedral, the equestrian statue of
Peter the Great and the Senate
Opposite below The Petropavlovsky
Fortress, St Petersburg
Right Drilling of recruits in the reign of
Nicholas I
Below The Fontanka Canal, which was
overlooked by Dostoyevsky's dormitory
at the Chief Engineering Academy

Above Ivan Turgenev aged twenty
Right Nikolay Nekrasov

Left Vissarion Belinsky
Above A. A. Krayevsky, publisher of
Dostoyevsky's second novel, *The Double*

'Two years after his father's death Dostoyevsky was commissioned in the lowest officer's rank, that of ensign, and received the privilege of living out in private lodgings while continuing his course at the Academy. Now that he had his own flat in St Petersburg he was less of a martial figure than ever, but was at least sufficiently conscientious for each succeeding summer to bring a new promotion.' In 1842 he became a second lieutenant. In 1843, still in this rank, he graduated from the Academy to employment as a War Ministry draftsman.

Though it seemed increasingly clear that Dostoyevsky was not one of nature's sappers or draftsmen, but rather a 'poet', as Russian novelists of the period liked to style themselves, there is now a significant change of tone in the many references to his major addiction contained in his letters. Invoked, in the youth's cadet days, as a clue to the Mind of the Universe, the French novelist Balzac now figures more prosaically in the junior officer's calculations as a source of hard cash. During the Christmas holidays of 1843 Dostoyevsky translated Balzac's short novel *Eugénie Grandet* somewhat hastily and sketchily, but showing a good grasp of French idiom.[20] In the following summer he had the satisfaction of seeing his translation published in a literary review, and of receiving a fee for this, his first venture into print. He also planned to finance ambitious publishing projects of his own, involving the translation of other French novelists: Eugène Sue and George Sand. But these enterprises collapsed after revealing in the young officer a flair for dazzling himself with potential profits that never began to materialize. Other cultural activities of the period included visits to the opera, the ballet, and to the extremely expensive concerts given by that flamboyant touring pianist Franz Liszt.

During his summer leaves Dostoyevsky would take the steamer to Reval: then belonging to the Russian Empire's Baltic provinces; now, as Tallin, capital of the USSR's Estonian Republic. Here he would spend a few weeks with his brother Mikhail, who had married a local German girl, Emiliya Ditmai, in 1842, and who obtained employment as a military engineer after graduating from his training institution. The Reval Dostoyevskys, and the children soon born to them, temporarily provided Fyodor with the domestic background that he craved. He relished the role of uncle, adored the babies, and was fascinated by the Gothic architecture of the ancient Baltic port and Hanseatic town. But he had already conceived his lifelong dislike of Germans and of the German atmosphere in the cosmopolitan Reval.

'Even in the early 1840s, as is confirmed by recently released material, Dostoyevsky was known to express an intense and uncontrollable loathing for non-Russians in general.' On one social evening at St Petersburg 'he let loose such a Philippic against foreigners' that certain horrified Swiss acquaintances retired in disorder, muttering that he was an '*enragé*'. He also begged his flat-mate Dr Riesenkampf, who reported this episode, never again to introduce him to foreigners. 'If I don't watch out they'll marry me to a Frenchwoman, and then it will be good-bye once and for all to Russian literature.'[21]

Now that Dostoyevsky was living in his own flat, money problems had become a permanent source of anguish. This was not the vague absentmindedness of the literary man who 'cannot be bothered' with financial details. With money worries Dostoyevsky most certainly could be bothered. Indeed, he saw to it by every means at his command that he *was* so bothered. After renting a flat beyond his means, and leaving two rooms empty because he could not afford to furnish them, he was openly plundered by his tailor, his shoemaker, his barber; and above all by his army batman, who kept a complaisant laundry maid and a whole family of hangers-on at Dostoyevsky's expense. Or he would genially rob himself by acts of charity disproportionate to his means. When the young German doctor Alexander Riesenkampf came to share the flat for a time, and held a surgery there for down-and-out patients, these unfortunates soon found their physician's landlord an unbelievably 'soft touch'. But he derived considerable benefits in return, since he was soon quarrying these experiences for his first novel *Poor Folk*, and other early works.[22]

Gambling was another means of frittering away his funds, whether at cards, billiards or dominoes. There were visits to expensive restaurants, and to rapacious usurers; there were 'loans', rarely repaid, to anyone who cared to ask for them. It was to save Fyodor from such foolishness that his brother Mikhail had induced him to accept Dr Riesenkampf as tenant, the plan being for some German thrift and self-discipline to rub off on the unruly young Russian. But after a few bewildered months the stolid Teuton moved out, leaving the Second Lieutenant as improvident as he had found him.

Though Dostoyevsky had a small salary as a military draftsman, and had earned a fee for translating Balzac, the bulk of his wantonly squandered funds was extracted from the estate of his deceased father through a series of letters—now whining, now arrogant, now self-pitying, now vaguely threatening. These were addressed to a new and somewhat formidable figure, Pyotr Karepin, who had married Fyodor's eldest sister Varvara (Varenka) in 1840. He was a self-made businessman, a quarter of a century Fyodor's senior, and was an executor, conveniently resident in Moscow, of the family estate.

To Dostoyevsky's impudent or self-pitying letters demanding cash Karepin would respond with magisterial silence. Or he would reply in the patient but at times abominably self-righteous tone of a man of the world dealing with a presumptuous young ass. On one occasion he solemnly recommended the fledgling genius, whom he had every possible excuse for not recognizing as such, to abandon Shakespeare and similar 'soap bubbles'. Fyodor Mikhaylovich should buckle to and make a go of his career: it would do him a world of good to be posted to some distant military backwater. 'The further away the better', adds Karepin with a gleam of pure malice.[23]

All this infuriated the Second Lieutenant, especially the disparagement of Shakespeare. 'That swine Karepin is as stupid as a grey gelding', he told his brother.[24] He probably drew on Karepin when creating his fullest fictional portrait of the smug, bourgeois man of affairs, the odious Luzhin of *Crime and Punishment*, and Karepin may also have inspired the villainous Bykov in *Poor Folk*. But despite the unctuous tone of his homilies the much-abused Karepin did yield again and again, whether through weariness or pity, to Dostoyevsky's demands. In 1844, for example, the young officer extracted the impressive sum of 2,412 roubles 50 copecks from the estate, as we know from the accounts; in which same year all three of his brothers received less than a thousand roubles between them, while the sisters received not a copeck.[25] Small wonder that Karepin rebuked Fyodor for taking more than his share.

It was all so much money down the drain. Receiving a thousand roubles one day, Dostoyevsky would repay his most urgent debts and squander what was left on restaurants, gambling, having his pocket picked, various hangers-on. Two separate thousand-rouble remittances disappeared in this way, each in a single day, in the winter of 1843–4.[26] These were sums on which a prudent person could live in reasonable comfort for nearly a year. The deceased doctor, we are reminded, had earned a mere six hundred roubles annually for his work at the Maryinsky Hospital—silver roubles, admittedly, worth over three times as much as the paper roubles mentioned above. But the son's funds, supplied via Moscow, were all wrung from the labours of the Darovoye and Cheremoshna serfs, including perhaps the recent murderers of the recipient's father.

One of Dostoyevsky's constant aims was to obtain from Karepin a settlement in full of his own share of the estate, and the suggestion has accordingly been made that his motive in requesting this was a high-minded urge to dissociate himself as quickly as he could from the exploitation of serf labour. 'We consider', a recent Moscow-published authority writes, 'that Dostoyevsky's renunciation of his inheritance was not a commercial decision, but a question of principle, a matter of his whole philosophy of life. It convincingly proves how closely in tune he was with the [notionally idealistic] spirit and aspirations of his age.'[27] Convincingly proves? Stuff and nonsense! Confronted with the actual spectacle of a weeping serf, the kind-hearted Dostoyevsky would of course part with his last copeck without hesitation. But when weeping serfs were several score in number and located at a distance of five hundred miles, their sweat and tears did not, so far as any available evidence goes, concern him in the slightest degree. He felt a desperate need for money. And that, so far as the evidence goes, was that.

As the years went by he became more and more irked by the demands of the Service. Of his work, after graduation, as a military draftsman in 1843–4 we know nothing beyond his own statement that it was 'as boring as potatoes'.[28] It was only, perhaps, to sustain the money flow from Karepin that he had persevered with the army so long. Eventually, in the summer of 1844, he took the plunge and resigned his commission. His brother-in-law was angry, but could do nothing about it; and was mercifully released from this tiresome financial involvement shortly afterwards when Fyodor at last extracted one thousand roubles, silver, as settlement of his inheritance in full.

In autumn 1844 Dostoyevsky was a free man at last. But freedom as he himself was to argue in some of his finest writings, is the heaviest of all the burdens that can ever be inflicted on man.

3

Apprentice Author

Poor Folk; The Double

During the winter of 1844–5 Dostoyevsky shared rooms with Dmitry Grigorovich, a former fellow-pupil at the Engineering Academy. He was an aspiring author whose two early stories, *The Village* and *Anton Goremyka*, helped to launch a long and not undistinguished literary career.

As the months went by Grigorovich noticed his flat-mate working on a mysterious manuscript about which he said nothing until, in May, he suddenly offered to read it aloud. It was a novel, *Poor Folk*, to which Grigorovich listened 'totally spellbound', uttering excited cries and restrained only by respect for his friend's reserve from repeatedly embracing him. When the reading was over the listener insisted on removing the manuscript 'almost by force', and took it to another literary friend: Nikolay Nekrasov. Also in his early twenties, Nekrasov had already embarked on what was to become a notable career as poet, editor and publisher. To him too *Poor Folk* was a revelation. He and Grigorovich finished the tale together in the small hours with tears streaming down their faces, and at once rushed off to the author's rooms to congratulate him.[1]

It was now four a.m., but Dostoyevsky was still awake after spending the night reading Gogol aloud with a few friends. According to his own version, recollected in tranquillity many years later, this had put him in just the mood of exaltation to appreciate all the embraces, exclamations and tears. But Grigorovich's account of the incident has him, more plausibly, as tongue-tied and embarrassed.[2]

The next stage was to submit the manuscript to Vissarion Belinsky, arbiter of literature and pioneer of Russian socialism. A veteran among these younger men, he was now thirty-three years old, his influence was enormous, and he remains Russia's most renowned critic to this day. When Nekrasov announced that 'a new Gogol' had arisen, Belinsky uttered a famous retort: 'Gogols sprout like mushrooms in your imagination.' But the novel itself removed his doubts. 'Bring him here at once!' he commanded, and so the awestruck author came to face one whose very commendations were a test of steadiness under

47

fire. Could Dostoyevsky himself, the 'blazing-eyed' critic demanded, truly comprehend the tremendous significance of what he had written? No, he could not, Belinsky 'shrieked' in answer to his own rhetorical question: he was too young and inexperienced. Such is Dostoyevsky's own account of the episode in his *Diary of a Writer* of 1877.[3]

One thing at least Dostoyevsky did understand, given Belinsky's reputation—that he himself had leapt straight into the leading ranks of Russian authors. It was just as well, to judge from his letters of the period when he was writing the novel, for they show him pinning all his hopes in life, financial not least, on the success of *Poor Folk*: he even threatened to hang himself, or throw himself in the River Neva, should it prove a failure. Instead of this he had experienced, in listening to Belinsky's praise, 'the most enchanting moment of my life.'[4] His novel became the talk of St Petersburg months before it was even published.

If the tears, the embraces, the exclamations, the blazing eyes should seem puzzling to a later and duller age, we may seek an explanation in the special situation of Russian literature at the time. The Russians had been slower, by several centuries, than the advanced countries of western Europe to acquire an internationally recognized literature, just as they were also backward economically, educationally and in many other ways. But they were determined to catch up. An impressive beginning had been made in the 1820s, when Pushkin emerged as the national poet, to be followed shortly by another important poet and novelist, Lermontov, and by a highly original writer of prose fiction, Gogol. Here were three major writers. They were not alone, but they were not enough. More were eagerly expected, and important new names indeed did appear almost simultaneously from the middle 1840s onwards. Turgenev, Goncharov, Herzen, Ostrovsky, as well as Grigorovich and Nekrasov, are some of the authors whose first influential publications belong, together with *Poor Folk*, to the years 1846–7. Tolstoy was soon to follow. It was, then, in the atmosphere of a literary boom that Dostoyevsky's first novel appeared, and everyone was ready to invest it with qualities for which the work itself at first seems to offer little evidence.

Poor Folk is a short novel consisting of an exchange of letters between a man and a young woman whom he loves from a distance. Both are victims, as politically-minded critics have repeatedly pointed out, of St Petersburg social conditions. The man, Makar Devushkin, is a virtuous, passive, downtrodden, poverty-stricken, middle-aged clerk. His correspondent, Varenka, is a virtuous, passive, downtrodden, poverty-stricken young spinster engaged in helplessly warding off various menaces ranging from frequent head colds to assaults on her chastity mounted by the lecherous landowner Bykov. The precise nature of her previous relations with Bykov is not revealed, for Dostoyevsky has already adopted one of his techniques as a mature novelist—that of spreading a delicious aura of vagueness over the misdemeanours, sexual or other, which his villains have allegedly committed in the period before the action of his narratives begins. Whether or not in the fullest sense the 'victim of a rich man's crime', the poor but honest Varenka suffers, at the end of the novel, a calamity severer even than the traditional fate worse than death: she is trapped by poverty into marriage with the monster Bykov, whose motive for making her his wife is not even lust for her body but a spiteful desire to disinherit an uncongenial nephew.

This is a black-and-white novel in which virtue and vice are polarized while vice triumphs. If it requires some effort to picture Grigorovich, Belinsky and even the successful businessman Nekrasov sobbing over so sentimental a tale, we must remember that such was the spirit of the age and country. Few modern readers, Russian or not, will find tears streaming down their cheeks at the point where, on the last pages of *Poor Folk*, the desperate Devushkin takes a tragic farewell of his beloved Varenka, who is now in the hated Bykov's clutches and whom he will never see again. As for the numerous still more pathetic minor characters and episodes in *Poor Folk*, it is tempting to remark that 'he must indeed have a heart of stone who can think of them without laughing.' Such is the piteously expiring consumptive student Pokrovsky whose coffin is driven off in an open cart in pouring rain while his poor old father totters after it weeping copiously.

And yet, if such things are to be done at all it is as well that they should be done skilfully, as they are in *Poor Folk*, for Dostoyevsky here seems to rival his older contemporary Charles Dickens with his Little Nells and his Bob Cratchits. Where opinions may differ on *Poor Folk*, and on similar features in Dostoyevsky's later novels, is on the degree of genuine compassion that the author may be thought to project. One extreme view is that of Belinsky, who wrote as follows of *Poor Folk*. 'Honour and glory to the young poet whose Muse loves those who live in garrets and basements, and speaks of them to the dwellers in gilded halls, saying "See, these too are men and your brothers." '[5] This verdict has been generally accepted by USSR-domiciled interpreters, who have Dostoyevsky, and indeed practically all other imaginative writers of all ages and countries, as a 'champion of the Little Man': that lowly, miserable yet noble victim of capitalist and other non-Marxist brands of persecution. But is Dostoyevsky's inspiration indeed as uncompromisingly philanthropic as Belinsky suggests? Does he not rather seem to enjoy the miseries that he

49

invokes with such skill and relish? The late nineteenth-century Russian critic and thinker N. K. Mikhaylovsky, who was almost as influential in his time as Belinsky, speaks of Dostoyevsky's habit of piling up an incredible mountain of misfortunes, calamities and insults 'simply in order to torment some Sidorov or Petrov created by himself, and to torment the reader at the same time.' That he was a fictional sadist, actively savouring cruelty and torture, was Mikhaylovsky's contention.[6]

Conflicting emotions

Pure love of his fellow men? Or out-and-out sadism? It is not, surely, from one or other of these opposing attitudes, but rather from the tension between them, that Dostoyevsky's first novel derives its by no means negligible merits. That his mind could not help simultaneously cultivating mutually exclusive attitudes and emotions is, indeed, its most striking specific. Moreover, 'poor folk', resembling in essence those of his first novel, continue to figure even in his mature work: effectively, but only as minor figures. The long line ends only with the death of Ilyusha Snegiryov in the last novel, *The Brothers Karamazov*.

Another of Dostoyevsky's staple themes is the assault on the virtue of young girls by elderly lechers, as represented in *Poor Folk* by Bykov. That this odious figure was possibly modelled on the author's middle-aged brother-in-law Karepin has already been noted. Like Bykov, Karepin was married to a 'Varenka' nearly thirty years his junior: Dostoyevsky's eldest sister. Other features from the author's life, briefly invoked in *Poor Folk*, include the scenery of Darovoye and nanny Frolovna. Childhood conversations with the poor patients at the Maryinsky Hospital in Moscow are quarried too, as are later contacts with St Petersburg's slum-dwellers.[7]

There are few indeed of Dostoyevsky's novels and stories in which such biographical echoes cannot be sensed, for his own experiences, his own nature, were always to remain his most potent inspiration. But whereas the biographical elements of *Poor Folk* are confined to externals and incidentals, those of his second novel, *The Double*, derive from the innermost core of his nature.

The Double, largely written in late 1845 immediately after *Poor Folk*, also attracted much attention before publication, especially as it differed strikingly from its predecessor. Though the hero, Yakov Petrovich Golyadkin, is another depressed clerk, he does not wrestle with mere poverty like his precursor Devushkin, but with the problem of retaining his dwindling sanity as it is menaced by repeated encounters with a duplicate of himself. This is another Yakov Petrovich Golyadkin: identical in name, clothing, appearance and every other respect, but with the striking exception of temperament. The original hero

(Golyadkin Senior) is timid, shy, awkward, socially inept and unsuccessful in all his undertakings. But his double (Golyadkin Junior) is impudent, self-possessed, assertive, arrogant and successful.

The rivalry of this sinister pair is developed with considerable art, not least through Dostoyevsky's 'deadpan' narrative: a technique whereby no one, except the unfortunate Golyadkin Senior, seems unduly surprised to find two exactly identical clerks so impossibly brushing shoulders in the same office. Nor does Dostoyevsky the narrator present Golyadkin Junior as a hallucination. Far from it, for that shameless personage soon becomes all too real, developing intolerable insolence towards his senior counterpart, while undermining his self-respect, his career, and through those his mental equilibrium. Pushful Golyadkin Junior filches Golyadkin Senior's written work and obtains the credit due to his counterpart from the head of the office where they both work. On another occasion, when the Doubles both chance to patronize the same café, the impudent Junior contrives to consume no less than ten pies; then craftily sneaks out, leaving his wretched twin to pay for them all. Meanwhile humiliation has been descending on Golyadkin Senior from other quarters too. For example, he has gatecrashed a ball, given in honour of a young woman with whom he has fallen secretly and ridiculously in love; and is there insulted by a tall, handsome officer as a prelude to being thrown downstairs. After all this it is not surprising to find the victim ignominiously removed to a lunatic asylum at the end of the novel.

These macabre twins represent a creatively distorted and split portrait of the Artist as a Young Man, as Dostoyevsky himself explicitly recognized by referring to himself, during the writing of the novel, as a 'real Golyadkin'.[8] And indeed he was in many ways a Golyadkin Senior. Ill at ease in company, he envied the wealth, the good looks, the social aplomb of others whom he simultaneously despised. He was inclined, like Golyadkin Senior, to toady to these envied persons; but he was simultaneously inclined, being arrogant as well as self-effacing, to trample on them with the impudence of a Golyadkin Junior. Golyadkin Senior was the miserable creature as which Dostoyevsky saw himself in bouts of self-abasement, whereas Golyadkin Junior was the triumphant dispenser of insults and injuries which part of Dostoyevsky was determined to become.

If at any time in his life Dostoyevsky behaved like a combination of his Doubles, it was in his relations with literary St Petersburg after the publication of his first novels. Instead of suppressing his Golyadkin-like traits with the appearance of *The Double*, he seems to have done the very opposite, for it is in the aftermath of its initial appearance that his touchiness and self-importance may be observed at their most pathetic. Life had first inspired art, and then proceeded to imitate it with redoubled fervour.

At least he could not complain of any lack of critical attention when his first two works appeared almost simultaneously in January 1846. *Poor Folk* came out in an almanac, *The St Petersburg Symposium* edited by Nekrasov; and *The Double* was published a few days later in a literary journal, *Otechestvennyye zapiski* ('Notes of the Fatherland') edited by A. A. Krayevsky. Such was the general interest that the author had traced no less than thirty-five reviews or critical mentions of his work in various periodicals by 1 April. 'Some praise me to the skies . . . others abuse me for all they're worth.' And the touchy Dostoyevsky was more inclined to brood on his detractors, those who denounced the novels as devoid of all merit, formless, unprecedentedly boring and the like. One critic claimed that all he could say after reading *Poor Folk* was: 'Poor Readers!' It was, according to one ugly image, like a soup containing lumps of sugar instead of beef stock. As for *The Double*, 'nothing more colourless, monotonous, tedious than this long, endlessly protracted and abysmally wearisome tale could be conceived.' Such were some of the hostile comments. Far more worrying, though, was the slowly dwindling enthusiasm of Belinsky and his set. Belinsky at first thought *The Double* superior to *Poor Folk*, in which he was surely right; as was the author himself when he claimed that his second novel was worth ten of his first. But then, as a preliminary to turning against Dostoyevsky's work as a whole, the critic began carping at *The Double* as repetitious, lacking artistic discipline and full of 'grotesque defects'. Soon Dostoyevsky was reporting that 'our lot, Belinsky and all, are fed up with me over Golyadkin.' Everyone, said Dostoyevsky, found *The Double* unbelievably boring and unreadable; and yet somehow, curiously enough, these same people seemed unable to put the novel down![9]

More painful still was the personal humiliation that Dostoyevsky was now bringing upon himself, in his social contacts with the Belinsky set, through a young man's understandable foolishness in letting his sudden glory go to his head. We can already trace the build-up of this attitude in the months preceding his novels' first publication, when he keeps bragging to his brother by letter; he preens himself on the 'incredible respect' accorded to him; says that his fame has reached its zenith; boasts that everyone is 'frightfully curious' about him. Moreover, some of these inquisitive persons are titled: Prince Odoyevsky, Count Sollogub. But how characteristic of the name-dropping young man that, after snobbishly congratulating himself on these eminent acquaintances in one sentence, he is already suspecting them, Golyadkin-like, of offensive condescension in the next. In November 1845, as we learn from a long letter to his brother Mikhail, Dostoyevsky is still obsessed with the devastating impression that he has made on the various literary figures whom he is simultaneously contriving to antagonize. Belinsky, whose 'love for me knows no limits', briefly dominated the young novelist, not only by adopting him as a literary protégé, but also by converting him to socialism and atheism—a theme to which we shall revert in the next chapter when considering Dostoyevsky's political involvements of the period. Another notability to fascinate the newly published Dostoyevsky was Turgenev, the future novelist so far chiefly known for his verse, who 'at once attached himself to me with such affection and intimacy that Belinsky says he's fallen completely in love with me . . . a poet, a great talent, an aristocrat —handsome, rich, intelligent, educated.' And Dostoyevsky for his part has 'almost fallen in love with Turgenev.'[10]

That these words were the prelude to a long and bitter quarrel between the two novelists will surprise no reader of *The Double*, and hostilities did indeed break out soon after their brief spasm of mutual affection. While Dostoyevsky, flushed by the success of his first works, was giving himself intolerable airs *à la* Golyadkin Junior, the urbane Turgenev was ingenious in helping him to make himself look even more foolish than he might have contrived unaided. He would provoke the passionate Dostoyevsky into heated arguments, tricking him into defending absurd and untenable theses. Turgenev also helped to write and circulate malicious verses lampooning Fyodor Mikhaylovich. He was described as a 'pimple on the face of literature'; as corroded with envy of Gogol; as the Knight of the Sorrowful Countenance. One of his many unfortunate social lapses, that of fainting or having a fit on being presented to a society beauty, was also commemorated in doggerel. And his ill-wishers spread the malicious and almost certainly unfounded rumour which had him so besotted with conceit over *Poor Folk* as to demand—unsuccessfully—that it be distinguished, in Nekrasov's almanac where it first appeared, by a special type and ornamental border.[11]

Rising to the bait and speaking the purest Golyadkinese, Dostoyevsky told Turgenev that he was not afraid of 'any of them'; his calumniators should 'just wait'; he would 'trample them all in the mud' one day. He also fell out with the all-powerful Belinsky, who had soon gone beyond finding minor faults in *The Double*, and was announcing that he and his friends had been deceived in thinking Dostoyevsky a genius. Dostoyevsky retorted that Belinsky understood nothing about literature. He also quarrelled with Nekrasov, describing him and his set as 'envious bastards', and even refusing to bow to them in the street.[12]

Dostoyevsky's tormentors behaved most unkindly. Granted that these clashes were partly his fault, it is still hard to pardon those who tried to goad him into becoming yet more of a double-dyed Golyadkin than he already was. On the other hand, had his associates been more friendly, he would have resented that as condescension. At this difficult stage of his life there was probably no way to avoid provoking in him either the one or the other Golyadkin, or even both simultaneously; especially as part of him seems to have enjoyed the very humiliations that he brought upon himself. There is also the hypothesis, which can neither be confirmed nor refuted, that he was impelled to court these humiliations by an unconscious, self-punishing drive to sabotage his very success even as it attained its greatest heights; just as he was inevitably compelled to squander money whenever he received a sudden windfall. And yet, appearances to the contrary, Dostoyevsky was no figure of fun. He was, rather, to be pitied for the nervous disorders that afflicted him. Not for nothing, it seems, did he have the biographically significant Golyadkin Senior removed to a lunatic asylum on the last page of *The Double*.

Dostoyevsky's doctor and personal friend S. D. Yanovsky claims to have seen him every day over a period of three years in 1846–9. He describes his patient as exhibiting the irregular pulse, nervous temperament and chronic hypochondria 'typical of women and neurotics.' Dostoyevsky repeatedly demanded that his tongue should be inspected; complained of hallucinations and dizziness; was continually borrowing medical tomes on diseases of the brain and the nervous system. Phrenology too fascinated him, and he would discuss his impressive cranial bumps with the doctor into the small hours.[13]

As will be shown below, Dostoyevsky was to become a martyr to epilepsy in the last half of his life. The condition was to be authoritatively diagnosed for the first time only in 1857, after he had already unwittingly suffered from it for at least six years. It was to 1850 or 1851 that he himself came to assign the onset of his affliction once it had been diagnosed. This dating is accepted by two of his biographers writing in English, the earliest and the most recent.[14] While not dissenting from their findings, I must also stress that the earlier Dostoyevsky is several times recorded as having suffered *pripadki* (fits, seizures, attacks) which, whatever their precise clinical nature may have been, came to be regarded with hindsight as epileptic by those who reported them.

One of these witnesses was the recently mentioned Dr Yanovsky. In July 1847 he found the young novelist shouting and suffering convulsions in one of St Petersburg's main squares, and treated him for what he describes, in memoirs published nearly forty years later, as his patient's first serious epileptic attack. Then again, if we go back a few years to 1844 or earlier, we find 'several seizures', implied to have been epileptic, recorded by Grigorovich as occurring in the period when he and Dostoyevsky were fellow-pupils at the Engineering Academy. Whatever their clinical nature, these 'fits' tended to be triggered by contact with death: by the sight of a funeral procession in a St Petersburg street, by the news of Belinky's passing in June 1848. Going back yet further in time, we find Dostoyevsky's first epileptic attack regarded by members of his own family as having been provoked by the news of his father's death in summer 1839, while one modern authority, who quotes no evidence at all, ascribes the first symptoms to the sufferer's seventh year.[15]

Retrospectively interpreted by so many witnesses as epileptic, these fits, attacks or seizures of the 1840s and earlier were never regarded as such by Dostoyevsky himself. He attributed the symptoms to an unspecified 'nervous disease', from which he claimed to have 'been cured' in Siberia.[16]

Among those who link Dostoyevsky's first epileptic attack with the death of his father in 1839 is Freud, who also suggests that the affliction was hysterical rather than organic in origin. Freud further links Dostoyevsky's epilepsy, and the periods of unconsciousness to which it gave rise, with certain strange, death-like, non-epileptic trances into which the young man (on the evidence of his brother Andrey) was also liable to fall. Fearful of being buried alive, he would leave written or verbal instructions that his inert body should not be moved until a period of several days had elapsed. Freud attributes these losses of consciousness to Dostoyevsky's determination to equate his deathlike self with the dead father for whose murder he felt responsible. But the trouble is that Freud, though possessing clinical qualifications not shared by most literary authorities, tends to misrepresent or misunderstand some of the humble and checkable facts on which he bases his diagnoses.[17]

Whether losing or retaining consciousness, the young author was equally liable to embarrass his associates. During a visit to Reval he somehow offended Mikhail and Emiliya Dostoyevsky, to whom he apologized by letter. There were times, he told them, when 'my nerves don't obey me'; his heart might be 'floating in love', but he somehow could not pronounce a single friendly word. On another occasion he wrote apologizing to the salon hostess Yevgeniya Maykova, for suddenly leaving her house after some unexplained outburst. 'I fled instinctively, anticipating the weakness of my nature, which cannot help erupting under extreme pressure, exploding hyperbolically in excesses. ... It's hard for me with my weak nerves not to rise to double-edged questions, hard not to lose my temper because they *are* double-edged.' Developing the theme of his culpability at inordinate length, he was of course soon apologizing for his apology. Far from callous and imperceptive, he was convinced that his nature was 'vile, odious, comic, repulsive', and resented being so much less master of himself than were the self-possessed mediocrities who mocked him.[18]

Dostoyevsky was no more adept at wearing civilian clothes than he had been at looking smart in army uniform. Though something of a dandy and a customer of fashionable tailors, he yet made the impression of a typical seminarist or theological student, that Russian byword for lack of sartorial grace. But unlike many a seminarist he had no taste for strong drink: as a keen sensation-craver, he perhaps shunned alcohol because it dulled that acute apprehension of reality or unreality which, however painful, he much preferred to self-oblivion. Yet he was no hermit. He liked the opera, he even enjoyed dancing. He also enjoyed company, but preferred associates—they were mostly young men with literary, and soon political, interests—whom he could address as if they were a public meeting, for he tended not to recognize that conversation can be a two-way affair. His manner of speech is graphically described in a recently published section of Alexander Riesenkampf's memoirs. 'Seizing on some subject and gradually becoming excited by it, he seemed all a-bubble. Thoughts arose in his head like the splashes from a whirlpool; he fell into a sort of frenzy; his natural eloquent delivery transgressed the canons of artistic discipline; his naturally hoarse voice became strident; he foamed at the mouth, gesticulated, shouted, spat in all directions.'[19]

What of his sexual experiences? Here we find few indications, despite the strong sensual urges that he was to develop in middle life. We have noticed his emotional friendships with other young men, and his reference to 'almost falling in love' with Turgenev. But Russian men repeatedly touch each other, and even kiss and embrace, without necessarily experiencing homosexual desire. Freud speaks of Dostoyevsky's suppressed homosexual proclivities, hints of which can indeed be adduced in quantity, but there seems to be no evidence whatever of homosexual practice. As for relations with women, Dr Yanovsky and Dostoyevsky's second wife both tell us that there was no serious love affair in his twenties. Nor did Dostoyevsky even cultivate the young man's habit of casually discussing the charms of attractive girls. 'He was fairly indifferent to the female sex and its allurements.'[20]

The pointers to heterosexual involvement, physical or emotional, are indeed few. Dostoyevsky's reference, in a letter of 1849 written in gaol, to the decline of his 'somewhat impure carnal urges' at least shows that he was capable of feeling such urges. And why 'impure'? Did he perhaps patronize the capital's brothels? His works abound in oracular references to these flourishing institutions, and his correspondence contains one intriguing passage bearing on them. 'The Minnushkas, Klarushkas and Mariannas [typical prostitutes' names] are deucedly pretty but also damnably expensive', he writes, adding that Turgenev and Belinsky have been 'giving me hell for my dissolute life.' Perhaps this was an empty boast designed to create an aura of picturesque debauchery, or perhaps he really did indulge himself in this way. We do not know, but it has been suggested that an unspecified 'local ailment', for which Yanovsky treated him, was possibly venereal disease.[21]

As for love on a less squalid level, Dostoyevsky claimed to have conceived a passion for the celebrated beauty and literary hostess Avdotya Panayeva, a member of the Belinsky set. But it was his friend and later enemy Nekrasov who made this delectable creature his mistress: not Dostoyevsky, who only worshipped from afar. Meanwhile, without his knowing it, Avdotya was summing him up in her mind, as she has recorded in her memoirs. 'One glance at Dostoyevsky showed you a frightfully nervous and sensitive young man. He was a short, fair-haired, thin little chap with an unhealthy complexion. His small grey eyes darted tremulously from one object to another while his pale lips twitched nervously.'[22]

Despite Panayeva's verdict it might be misleading to dismiss the young Dostoyevsky as unattractive to the other sex. There are women who dote on neurotics, and his peculiar temperament would, to some, have proved a positive attraction. But how could this nervous, twitching creature, this fainter at phantoms and beautiful girls, conceivably have coped with an actual woman? Inadequately, one surmises, at this stage of his development. And so he remained in some ways a lonely young man. But from the autumn of 1847 his loneliness was at least relieved by the arrival of his brother Mikhail. That translator of Goethe now gave up his career as an engineer, left Reval and moved his family to St Petersburg, where he set up a cigarette factory.

After the publication of *Poor Folk* and *The Double*, Dostoyevsky remained a moderately prolific author, but failed to fulfil his early promise. In the next four years, 1846–9, he wrote ten short stories, and also a longer work, *Netochka Nezvanova*; which, though he called it a novel, in fact consists of three linked stories. It was in this last work, interrupted by his arrest and never finished, that he invested his chief

More Books

ambitions. He intended it as a crushing retort to certain 'friends' who were 'set on burying me alive', but who were going to find 'their noses thoroughly put out of joint.'[23] Alas, these brave predictions were vain. Neither *Netochka Nezvanova* nor any of the ten lesser items attains even the modest level of *Poor Folk*, let alone that of the profoundly disturbing *Double*, and they provoked a generally hostile reception. Can it have been Dostoyevsky himself, rather than his envious friends, who was determined to bury his career alive? And was it perhaps to further this same self-destructive urge that he had now 'sold himself into slavery' by accepting so many advances from his new publisher? This was Krayevsky, editor of *Otechestvennyye zapiski*, to whose side Dostoyevsky had rallied after Krayevsky too had quarrelled with Nekrasov and Belinsky. Dostoyevsky sent his new publisher frenzied, itemized letters explaining why, owing to special circumstances certain never to recur, yet more and more advances were urgently and instantly required. But the more he struggled to extricate himself from this self-sprung trap, the worse confounded did the harassments of financial chaos become.

Though the minor items of 1846–9 have less than *The Double*, or even *Poor Folk*, to offer the general reader, they by no means lack significance. The variety of theme and treatment confirms the seriousness of Dostoyevsky's vocation and his determination to persist with experimenting until he finds his true level. But he also clings to certain positions previously adopted. However varied the method, humanity under strain remains the major interest. And much of the work continues to be set in St Petersburg, further staking his claim to be Russia's premier metropolitan novelist and a chronicler of town life who ventures rarely, and with apparent reluctance, into the fields and forests hymned by Turgenev and Tolstoy. Dostoyevsky also creates several new variants of the self-portrait hero. These are shy, retiring, lonely, introverted, hypersensitive, garret-domiciled, Golyadkin-like young male St Petersburgers: all in a sense untalented Dostoyevskys. The most significant of them, biographically, is Vasya Shumkov, hero of *A Weak Heart*. Happy in a love which is, for once in Dostoyevsky's early work, reciprocated, this humble, grateful young man is equally happy in his work, though it consists only of copying documents. But Vasya ends by going out of his mind simply because he cannot endure such ecstasy. Was it, then, to protect his own sanity that Vasya's creator continually ensured, through self-sabotage, that he himself did not find comparable satisfaction in work or love?

Illuminating for the insights which it provides into its creator's character, *A Weak Heart* is not impressive as a work of art. Even less impressive are some of the other short writings of the period. Belinsky, now thoroughly disillusioned with Dostoyevsky, called the story *Mister Prokharchin* 'grotesque, affected, incomprehensible'; and he said that another story, *The Landlady*, was 'a sort of monstrosity'.[24] From these judgements posterity has not notably dissented.

With the unfinished 'novel' *Netochka Nezvanova*, Dostoyevsky so far abandons the self-portrait hero as to make his chief character a little girl. Netochka is the narrator of all the three short stories of which the work consists, and as such imparts to it such unity as it possesses. The choice of narrator reflects Dostoyevsky's abiding interest in children, who attracted him throughout his life, and who were to play a significant part in his mature fiction. Precocious, like most other Dostoyevskian infants, Netochka analyses her complex relations with her stepfather, an unhinged violinist; with a little rich girl, Princess Katya; with her benefactress Aleksandra Mikhaylovna. The preoccupations are characteristic in that the perversity of human reactions is everywhere stressed. Just as in the mature works, intricately intermeshed love and hate dominate the various relationships. But the method is static and analytical; there is little of the dynamic pressure and dramatic dialogue with which the mature author was to develop these same themes.

The topic of infantile sexuality, an abiding obsession of Dostoyevsky's, is well represented by the nymphet and emotional vampire Netochka, and also by some of her small and sadistically inclined friends. The same theme also figures in a shorter work of the period, *The Little Hero*; here the protagonist and narrator is again a child, an eleven-year-old boy precociously sensual in his attitude to the attractive adult heroine. As this reminds us, all Dostoyevsky's children are apt to be emotionally and, in potential, sexually precocious. They often behave like little adults, whereas his adults, by contrast, are often found behaving like overgrown children. His very greybeards are subject to those sudden gusts of irrational, impotent and uncontrollable passion which are generally associated with infancy, for Dostoyevskian tantrums are by no means confined to those of tender years. All his characters, of whatever age, thus tend in a sense to be equals: a persistent trait in his work of which *Netochka Nezvanova*, *The Little Hero* and other early works serve notice.

4

Political Criminal

The months from April to June 1847 witnessed Dostoyevsky's first significant excursion into journalism, four articles published under the heading 'St Petersburg Annals' in the daily newspaper *Peterburgskaya gazeta* ('The St Petersburg Gazette'). Trifling in themselves, these short items are yet important as foreshadowing his extensive journalistic writings of the 1860s and beyond. Already, in 1847, he is invoking a controversy which was later to dominate much of his thinking: that between Slavophilism (emphasis on the special role of the Slav peoples headed by Russia) and Westernism (the tendency to play down Russian nationalism, while claiming that Russia should copy the cultural, social, economic and political practices of western Europe).

It is a definite Westernist stance that the Dostoyevsky of the 1847 articles adopts; but with certain reservations hinting at the change of course which would one day turn him into a thorough-paced Russian nationalist. That his journalism of 1847 reveals him as unmistakably 'very much dissatisfied with the existing arrangements of socio-political life in his fatherland' has been recently maintained.[1] As will be shown below, this claim is supported by evidence independent of the 1847 articles. However, those articles themselves, taken in isolation, can only be interpreted as reflecting such acute dissatisfaction by straining a little too hard to read 'between the lines'.

Difficult though it may be to read social and political disaffection into the 1847 articles, there can be no doubt at all that their author was beginning to experiment with the posture of opposition to the all-powerful autocratic state. It was at about Easter time in the same year that he first began to attend the Friday meetings of the circle informally headed by M. V. Butashevich-Petrashevsky, an official of the Ministry of Foreign Affairs who was also a political dissident.

At Petrashevsky's flat, over tea and through dense clouds of tobacco smoke, political and social problems were discussed by a varied and shifting group of young men—university graduates, guards officers, present or future writers, scholars and editors. Debating serf emancipation, legal reform, socialism, revolution and kindred topics, they made no secret of their activities. But they would have been wise to do so, for they were hazarding their liberty, and even their lives. Though they themselves seem to have been unaware or careless of the risks that they ran, the fact was that attempts to curtail the Tsar's authority, and to alter the prevailing system of government, were defined in the new Legal Code of 1845 as crimes carrying the death penalty. So too was the mere expression of such urges, and even the 'failure to denounce' to the authorities the expression of them by others.[2] In Russia of the late 1840s there might, accordingly, prove to be little distinction between a casual discussion group and a nest of traitors undermining the very foundations of the state.

Nor must the harsh mentality of the Emperor Nicholas I be forgotten. On the very day of his accession in 1825 he had quelled a revolutionary *coup d'état*, that of the Decembrists. Much later, when the Petrashevsky group had already begun to meet, the sovereign's fears of political upheaval were intensified by the anti-monarchical revolutions of 1848 in France and other European countries. To detect and crush some sort of Russian political conspiracy evidently seemed a salutary operation to the Tsar and his political police at this sensitive and dangerous juncture. And here was the Petrashevsky circle to provide, if nothing better, at least the semblance of a treasonable plot. This was all the more welcome to the authorities in that the country now possessed a pervasive political police, directed by the 'Third Section' of the Imperial Chancery and including a network of spies and informants. There was everything, in fact—except a sufficiency of political offenders—to justify so impressive an organization. In the end it was an undercover agent of the ordinary, less prestigious, non-political police who penetrated the Petrashevsky group. Secret preparations were made for the arrest of those implicated, including Dostoyevsky, and they were seized from April 1849 onwards, being held for up to eight months in solitary confinement. After repeated interrogations they were tried and sentenced in their absence by a special military court, though they were mostly civilians.

Dostoyevsky was more deeply involved in these supposedly subversive political activities than many of the other Petrashevskyites, especially as he helped to establish the so-called Durov circle. This took its name from S. F. Durov, a translator and minor poet. Its reasons for meeting independently of the parent group included an interest in art transcending the narrowly political and utilitarian preoccupations of the Petrashevskyites in general, together with a fear—well-founded, as it was to prove—that the larger group was more vulnerable to police surveillance. Though the activities of the Durov group still remain obscure, it seems to have been more conspiratorially inclined, in the practical sense, than the parent body—at least to the extent of acquiring and assembling a secret printing press. The installation was never used, and it was spirited away before the police could find it. As this reminds us, the eventual charges against Dostoyevsky were to include that of plotting to acquire and use a lithographic press. But this was, fortunately for him, a less serious offence in two respects than that which he had committed and which he managed to conceal from his judges: the actual (not merely projected) acquisition of a printing (not a mere lithographic) press. An illicit press was later to play a role in Dostoyevsky's novel of 1871–2, *Devils*, where he extensively exploits his experiences as a political dissident in 1847–9.

In any case the main charge against him was that of orally disseminating a notorious subversive document, Belinsky's open *Letter to Gogol* of 1846. In this magnificent tirade the great critic and revolutionary atheist denounces Gogol, who had recently horrified the left by revealing himself as a religious fanatic and political reactionary of the blackest hue. While attacking Gogol, and incidentally producing one of the most important documents in Russian cultural history, Belinsky also denounced the basic assumptions, political and religious, on which the Imperial Russian state rested. For this reason his *Letter to Gogol* was to be described in the trial records as a 'felonious missive . . . full of impudent expressions directed against Supreme Authority and the Orthodox Church.' Dostoyevsky's crime was not only to have read it aloud both in Durov's and in Petrashevsky's circle, but also to have failed to report the dissemination of it to the proper authorities.[3] It was for these offences that he heard himself sentenced to death on Semyonovsky Square on 22 December 1849, as described at the beginning of this book.

Dostoyevsky was one day to become the very opposite of a revolutionary. Like Gogol before him, he was to emerge as a militant conservative, a pillar of throne, church and state. And since he was a creature of extremes and opposites it is tempting to see him, in the late 1840s, as a dedicated revolutionary and atheist—that is, as the diametrical opposite, and therefore in a sense the identical twin, of what he was later to become. But the evidence of his contemporaries is conflicting. One member of the Durov group, Aleksandr Palm, cites him as directly advocating peasant revolt if emancipation could not be achieved by non-violent means. Another witness, Pyotr Semyonov, claims that Dostoyevsky was only a revolutionary to the extent of being subject to emotional brainstorms during which he was capable of sallying out into a public square waving a red flag.[4] Nor, well over a hundred years later, are authorities on Dostoyevsky in his own country agreed on the extent of his commitment to revolution. Leonid

Grossman denies in his biography (Moscow, 1965) that the young Dostoyevsky was a revolutionary at all. But the editors of the two-volume anthology of memoir material by Dostoyevsky's contemporaries, published in Moscow in the previous year, incline to a more militant interpretation.[5]

What of Dostoyevsky's own account of his political involvements of the period? Typically of their author, they are no model of consistency. Commenting a quarter of a century later (in *The Diary of a Writer* of 1873) on aspects of his early life, he offers several statements on his period as a political dissident. 'The most definite relate to Belinsky who, in 1846, 'immediately set himself . . . to convert me to his creed. . . . He was a passionate Socialist when I met him and he started me off with atheism straight away.' This assault was completely successful, according to Dostoyevsky: 'I passionately accepted his entire doctrine at the time.' As we remember from the previous chapter, Dostoyevsky quarrelled with Belinsky over literary matters shortly after becoming converted to his philosophy. But we have no evidence on the effect which this estrangement may have had on dislodging or modifying the socialist and atheist creed which the famous critic temporarily implanted in his protégé. Elsewhere in *The Diary of a Writer* Dostoyevsky invokes the notorious Sergey Nechayev, a violent revolutionary of the younger generation who had been only one year old at the time of the Petrashevsky affair. Active from the late 1860s, Nechayev was an out-and-out political terrorist. Yet Dostoyevsky can say of himself, again in his *Diary of a Writer*, that 'I could probably never have become a *Nechayev*. But a *Nechayevite*? Though I can't be sure, I possibly might have become one in my young days.'[6] 'Probably', 'can't be sure', 'possibly', 'might have': these equivocations do not necessarily conflict with the 'passionate acceptance' of Belinsky's creed earlier noted, for one may embrace a doctrine with oscillating degrees of fervour and without necessarily acting out its consequences.

Whatever Dostoyevsky's degree of commitment to Nechayevism, Belinskyism, revolution or reform may have been—and it may be supposed to have fluctuated considerably—there is at least some evidence that he suffered deeply on behalf of the exploited common people of his country. 'He always spoke out energetically against measures in any way liable to hamper the people, and was particularly outraged by the ill usage suffered by the lower classes and by young persons at school or college.'[7] His feelings were also outraged by an episode of which the sources tell us little, and which he may have witnessed personally. It was the savage collective flogging, in accordance with Russian military tradition ('running the gauntlet') of an unfortunate army sergeant-major of the Finland Regiment, who had in some way taken reprisals against an officer for brutality towards the victim's comrades. Alluding cryptically to this barbarous affair, I. M. Debu (a fellow-member of the Petrashevsky circle) recalls Dostoyevsky's vivid indignation when he spoke of it, and also invokes him as denouncing 'the treatment of the enslaved peasantry by their owners.'[8]

This is important testimony. But is it sufficiently impressive, and is there enough of it, to justify the following claim, made by a recent authority? 'Nobody could have the slightest doubt that Dostoyevsky was filled with a burning urgency to remedy the intolerable social injustice in whose midst every Russian was forced to live.'[9]

The strength of Dostoyevsky's compassion for individual victims of ill-treatment, particularly when he could see them with his own eyes, is not in dispute. But we must surely be more cautious in attributing to him a generalized social conscience about large sections of the community whose sufferings were not in the immediate foreground of his vision. Still more must we beware of attributing to the Dostoyevsky of the 1840s any sustained commitment to the cause of sweeping social and political reform. Nothing of the sort is expressed in the main body of evidence on his sentiments of the period—his letters, totalling over a hundred pages and covering the years 1837–49; and I regard the omission as significant despite the fact that even Dostoyevsky presumably exercised some caution as a correspondent, since he was writing in a country where the mail was liable to be monitored by the political police. As for the intense compassion for the underdog or 'little man' seemingly implied in some of the fiction discussed above, this lends itself, as has already been argued, to conflicting interpretations.

That the young Dostoyevsky may have had a social conscience I do not deny, but I find little evidence of it in the sources.

One marked feature of Dostoyevsky's dissident phase in the late 1840s was his tendency to submit to the moral domination of others. After Belinsky, his first tutor in revolution, had become estranged from him and had died in 1848, a more formidable supervisor took over: Nikolay Speshnev, an early student of Marx and perhaps the most committed revolutionary in the entire Petrashevsky group. The cool, self-contained, handsome, strong-willed Speshnev, a devastating ladies' man, was to be sentenced on the Semyonovsky Square with Dostoyevsky and was to provide the main model for Dostoyevsky's most tantalizing hero, the revolutionary dictator-in-potential Nikolay Stavrogin of *Devils*. Once described by Dostoyevsky as his 'Mephistopheles', Speshnev does indeed seem to have exercised some kind of demoniac control over Dostoyevsky from 1848 onwards. 'Now I am

Left Dostoyevsky's elder brother Mikhail
Mikhaylovich
Below Dostoyevsky in 1847
Bottom The Alekseyevsky Ravelin of
the Petropavlovsky Fortress, where
Dostoyevsky was held in solitary
confinement for eight months

Left The dissident M. V. Butashevich-Petrashevsky
Below Nikolay Speshnev, one of the main models for Stavrogin in *Devils*
Opposite A marching party of convicts passing a train of freight sledges

Below The 'execution' of the first three Petrashevskyites in Semyonovsky Square, St Petersburg, on 22 December 1849

Overleaf East-bound convicts at the boundary post between European Russia and Siberia

in his clutches', Dostoyevsky wrote of Speshnev at this time. One reason for this was that Speshnev had made Dostoyevsky the sizeable loan of five hundred silver roubles.[10]

Of all Dostoyevsky's comments on his period as a revolutionary conspirator the most revealing is surely the brief and casual aside that he let fall in a letter of 1856 from Siberia. Here he describes the whole business of his involvement in the Petrashevsky case as no more than an 'accident'. If so, it was indeed an unlucky accident, for it was to rob him of ten years of liberty after menacing his very existence.

In an album entry of 1860 Dostoyevsky has described his arrest, at his lodgings in the small hours of 23 April 1849, by a small party of combined criminal and political police headed by a polite sabre-clinking officer in the sky-blue uniform of a lieutenant-colonel of gendarmes.[11] After removal to the Petropavlovsky Fortress, a regular place of incarceration for the Empire's political offenders, the criminal was kept in the especially dreaded Alekseyevsky Ravelin in solitary confinement punctuated by interrogations.

Seeking to avoid implicating his colleagues or himself more than was inevitable, Dostoyevsky contrived, as we have noted, to conceal some of the most incriminating details in his record as a subversive. His extensive written submissions, composed at the behest of the Commission of Investigation, are a model of intelligent reserve. Giving away no more than he has to, he admits among other things to being a disciple of the French non-violent socialist thinker Fourier. But it must be added that socialist ideas, whether Fourierist or non-Fourierist, play no role whatever either in his pre-arrest fiction or in his correspondence of the period. Nor does the atheism to which Belinsky allegedly converted him. Nor yet, for that matter, do we find any foretaste of his later religious thinking as an apostle of Orthodox Christianity. For the absence of political and religious themes the strict literary censorship of the period would partly account—but only partly. However strongly Dostoyevsky may have been drawn to socialism and atheism in his twenties, he is not recorded as ever having taken the most tentative step towards erecting these doctrines into a system of rigid dogma comparable to that which he was later to evolve in order to express the extreme rightist views of his maturity.

We have observed Dostoyevsky utterly demoralized by his triumphs, and shall therefore be the less surprised to find, as we now do, that the disaster of his arrest and imprisonment had the effect of raising his spirits. This may be traced in four long letters to his brother written in the Petropavlovsky Fortress. Here, while complaining of piles and of troublesome 'nerves', he yet stresses again and again the enormous resilience which he feels welling inside him. Only now can he truly gauge, from first-hand experience, man's 'infinite toughness and vitality'. 'I had expected much worse, and now see that I possess an inexhaustible stock of vitality.' Far from abandoning his literary plans, he has not only been working out the ideas for two novels and three stories, but has even written one story, *The Little Hero*.[12] Composed in his dungeon, this is yet the most buoyant in tone of all his pre-Siberian works.

We have already watched Dostoyevsky taken from his cell on 22 December 1849 to face execution by firing squad as countermanded at the last moment by prior arrangement. Sentenced instead to four years' *katorga*, to be followed by compulsory military service in exile, and also stripped of his status as a member of the gentry, he was temporarily returned to the Petropavlovsky dungeons to await transportation to Siberia. There, immediately after surviving his great ordeal, he wrote the last and most revealing of his four letters to his brother Mikhail from the fortress, a letter in which the accent is more than ever on the prisoner's resilience. 'Never did such abundant and healthy reserves of spiritual life seethe inside me as now', he asserts. Though he also claims to be suffering from scrofula, his worst fear is that he may never take a pen in his hand again. That all literary activity will be excluded during the four years of his prison sentence he is well aware, and the thought fills him with despair. 'I'm lost if I can't write. Better fifteen years in prison with a pen in one's hands.'[13]

All these experiences confirm an aspect of Dostoyevsky on which we have not yet insisted—the impressive reserves of mental and physical toughness on which this neurotic, hypersensitive, habitually over-reacting, never-relaxing man could draw throughout his life. Many a 'normal', healthy, un-neurotic person has collapsed under a hundredth part of the burdens that Dostoyevsky heaped upon himself. Of this buoyancy further evidence is supplied by Aleksandr Milyukov, writer, critic and friend of the Dostoyevskys, who was present at the half-hour farewell meeting permitted to the brothers Fyodor and Mikhail by the Commandant of the Petropavlovsky Fortress. Though this occurred only a few hours after the ordeal of the 'mock execution' on Semyonovsky Square, 'Anyone witnessing the parting of the Dostoyevsky brothers would have noticed that the one who suffered the more was he who remained in freedom in St Petersburg, and not he who faced the journey to Siberia and the *katorga*. There were tears in the elder brother's eyes and his lips trembled, while Fyodor Mikhaylovich was calm and sought to comfort him.'[14]

5
Convict and Exile

Uncle's Dream; The Village of Stepanchikovo

On Christmas Eve 1849, at midnight, Dostoyevsky had fetters weighing ten pounds fixed to his ankles, and left the Petropavlovsky Fortress to begin his arduous two-thousand-mile sledge journey to the military prison at Omsk in western Siberia.

Of his emotions and sensations we are informed in a long letter written to his brother Mikhail in February 1854, shortly after the expiry of his sentence made it possible to resume a correspondence forbidden to him during his *katorga* term. It was, we learn, in an open sledge, part of a convoy of four, that he quitted the capital in the freezing small hours of Christmas morning. In the leading vehicle rode the imperial courier in command of the party, while the other three sledges each bore a single shackled prisoner escorted by an armed gendarme. All three deportees were casualties of the Petrashevsky affair. They were, besides Dostoyevsky himself, I. L. Yastrzhembsky, a lecturer in political economy; and S. F. Durov, to whose small 'circle' within the Petrashevsky group Dostoyevsky had belonged before his arrest.[1]

As their convoy swept unnoticed through the capital more fortunate St Petersburgers were deep in the seasonal festivities, and it was a poignant moment for Dostoyevsky when he sped past the brightly-lit home of his publisher Krayevsky. Here, as he knew, his brother Mikhail's wife and children were now celebrating Christmas.[2]

Shivering in the cold, undermined in health by eight months in the dungeons, shaken by the recent ordeal of the mock execution, Dostoyevsky yet felt a surge of high morale, his natural response to total disaster; he experienced 'great serenity', and 'the vitality and buoyancy that commonly precede any new step in life.' He enjoyed the fresh air after the stale stink of his cell, and was soon counting other small blessings. The courier in charge of the convoy was friendly, and he obtained closed sledges in place of the open vehicles in which the journey had begun. This afforded some protection against the cold; it was bitter even by the standards of a Russian winter, and sank to forty degrees of frost in Perm Province.[3]

One night the travellers approached, in a raging blizzard, the point of the Ural mountain range dividing Russia-in-Europe from Russia-in-Asia. As they did so their sledges got stuck in the snow and had to be hauled out, while Dostoyevsky could not hold back his tears. When, if ever, would he traverse this sinister landmark from the opposite direction? Even when freed from the unspecified term of military service that was to follow four years' *katorga*, he would depend on the Emperor's clemency for release from the wilds beyond the Urals.

On 11 January 1850, after eighteen days on the road, Dostoyevsky's party reached Tobolsk in western Siberia. Here the three 'Petrashev-skyites' were held for six days in the local staging prison from which they and other members of their group were to be distributed among scattered Siberian places of confinement. Dostoyevsky comforted his demoralized companions, handing round cigars that he had secreted in his belongings. Further solace was provided by veteran exiles from European Russia, the wives of participants in the Decembrist con-spiracy of 1825. These heroic women had long ago voluntarily followed their husbands to Siberia. And such were the occasional relaxations permitted by the penal system that they were now able to offer Dos-toyevsky and his companions words of consolation at a meal in the quarters of the Tobolsk prison governor. They also gave each prisoner a copy of the Gospels with a ten-rouble note concealed in the cover. Dostoyevsky always treasured this, the only book permitted to a convict. He was to keep it on his desk in later life, and consulted it as he lay dying. The episode acquires symbolic significance when we remember that his Christian faith, only a minor preoccupation at the time when he received the book, was to become an obsession in his last years.

Though Dostoyevsky might feel encouraged by the kindness of the Decembrist wives, he could be under no illusions about his present discomfort and menacing future. Surveying Tobolsk gaol, he could see about three hundred men, women and children huddled together. Heads were being half-shaved, in accordance with regulations. Fetters, such as he himself already wore, were being hammered on to others' ankles, and convicts were being chained or 'threaded' on a long iron rod as a means of keeping them in line.[4] Here was a foretaste of what awaited him at Omsk, a town situated on the River Irtysh some three hundred miles to the south-east.

Omsk was the military and administrative capital of western Siberia, and as such the seat of a Russian Governor-General; but it was a remote and barely civilized backwater to any Muscovite or St Peters-burger. Founded in the early eighteenth century as a stockaded outpost, it had kept some of its original character, and the surrounding steppes were still the dwelling-place of sparse, semi-nomad Asian peoples. In some ways, for all its stone-built administrative buildings, Omsk resembled a log-cabin town in the American West.

Reaching Omsk prison after a three-day sledge journey from Tobolsk, Dostoyevsky found himself surrounded by enemies of different calibre from the sardonic, teasing Turgenev and the exploiting Krayevsky. No longer the victim of subtle innuendoes and financial chicanery, he was jostled by condemned murderers who seemed capable of bashing out his brains at the prompting of psychopathic impulse. No less menacing was the prison staff. Disciplinary punish-ments included floggings so severe that they sometimes proved fatal. With this prospect Dostoyevsky was threatened immediately on arrival by the purple-faced, bloodshot-eyed Major Krivtsov, the assistant commandant. 'This thorough-going bastard, this primitive, niggling, drunken mediocrity' (Dostoyevsky's own words) roughly abused his new intellectual prisoner, called him an imbecile, and threatened to have him beaten for his first infringement of the rules. Fortunately this revolting bully, known as 'Old Eight-Eyes', was himself to be court-martialled and cashiered half-way through Dostoyevsky's term of imprisonment.[5]

As fully-fledged convicts, Dostoyevsky and Durov—still his com-panion in misfortune—had their heads half-shaved, and were equipped with regulation dress. It consisted of a jerkin, half-black and half-grey with a yellow lozenge on the back; a flat, pancake-shaped cap; a sheep-skin coat. Like the other convicts, they were to wear their new, lighter ankle-fetters, which were now fitted, throughout the term of their sentences—when waking and sleeping, when working and resting, when lying in the prison sick-bay, when taking part in the occasional amateur theatricals, and even when undergoing the periodical collective steam-baths.

Dostoyevsky's new dwelling was a military prison of modest size, housing about a hundred and sixty convicts. The gaol was part of an original fortress, which had been built, complete with moat and rampart, in the early eighteenth century: it consisted of a rough hexagon some two hundred yards long at its widest part, and sur-rounded by a formidable fence of thick-set pointed palings about fifteen feet high. Beside its guard-house and offices it contained the crude, disintegrating log huts in which the prisoners lived, and which have been vividly described by their most distinguished inmate. 'Picture an old, decrepit, obsolete, wooden structure . . . intolerably stuffy in summer, unbearably cold in winter. All floors rotten and several inches deep in mud on which you can slip and fall. Small windows so frosted that you can barely read all day. Several inches of ice on windows. Drips from ceiling, leaks all over the place. We're jammed like herrings in a barrel. Six logs in stove, but no heat. Ice barely thaws in room. Intolerable fumes. So it goes on all winter.'[6]

What with men washing clothes and splashing water there was no room to turn, Dostoyevsky complained. They all 'stank like swine', they slept on bare boards with a single pillow and no blankets, huddled inside their short sheepskin coats. 'You shiver all night long. Fleas, lice, cockroaches by the bushel.'[7] Shivering in winter or sweating in the surprisingly hot Siberian summer, the convicts might well feel that this was a hell on earth. The shouts, the curses, the eternally clanking chains combined to confirm that impression. These filthy, swearing, lice-ridden, fetter-jangling, diseased, illiterate wrecks of humanity, some hopelessly brutalized, others astonishingly kind, and all locked in at night with a large bucket, their communal lavatory: they were as far removed as possible from the genteel sophisticates of St Petersburg salons whose mockery, real or imagined, had so tormented the young author. But all were human beings, and Dostoyevsky had long set himself to probe humanity in its full range from the sublime to the lowly, oppressed, degraded and vicious.

In the mornings the convicts were marched out to work under armed guard. Dostoyevsky told his brother that the work was 'heavy, but not always of course, and I was sometimes at the end of my tether, in foul weather, in the damp and slush, or in the intolerable winter cold. I once spent four hours on an emergency job when the mercury had frozen and there must have been forty degrees of frost.' On another occasion he and his mates dismantled a dilapidated barge, knee deep in the River Irtysh. There was also relatively light labour: painting, plastering, shovelling snow, firing bricks.

From the rigours of manual toil the prison sick-bay provided occasional relief. Dostoyevsky suffered from stomach trouble as well as from attacks later to be diagnosed as epileptic, but was also sometimes permitted to rest in the sick-bay when he was well, through the connivance of the medical officer. Here he took the opportunity to read Vvedensky's translation of Dickens's *David Copperfield* and *Pickwick Papers*, which chanced to be available and was to have some influence on his writings. He also made brief jottings on prison conditions. Known as his 'Siberian Notebook', they have survived and were to become the nucleus for *Memoirs from the House of the Dead*, describing Omsk prison and published a decade after his ordeal.[8]

The worst of his sufferings was lack of solitude. 'I was never alone for one hour. To be on your own is as normal a requirement as eating and drinking, otherwise the enforced communism [*sic*] will make you a misanthrope. Human company becomes a poison and infection, and it was from this intolerable martyrdom that I most suffered during the four years.'[9] Yet this same enforced company also fascinated Dostoyevsky by displaying the common people's traditional flair for evading official regulations. Though money was officially forbidden it was in common use, and the prisoners had their own usurers, bankers and financiers. Thriving gambling schools and a lively traffic in smuggled liquor are other features recorded by Dostoyevsky, who claimed that there was no surer way for a convict to earn general esteem than to parade the gaol helplessly inebriated. Nor were sexual amenities lacking, for prostitutes were occasionally smuggled in and it was even possible for an enterprising convict to bribe the warders, to slip through the stockade, and to sample (still fettered?) the stews of Omsk.

Other breaks in routine included the collective saunas into which Dostoyevsky and his fellows were periodically herded. It required much skill to remove one's underclothes through the fetters before blundering into the blinding steam of a bath-house about twelve yards square where up to a hundred convicts floundered in the mud, jostling, yelling, jangling their chains and fetters, sluicing themselves from pails and lashing themselves with the traditional birch switches. 'Fifty switches rose and fell in unison on the shelf as all lashed themselves till they felt drunk. The steam came faster and thicker. This was more than heat, it was a fiery furnace, with everyone yelling and cackling while a hundred chains dragged clanking on the floor.'[10] The description is Dostoyevsky's own, and comes from *Memoirs from the House of the Dead*, where he evokes the steam-bath inferno in a scene that has been acclaimed by Turgenev as 'Dantesque'.

As for the threatened floggings, Dostoyevsky probably escaped them; on one occasion through the intervention of the humane prison commandant after the prisoner had been detected, by the atrocious Major Krivtsov, as absenting himself from work when ill. In early 1852 the same kindly commandant also applied for Durov and Dostoyevsky to be exempted from fetters, and to be assigned to a less arduous category of imprisonment in recognition of two years' good conduct. But this application was turned down by the Emperor Nicholas, who would not relax the explicit orders that he had personally given at the outset—for the 'Petrashevskyites' to be treated exactly like the common criminals with whom they were imprisoned. According to another report, which I incline to doubt, Dostoyevsky did once suffer the appalling ordeal of flogging—to the horror of friends who realized what a shattering effect this must have 'on one with his

nervous temperament and self-importance.' They could soon observe
the catastrophic result: the victim's first epileptic fit which this witness
(his old St Petersburg flat-mate, now practising in Siberia, Dr Alexander
Riesenkampf) places in 1851.[11] However, as indicated above, there is
no general agreement about the precise date on which Dostoyevsky
first became afflicted with epilepsy, and Riesenkampf's testimony
contradicts that of others. The most authoritative report was to be
made on 16 December 1857 by Dostoyevsky's battalion medical officer
at Semipalatinsk, who is presumably quoting his patient's own account.
'His first epileptic attack occurred in 1850, the symptoms being:
shrieking, loss of consciousness, convulsions of the extremities and
face, foaming at the mouth, hoarse breathing and a weak, rapid . . .
pulse rate. The attack lasted fifteen minutes, being followed by general
weakness and the recovery of consciousness. In 1853 it was repeated,
and has since occurred at the end of each month.'[12]

Before his imprisonment Dostoyevsky had encountered the *narod*
(common people) chiefly as serfs or servants—coachmen, maids, wet-
nurses, porters, waiters and the like. Himself one of the élite, for all
his complaints of poverty and ill usage, he had so far stood on the other
side of the vast and seemingly unbridgeable rift separating Russia's
educated, privileged minority from the mass of her unwashed peasant
illiterates. But now, as one more shackled convict, he had become as
intimately merged with the *narod* as an ex-gentleman could. Not that the
rank and file regarded him as their own. But at least he could claim to
'know the *narod* as perhaps few others know it';[13] by 'others' he of
course meant other Russian gentlemen. We must briefly qualify this
assertion. First, it was not only the Russian 'people' but a cross-section
of the multi-racial Russian Empire, including Tatars and sundry
Caucasian tribesmen, that Dostoyevsky knew so intimately at Omsk;
there were also a few Polish intellectuals. Secondly, his new contacts
were not a typical cross-section of any social group, in that all had been
sentenced as common or political criminals.

Comments on the *narod*, volunteered by Dostoyevsky immediately
after his prison term, show great ambivalence. There are eulogies
foreshadowing the idealization of the 'people' that he was to embrace
in middle age. 'Deep, powerful, beautiful characters' were to be
found among them, he reported to his brother Mikhail. 'How ex-
hilarating to discover the gold beneath the crude husk. . . . What a
marvellous *narod*.' He had met so many folksy types, heard so many
stories of tramps and highwaymen, learnt so much of the common
people's tribulations that, from an author's point of view, his time in
gaol had not been wasted. Yet he also voices a violently hostile attitude
elsewhere in the same letter, speaking of the common people as rough,

Below Tobolsk Prison
Bottom 'Christmas in Omsk Prison': oil
painting by K. Pomerantsev, 1862.
Dostoyevsky is depicted in the centre

Above An illustration (c. 1890) to *Memoirs from the House of the Dead*
Right A Siberian prison executioner

Below The guard-house at Omsk Fortress
Bottom A street in Semipalatinsk

Below Dostoyevsky's first wife Mariya
Dmitriyevna
Right Dostoyevsky in ensign's uniform,
Semipalatinsk, 1858
Bottom House in which Dostoyevsky
lived at Semipalatinsk

irritable, embittered. The *narod*'s attitude towards former members of the gentry such as himself was, said he, utter hatred and delight in their misfortunes. 'They'd have eaten us alive if they could.' He calls his fellow-convicts 'a hundred and fifty enemies never tired of persecuting me', and he even refers to the 'moral superiority' of the few ex-gentlemen, including himself and Durov, in the gaol. 'They [the *narod*] always recognized us as their superiors.' This remark contrasts violently with his later acclamation of the Russian peasant masses as morally superior to the privileged classes. It also helps to explain how a Polish prisoner, S. Tokarzewski (one of the few witnesses to Dostoyevsky's life in gaol other than himself), could accuse him of snobbishness and rabid nationalism. Dostoyevsky charges his Polish fellow-convicts with these same vices in *Memoirs from the House of the Dead*, but it does not follow from this apparent conflict of evidence that either side was wrong in levelling its accusations.[14]

By another memoirist, P. K. Martyanov, Dostoyevsky's attitude in gaol has been described as glum, taciturn, unsmiling and reserved. He suspected even those who wanted to help him; he was like a trapped wolf. But though he was unpopular with his fellows, they at least respected the moral authority that he ascribed to himself. More surprising, perhaps, is his physical robustness. In his prison dossier his physique is described as 'powerful'; and Martyanov too speaks of his rugged look. Dostoyevsky also made an alert and soldierly impression, by contrast with his cadet days. These comments show that he was no wilting, ailing, typical 'intellectual', and accord with the toughness of moral fibre that helped to bring his highly strung nature into balance.[15]

When his four years' *katorga* were over, he could congratulate himself on having survived an atrocious ordeal. He was primed with new knowledge, unique among major contemporary Russian authors, of Russia's lower depths. But his abiding impression was of sheer horror. 'Shut in my coffin, buried alive for four years'—thus he summed up the experience to his brother Andrey shortly after his release.[16]

March 1854 saw Dostoyevsky freed from gaol and despatched under escort to serve as a private soldier in the Seventh Siberian Battalion of the Line, stationed at Semipalatinsk.

The town lies about five hundred miles south-east of Omsk, upstream on the River Irtysh. Like Omsk, it had originally been founded as an early eighteenth-century Russian outpost, and it was now a minor administrative centre with about five thousand inhabitants. But despite its 'Russian quarter', its law courts, its government offices and the garrison in which Dostoyevsky served, the place was markedly more provincial than Omsk; it was also more Asian in character, and now comes within the boundaries of Kazakhstan. Set in sand and thistles, dotted with minarets, with a Russian cantonment and a Muslim shanty town, Dostoyevsky's new abode was the focus for a thriving camel-borne freight trade, but for little else.

Dostoyevsky was now exhausted by four years' *katorga*, and conditions in the local barracks did little to relieve his moments of despair. 'In my soldier's cloak I'm as much a convict as ever . . . it will soon be five years since I . . . spent one hour on my own.'[17] Still, minor reliefs were at hand. One was restoration of contact with the family from which he had long been cut off. Correspondence with the homeland was vital to him, especially letters from his brother Mikhail, who sent books and information on literary developments, besides lending money and soliciting loans on Fyodor's behalf. But the turn-round for letters was at least two months, and those sent through the regular mail were liable to interception by the authorities because they concerned someone under sentence for a political offence.

Delighted to resume old contacts by letter, but also needing a local kindred spirit, Dostoyevsky was fortunate to meet a twenty-one-year-old lawyer, Baron Aleksandr Vrangel, who arrived in Semipalatinsk to become District Public Prosecutor in November 1854. By now Private Dostoyevsky had permission to live out of barracks, and was happy to rent a poorly lit, cockroach-infested room in a wretched hut among the sand and thistles. Thus Vrangel describes it in his memoirs, adding that the tenant was a grim, pale-faced, freckled soldier wearing the usual tunic with a high red collar and red epaulettes, and a grey military cloak. At first extremely reserved, as was his custom with strangers, Dostoyevsky soon accepted Vrangel as a trusted intimate. By now the reluctant infantryman, not overburdened with military duties, had resumed reading and writing, despite the gloom of lodgings where he was to be found smoking his long pipe, talking to himself, declaiming Pushkin and singing snatches of opera.[18]

Vrangel did much to entertain the exile, renting a summer cottage and introducing him to gardening, angling and swimming in the River Irtysh. But Dostoyevsky turned out indifferent to natural scenery, being exclusively obsessed with human beings and their behaviour. Here too Vrangel helped, by introducing him to the cream of Semipalatinsk society. He was now meeting his own commanding officer, Lieutenant-Colonel Belikhov, on social occasions, together with the local judge, the district Governor and other worthies. These were the cultural élite of a Central Asian dump largely given over, Vrangel complains, to trade, card-playing, drunkenness and gossip. By no means the proverbial 'one-horse town', Semipalatinsk was literally a one-piano town, and there were only a dozen individuals who subscribed to papers or periodicals.[19]

Vrangel unfortunately left Semipalatinsk at the end of 1855, but continued to encourage and assist Dostoyevsky's struggle for rehabilitation by interceding for him in St Petersburg. Meanwhile the exile was not permitted to publish anything that he might write, and his chief concern was to secure the removal of that ban. His method was to bombard St Petersburg with jingoistic verses destined for the ear of the Emperor himself, and so effusive in their expressions of devotion to Russia and its ruling house that they might seem to clamour for publication. The manœuvre failed, but at least helped Dostoyevsky to achieve promotion in the army: to corporal in 1855, and to ensign (the lowest commissioned rank) in the following year. Even these reliefs would probably not have been permitted but for the providential death of the tyrannical Nicholas I in February 1855; this helped to console the country for imminent defeat in the Crimean War, an event that inspired Dostoyevsky's first patriotic ode. Nicholas's successor Alexander II still withheld permission to publish, ordering that the new ensign should be put under secret surveillance to establish whether he had become sufficiently 'trustworthy' to appear in print.[20] Still, it was something that the Tsar had sanctioned the ex-convict's promotions within the army—a faint indication, even to remote and sleepy Semipalatinsk, of the hopes and relaxations that characterized the early years of the new reign more markedly in European Russia and especially in St Petersburg and Moscow.

Even as Dostoyevsky yearned to escape from army service and Siberian exile, he was taking on the new burden of association with a woman, Mariya Dmitriyevna Isayeva, who might have been designed to aggravate his troubles. She was the twenty-six-year-old wife of an impoverished, ailing, drunken, affable, out-of-work former schoolteacher, Aleksandr Isayev. They had a nine-year-old son, Pavel, known as Pasha. By the standards of Semipalatinsk Mariya Dmitriyevna was a highly educated woman. Vrangel calls her a beautiful blonde of medium height, kind, vivacious, impressionable, passionate and highly-strung. On Dostoyevsky, who was now in his early thirties, and who had never been seriously in love, she made a devastating impression.[21] But though he had a strong sexual appetite, at least in later life, he appears to have been captivated less by her feminine charms, physical or spiritual, than by her pathetic predicament as a young mother tied to an ailing, penniless drunkard whom she did not love and who could not support her; besides, she was herself in poor health, and later turned out to have contracted tuberculosis. 'Seductive to him as an object for pity, she was doubly so through her perverse temperament. This might have repelled another man, but he was overjoyed to find so accomplished a sufferer and purveyor of suffering.'

Mariya was 'not the least in love' with Dostoyevsky, says Vrangel, but she welcomed his advances. Whether they became lovers in Semipalatinsk we do not know. In any case May 1855 saw the Isayevs leave for Kuznetsk, yet another Siberian log-cabin town about four hundred miles to the north-east, where Mariya's husband had been offered a post in the excise service. Before they went Dostoyevsky was able to take farewell of his beloved in private after Vrangel had obligingly incapacitated her husband with champagne. When she was gone Dostoyevsky could not eat or drink, but miserably chain-smoked his pipe, comparing the blow of parting with that of his arrest in 1849.[22]

In August Mariya wrote from Kuznetsk to tell Dostoyevsky that her husband had died, leaving her and their small son destitute. He was horrified, but was prevented by his army duties and his own poverty from rushing to her side, and could only send her money borrowed from Vrangel. He had soon decided to make the helpless widow his wife, and began wooing her with passionate love letters. But though Mariya's position indeed was desperate, it was somewhat less so than Dostoyevsky supposed, since she received money from her father, an official in the town of Astrakhan. In any case she was in no hurry to yield to her distant suitor. While he pined in Semipalatinsk, she wilfully increased his torments by writing that a rich elderly man wanted to marry her. Would Dostoyevsky advise her to accept this advantageous proposal? In the end she turned out to have invented her elderly suitor in order to make him jealous.

When Dostoyevsky at last contrived to meet Mariya, at Kuznetsk in June 1856, she told him that she was now in love with someone else, a poor schoolteacher younger than herself called Vergunov. This new association was not imaginary, for Vergunov indeed did exist. Dostoyevsky met him, but showed no aggressiveness towards his successful rival, seeking rather to further the other's suit—another self-tormenting device. He tried, for example, to help the younger man by putting a better-paid post in his way. But Vergunov remained an even worse marriage prospect than Dostoyevsky himself, whose future began to look brighter when he was promoted to ensign in October 1856.

Eventually preferring the officer to the schoolteacher, Mariya married Dostoyevsky at Kuznetsk on 6 February 1857, and they at once left for Semipalatinsk. But while staying in transit with friends in the near-by town of Barnaul they suffered an experience of ill omen for their domestic future. A severe fit prostrated the bridegroom for four days; and it was only now that his seizures, previously dismissed by doctors as merely 'nervous', were at last authoritatively diagnosed as epileptic. As he wrote to his brother shortly afterwards, 'had I known that I had genuine epilepsy, I would never have married.' Nor presumably would Mariya, who had had even less cause to suspect that he suffered from so distressing an affliction.[23]

After the horrors of their honeymoon Fyodor and Mariya settled down to a humdrum life in a small flat in Semipalatinsk, Dostoyevsky's newly acquired stepson Pasha being dispatched to the Siberian Cadet Corps in Omsk. Far from living up to the husband's fervent expectations, the marriage soon became a matter of obligation, responsibility and domestic irritation. Within a few years he and Mariya were partially estranged, but never formally separated. He never ceased to provide for her, or to care for her as she progressively succumbed to tuberculosis, but his romantic zeal seems to have lapsed almost with the wedding ceremony. The eulogies to Mariya's beauty and intelligence, with which his previous letters had been saturated, significantly cease at the moment when he becomes a husband.

Mariya seems never to have realized that the man whom she had married, partly as a support to herself and her son, possessed special gifts, and greatly needed the loving help that a different wife might have provided. So much for the sensitivity of the most cultivated woman in Semipalatinsk! As for the obsessive urge that originally drove Dostoyevsky into her arms, it is tempting to link this with the lust for anguish testified by other episodes in his life and lavishly illustrated in his fiction. 'My relations with Mariya have obsessed me for the last *two years*', he wrote to Vrangel shortly before his marriage, adding a significant comment: 'At least I've *lived*; I may have suffered, but I have lived.'[24] Intense feeling, albeit painful, still retained for Dostoyevsky a lure such as no emotion, however pleasurable, could ever hold if experienced in moderation.

We now turn to Dostoyevsky's literary activities after his release from gaol. His first concern was to catch up with his reading, as may be seen from letters of 1854 in which he calls books 'my life, my food, my future', clamouring for numerous works to be sent from St Petersburg. He demands 'historians, economists, *Otechestvennyye zapiski*, the Church Fathers, church history. . . . Send the Koran, Kant's *Critique of Pure Reason* . . . Hegel, especially the *History of Philosophy*—my whole future's bound up with it.' He also calls for Herodotus, Thucydides, Tacitus, Pliny and Plutarch.[25] Most of all he was interested in his

Russian contemporaries, and though he may have neglected Hegel, he eagerly read new works by Turgenev, Ostrovsky, Pisemsky, Aksakov and Tolstoy.

Works In Army

Though Dostoyevsky continued jotting down his prison memoirs and was toying with the idea of a 'comic novel', his attitude to creative writing remained desultory for a while. But then, in August 1857, for the first time in eight years, a work of his achieved publication. It was the half-forgotten short story *The Little Hero*, originally written in the Petropavlovsky Fortress in 1849, and it came out under a pseudonym in *Otechestvennyye zapiski*. This was only a minor event in itself, but it was a sign that the long embargo on publication had at last been lifted, and by early 1859 he was ready with two new novels. The shorter, *Uncle's Dream*, appeared in the journal *Russkoye slovo* ('The Russian Word') in March of that year, and the longer, *The Village of Stepan-chikovo* in *Otechestvennyye zapiski* for November and December. The placing of these publications involved complex financial negotiations, and it was fortunate that Mikhail Dostoyevsky could act as Fyodor's literary agent in St Petersburg.

Uncontroversial light hearted

Both novels fall outside the main stream of Dostoyevsky's work, being deliberately designed for light entertainment. As a former political prisoner still exiled to Siberia, he wanted to re-establish his name in print without raising sensitive issues that might trouble the censor. 'It was my first work after *katorga*', he wrote of *Uncle's Dream* in 1873, and it had been 'written with the sole purpose of restarting my literary career and in terrible fear of the censorship's attitude to . . . an exile, which is why I involuntarily wrote something blissfully innocent.' He also said that *Uncle's Dream* was 'no good'.[26]

Few will dissent from the author's own verdict on this farcical study of attempts to trap a rich, senile, imbecile prince into marriage. Yet *Uncle's Dream* does not lack all merit. The imaginary town, Mordasov ('Mugsville'), where the action is set, is based on Semi-palatinsk, and Dostoyevsky offers an amusing satire, somewhat in Gogol's manner, on that provincial backwater. The novel has pace and verve, also testifying to the author's continuing obsession with *skandal* scenes.

These last features also distinguish the second, longer Siberian novel. But *The Village of Stepanchikovo* is a more impressive achievement, as the author knew. In May 1859 he informed his brother that, despite its 'enormous defects', the novel had 'great merits, and is my *best work*.' All his hopes for the future were bound up with it. 'I have put my soul, my flesh, my blood into it. . . . It contains two colossal and typical characters that I've spent five years *conceiving* and *recording* . . . characters wholly Russian.'[27]

86

The two colossal and typical characters are Colonel Rostanev, a country landowner of herculean stature with 'the spirit of a mouse', and the sanctimonious Foma Fomich Opiskin, attached to the Colonel's household as one of those 'hangers-on' so prominent in the annals of nineteenth-century Russian estates. Here it is the parasite who dominates the nominal master of the house. Foma Fomich bullies the gentle giant, patronizing, abusing and mocking him so viciously that unbearable tension is established. Will the worm turn? This eventually happens when Foma Fomich overreaches himself by insulting the innocent governess whom the Colonel wishes to marry. At last the colossus arises enraged, seizes his tormentor by the shoulders and hurls him through some french windows as a climax to the finest of Dostoyevsky's many *skandal* scenes to date.

The success of this scene, the skill with which it is prepared, the clash of memorable characters, the novel's dynamic thrust—such features justify Dostoyevsky's own view that here was his best work to date. The novel also further explores major themes of his first two decades as a writer, those of status-seeking and humiliation. *The Village of Stepanchikovo* also has Dostoyevsky mocking a former idol. Having long creatively imitated Gogol, he now uses Foma Fomich's sententious harangues to parody the language of Gogol's widely disliked homiletic work *Select Passages from a Correspondence with Friends*. By deriding his former master Dostoyevsky was serving notice that he intended to be an innovator. He was now well embarked on his second apprenticeship to the self-taught craft of creative writing, and it is a sign of his success that he could at last formally dissociate himself from the main inspirer of his early work.

Had Dostoyevsky's outlook been dramatically transformed by Siberian imprisonment and exile? To present him as a fanatical young revolutionary atheist of the 1840s who, purged in the crucible of suffering, suddenly emerged in the 1850s as his very opposite, a passionate Christian and patriot—this temptingly sensational picture would be most misleading. As we have seen, his general outlook of the late 1840s did indeed embrace a marked degree of sympathy with the political left, but it also tended to be unstable and elusive, while its details are in any case largely a matter for dispute and conjecture. That he held his 'views', whatever they were, passionately is not to be doubted, for he was incapable of entertaining any idea other than passionately. But (as is noted above) the views remained unadvertised at the time by their author and have later been conflictingly recorded by himself and others; they thus stand in sharp contrast with the system of dogma that he was to evolve in his maturer years, a system trumpeted to the world again and again by Dostoyevsky himself. The transformation, for a transformation indeed was eventually accomplished, involved a complex process spread over a quarter of a century. In Siberia, Dostoyevsky certainly did cease to be a fiery young radical in so far as he ever had been such a thing. But he was not yet the mature Dostoyevsky—the apostle of the 'Russian Christ', the militant Slavophile, the passionate believer in the innate virtues of the Russian people.

Not yet a folk-fancier, he had even bragged of his 'moral superiority' to the common people, as is also noted above, but was already subject to contrary tugs in which the later motifs of folk-worship can already be discerned. As for patriotism, there are suggestions in his letters that the emotions behind his false-sounding loyalist odes may have been partly genuine. On 18 January 1856 he claims always to have 'been a true Russian. ... I share the idea that Russia is destined to carry Europe and her destiny to its conclusion.'[28] However, he was still far from the extreme nationalist sentiments of his maturity, as is testified in a letter of October 1870 referring to his Siberian period. 'I didn't consider myself illogical in feeling Russian.' Such is the lukewarm formula in which the older man sums up his patriotic sentiments of the 1850s, going on to explain that he was then 'still heavily polluted by mangy Russian liberalism as propagated by the dung-beetle Belinsky and shits of that ilk.'[29]

So much for love of country. What of the fanatical belief in Russian Orthodox Christianity that was to distinguish Dostoyevsky in later life? There are few indications of it in his Siberian period. How uncertain his religious faith was may be judged from a much-quoted letter of February 1854 to Madame N. D. Fonvizina, one of the Decembrist wives who had befriended him on his first arrival in Siberia. 'I'm a child of the age, a child of unbelief and doubt to this day, and even, I'm certain, till the day I die. What appalling sufferings it has cost me, and still does cost me—the craving to believe.' But he adds that 'the greater the arguments against that craving, the mightier does it become.' He also adds, in yet more sibylline style, that 'if anyone should prove to me that Christ was outside the Truth, and if it *really* was the case that the Truth was outside Christ, then I'd rather remain with Christ than with the Truth.'[30]

These are not the words of a believer, nor yet of an unbeliever, but reflect conflicting urges such as always tended to be present in Dostoyevsky's mind when questions of faith were concerned. But the main point about his beliefs in the Siberian period is that, hesitant or not, they were not yet to him the matter of desperate concern that they were later to become.

6

Memoirist and Journalist

Insulted and Injured; Memoirs from the House of the Dead;
Memoirs from Underground

March 1859 marks two further steps in Dostoyevsky's rehabilitation. First, he was permitted to resign from the army for health reasons, with the rank of second lieutenant. And secondly he received permission to reside in European Russia. But he was expressly forbidden to live in either Moscow or St Petersburg, and so he went to Tver, a provincial city conveniently situated on the newly-built railway line connecting the two metropolises. He arrived in mid-August, and was visited shortly afterwards by his brother Mikhail, now more active than ever as his literary agent. But Dostoyevsky soon found Tver 'a thousand times viler' than Semipalatinsk,[1] and urgently sought permission to move to St Petersburg. This, after approaching the Emperor through the friendly Governor of Tver Province and other exalted intermediaries, he obtained in December 1859. Towards the end of the month he at last returned to the city that he had left in fetters ten years earlier.

Restored to the capital, where he was to occupy a succession of rented apartments during the next seven years, Dostoyevsky had reconstituted conditions similar to those of his previous residence. But he had also brought new disadvantages with him. As a former political prisoner he remained under secret surveillance by the security police at the Emperor's express order; he was established as a chronic sufferer from epilepsy, attacks of which occurred at unpredictable intervals, leaving him exhausted and depressed for days on end; he was burdened by an ailing, irritable wife. On the credit side was the vitality with which he assaulted metropolitan life anew.

This was not the St Petersburg that he remembered from the 1840s. Five years had passed since the death of the despotic Nicholas I— years of relaxation suggesting that Russia had embarked on a new and glorious epoch. Political prisoners, including the surviving Decembrists and Dostoyevsky himself, had been restored from Siberian exile; foreign travel had been made easier; educational restrictions had been relaxed. But this was nothing beside the prospects for political and social reform. In 1856 the new Tsar Alexander II had announced his intention of emancipating the serfs, and was to implement this in 1861. Other reforms were also pending: of the judicial system, of local government, of the army. Nowhere was the new spirit more evident than in Dostoyevsky's own profession. Literature, which had prospered even under the severe restrictions of the previous reign, was flourishing more vigorously than ever under the easier censorship policy of the new era. Literary journals enjoyed increased vogue now that they could engage more openly in political polemics, though still hampered by many residual taboos and limitations. Dostoyevsky, who had long wished to be a literary entrepreneur, took advantage of these conditions to found a new literary monthly, *Vremya* ('Time'). After all the necessary permissions had been obtained it began publication in January 1861, the editor and financial manager being his brother Mikhail. Fyodor was ineligible for the post owing to his political past, but was all along a fully engaged co-editor in all but name. He was also the journal's foremost contributor.

Before considering *Vremya* and its role as a vehicle for his philosophical journalism, we shall examine his two major works of belles-lettres to be serialized in the review. They are the novel *Insulted and Injured*, with which *Vremya* made its début in January 1861, and which was concluded in July of that year; and the non-fictional *Memoirs from the House of the Dead*, which appeared between April 1861 and December 1862, after another periodical had abortively published some early chapters in 1860. Both works are of cardinal importance in his evolution. They are saturated with material from the previous fifteen years of his life, drawing heavily on his Siberian experiences and quarrying his adventures as a young writer in St Petersburg of the 1840s.

When planning *Insulted and Injured* Dostoyevsky reverted to the formula that had gained him most fame in the past: he had decided that his new novel was to be 'like *Poor Folk*', which meant that it would present an array of pathetic characters in a St Petersburg setting.[2] Work began in early 1860 and was completed on 9 July 1861, the novel being written under intense pressure to meet the needs of serialization. It is typical of his fiction in that early sections appeared long before the rest of it had been written. As he explained at the time, 'I've often had the beginning of a chapter . . . already at the printers and being set while the end was still lodged in my head, but must be written *without fail* by the morrow.'[3]

Insulted and Injured is twice as long as *The Village of Stepanchikovo*, his previous most extensive work. The new work is also the most autobiographical of all his novels, for the hero and narrator Ivan Petrovich comes closer to a deliberate self-portrait of the author than any other character in his fiction. Ivan Petrovich depicts himself as a young author whose first novel had enjoyed a great success in St Petersburg. Not named, but from its description resembling *Poor Folk*, it had delighted 'the critic B' and caused friction with the literary 'entrepreneur K'; by which initials Belinsky and Krayevsky are unmistakably designated. Then again, Ivan Petrovich's amatory involvements are patently based on his creator's wooing of Mariya Isayeva in the depths of Siberia in the mid-1850s. Ivan Petrovich (Dostoyevsky) is in love with Natasha (Mariya), who is in love with Alyosha (Vergunov). Far from treating Alyosha as a hated rival, Ivan Petrovich copies Dostoyevsky in assisting the other man's courtship, running errands for him and delivering his messages. But Dostoyevsky has not reproduced his Siberian amours in detail, for the novel's Alyosha is a wealthy young aristocrat, not an impoverished schoolteacher. It is less in the narrative than in the psychological pressures that we see the author reworking his own experiences.

Nothing more distinguishes *Insulted and Injured* from all Dostoyevsky's past and future works than intense concentration on the theme of love. But the more his characters love, the greater their anguish. 'We must somehow suffer our way . . . to our future happiness. We must purchase it by new torments. All is purified by suffering.' Such are Natasha's words to Ivan Petrovich, who has an unrequited passion for her while she burns with unreciprocated love for Alyosha. To love is to suffer and to inflict pain. That love could ever, under any circumstances, bring emotional and physical satisfaction, that there is such a phenomenon as sexual desire and its fulfilment—of these features of human nature *Insulted and Injured* provides few indications indeed.

To deny that love can ever generate pain would be as perverse as to claim, which Dostoyevsky does by implication, that it consists of nothing but hurting and being hurt. Yet, if he has not done justice to the full range of human potentialities in love, it does not follow that he has offered no stimulating insights. How often a novelist or poet succeeds precisely because the very distortion of his vision emphasizes some hitherto neglected aspect of human nature. Dostoyevsky's vision of love, in *Insulted and Injured* and elsewhere, is not instructive because it is universally valid, but because it is partly so.

The emotional perversities portrayed in *Insulted and Injured* include the tantrums of an adolescent girl, Nelly, whom Ivan Petrovich protects from an evil procuress. Here is another echo of *Poor Folk*. But the novel pioneers new territory with Prince Valkovsky, an assured, worldly, depraved middle-aged man who radiates wickedness, and even takes part as devil's advocate in a philosophical debate denouncing Ivan Petrovich's romantic idealism. These features foreshadow the great villains of the author's maturity—Svidrigaylov, Stavrogin, Versilov and Ivan Karamazov.

Insulted and Injured is a fascinating document but an ineffective novel. The lessons so well absorbed, it had seemed, by the author of *The Village of Stepanchikovo* now appear to have been forgotten. Where is the taut plot, the suspense, the pace? Where, above all, is the riotous humour? Of that commodity, so common in Dostoyevsky's *œuvre*, we find none in *Insulted and Injured*. Nor did that novel fulfil its author's hopes, as expressed when he said (as he usually did say of any fiction in progress) that his 'whole future' depended on its reception.[4] How fortunate that this was not so, for the work was coolly received by the public, and mostly condemned by its few reviewers. There was a notable exception—the radical critic N. A. Dobrolyubov, whose article 'Downtrodden People' acclaimed Dostoyevsky's latest work, together with the whole corpus of his published writings, as social criticism of the existing order. To be saluted in one of these now traditional radical sermons was an accolade of a sort; but there is little evidence that Dostoyevsky had directly aimed, here or elsewhere, at purveying the sort of social criticism that the critic discerned.

Despite the autobiographical links indicated above, *Insulted and Injured* is basically an imaginative work, whereas Dostoyevsky's next major publication consisted largely of autobiographical material. *Memoirs from the House of the Dead* is in effect the author's reminiscences of his four years as a convict at Omsk. Formally speaking, this too is a novel: it is presented as the memoirs of a fictional character, Aleksandr Petrovich Goryanchikov, who had served ten years for murdering his wife. But after presumably adopting this device to appease or bemuse the censor, Dostoyevsky seems to forget his imaginary narrator as the work proceeds. It consists, to the considerable extent to which it can be independently checked, of his own recollections somewhat sensationalized.

The House of the Dead is by far the most impressive work yet to have come from his pen. Yet here is a contribution, and from the most creatively imaginative of all Russian authors, which owes less to the creative imagination than any of his other essays in belles-lettres. The author thus presents a paradox that would have misled anyone attempting to forecast his future: he fails with his most ambitious imaginative work, but succeeds with a study where his soaring fancy is curbed by the discipline of reporting hard facts.

To preserve an objective approach was the author's express intention. 'My personality will disappear', he had announced when planning the *Memoirs*,[5] and the change of policy seems long overdue. So far, we remember, his novels and stories had often viewed the world through a haze of author's narcissism, featuring so many distorted Dostoyevskys in a leading role. But now he was experimenting with a new approach: less concerned with himself, he was observing others more closely. The convicts of *The House of the Dead* serve as the raw material of human nature, which he is determined to probe. Approaching them in a spirit of enquiry, he is an asker of questions, not yet a purveyor of answers. Here is a brief intermediate stage, that of empirical observation, dividing the narcissism of the author's youth from the prophetic utterance of his maturity.

Describing his fellow-convicts as he remembered them, Dostoyevsky did not of course offer a dull catalogue of facts. He processed his subjects intellectually, ranging them in categories corresponding to some of his fictional preoccupations. They accordingly tend to be polarized into the excessively active and the excessively passive. Obsessed by the criminal mentality, he was above all impressed by the will-power enabling certain 'strong personalities' to commit their crimes casually, without any pangs of conscience. He was also fascinated by their opposites—the gaol's kindly, saintly, universally trusted inmates. But the most exciting of all were those who abruptly switched from one category to another, performing a dramatic volte-face reminiscent of his own fictional *skandal* scenes. Such is the meek, Bible-reading convict who suddenly emerges from a trance of passivity to assault a prison officer with a brick, is flogged, and dies three days later saying that he wishes no one any harm. He had only 'wanted to suffer.'

Dostoyevsky had already moved closer to idealization of the common people, later a basic feature of his philosophy. By contrast with the previously asserted 'moral superiority' of the educated classes over the common herd, we now read that 'our sages haven't much to teach the common people, but themselves ought to learn from the *narod*.'

The House of the Dead was well received, and did more to make Dostoyevsky famous than any preceding work. The triumph owed something to his sensational subject, for never had the *katorga* been so directly presented in print. But the main credit was due to the impact of his surging prose. Favourable contemporary reactions included a long critical article, 'The Damned and the Doomed' (1866) by another radical critic, D. I. Pisarev; he derives from the work the lesson (diametrically opposed to Dostoyevsky's later teaching) that crime is the product of environment. As for the censors, they imposed only minor cuts and alterations; they also expressed concern that the work might, presumably by dwelling on the sexual and alcoholic orgies staged in gaol, provide too 'seductive' a picture, thus reducing the value of the *katorga* as a deterrent.

The House of the Dead had created 'a veritable furore', Dostoyevsky boasted. 'I have revived my literary reputation.' It also helped to put *Vremya* on a sound footing. With 2,300 subscribers in its first year of publication the journal had not quite broken even. But in the following year, 1862, the list soared to 4,300; and all subscriptions above 2,500 represented a profit of about ten roubles.[6]

Dostoyevsky was now a celebrity who dominated the regular Tuesday evening meetings at the home of the literary critic Aleksandr Milyukov, a friend from pre-exile days. Here he met another old friend, the poet Appollon Maykov, and a young literary critic, Nikolay Strakhov. It was not any aura of martyrdom, says Strakhov, but Dostoyevsky's ebullient ideas and dynamic manner that made him the centre of attention. Bearded, bewhiskered, with his large forehead, plebeian features, and the air of a common soldier acquired from some fifteen years under military discipline, he was yet mild-mannered. He would begin talking in a whisper, being gradually swept away by his ideas until he was haranguing his hearers at the top of his voice.[7]

Such is the forty-year-old Fyodor Mikhaylovich as he appears in the memoirs of Strakhov, now chief literary critic of the new journal *Vremya*, and second only to the Dostoyevsky brothers in moulding that publication's personality. As this may remind us, readers of the intellectual reviews positively insisted on commitment to a cause which must be identifiable despite all evasions imposed by censorship. And that cause must above all embrace the interpretation of Russia, her past, present and future. Within this basic requirement a wide range of overlapping options remained open: socialist, liberal, conservative, Westernist, Slavophile.

What then of *Vremya*'s profile? Dostoyevsky's early background made a committed left-wing posture seem probable, whereas those familiar with the fanatical Russian nationalism of his later years will expect, with hindsight, to find him and his journal in a rightist role. And yet, for once in his life a middle way was chosen: the brothers tried to hold a balance between progressivism and traditionalism. It was to reconcile the social classes, to bring educated society into harmony both with itself and with the untutored masses, that *Vremya* aimed; it also sought to reconcile left and right, Westernist and Slavophile. Friendly relations were accordingly maintained with the leading left-wing journal *Sovremennik* ('The Contemporary'), and major writers of the radical left, including Nekrasov and the satirist Saltykov-Shchedrin, were enlisted as contributors to *Vremya*. But Strakhov was a firm Slavophile, while another influential contributor, the engagingly original critic Appollon Grigoryev, tended to be mistakenly assigned to that category. The balance between conflicting policies was hard to sustain in practice, for it was with conservative and Slavophile thinking that *Vremya* and its most famous contributor became increasingly identified; and though Dostoyevsky himself wrote articles abusing aspects of Slavophilism, he was more and more leaning in that direction. Such a view was inherent in his journal's original manifesto. It proclaimed a metaphysical attachment to the Russian soil (*pochva*) as the basis of its policies, for which reason the *Vremya* group became known as 'soil men' (*pochvenniki*).

Dostoyevsky's own articles in *Vremya* are remarkable for his advocacy of extreme Russian nationalism, a topic never previously prominent in his writings. Now, in the misleadingly named *Series of Essays on Literature* (1861), he assaults the theme with fervour exceptional even in a nation of obsessed self-observers. Russia is unique, he tells *Vremya*'s readers; but it is also the least understood nation in the world. It has outlived all western European influences, it now stands on the threshold of a new era. Appearances to the contrary, there is no fundamental disharmony between the country's social classes; they are being, have been or are just about to be fused together through a uniquely peaceful process beyond the ken of peoples less co-operatively inclined. Anticipating his later *Diary of a Writer*, and especially its most famous single item (his 'Pushkin Speech' of 1880), Dostoyevsky the journalist of 1861 goes on to claim for his fellow-countrymen the special quality of 'omnihumanity', denied to other nations. The Russian can understand and adapt to them, whereas they, hampered by their inhibitions, cannot understand and adapt to him. Russians never take offence, as other peoples do. Russians can speak all languages. They possess in Pushkin a poet of such colossal significance that other peoples are precluded by congenital insensitivity from comprehending so elevated a phenomenon. Pushkin's 'purport in the evolution of Russia is profoundly portentous. He is, for all Russians, the incarnate exegesis, in full artistic measure, of the essence of the Russian spirit, of the focus of all Russian strivings, of the precise nature of the Russian ideal. The phenomenon of Pushkin is proof that the tree of civilization has reached maturity and that its fruits are not rotten, but magnificent, golden fruits. All that we could learn about ourselves through knowing Europeans we have already learnt. All that civilization could explain to us we have explained to ourselves, and that knowledge has manifested itself to us in its fullest and most harmonious form in Pushkin. In him we have come to realize that the Russian ideal is total integrity, universal reconcilability, omni-humanity.'[8]

Dostoyevsky also claims that Russians never boast, as other peoples do.

If it is surprising that a personally modest man should have indulged in such bombast on behalf of his nation, it is no less remarkable that he should have kept his harangues compartmented. When writing as an artist, not as a publicist, he adopted a different tone. Neither the misconceived *Insulted and Injured* nor the powerful *House of the Dead*, both composed at about the same time as the *Series of Essays on Literature*, could have suggested to readers that their author was, in part of his nature, a ranting fanatic. Even as a ranter, however, Dostoyevsky was magnificent. Polemically impassioned by nature, he needed to feel menaced by ideological enemies whom he cheerfully pulverized with his sarcasm and mocking humour.

Behind the stinging rhetoric we discern a compulsive need to hate—not personally, but philosophically—and his nationalist fervour helped to feed this compulsion by providing a target: foreigners and their knavish tricks. Of another key phobia of the future, Russian 'progressives', his 1861 writings reveal little. But that emotion lay near the surface, and was soon to flourish in the atmosphere of disillusionment and tension provoked by the Emancipation of the Serfs. Signs of demoralization were accumulating in Russian society as peasants, frustrated by the terms on which they received their liberty in 1861, celebrated it with riots. In autumn of that year students launched protest demonstrations in St Petersburg, helping to found a tradition of Russian university unrest destined to outlast the Empire.

In the following year, 1862, the campus revolutionaries of the era, and the politically disaffected younger generation as a whole, were first labelled 'Nihilists'—in Turgenev's influential novel *Fathers and Children*. The word caught on and became a term of abuse. It was largely used by moderates and conservatives, who applied it to the opposition movement as a whole, from revolutionary assassins to those many young people whose most dastardly crime was to fail to clean their finger-nails and to hector or patronize their elders. Male Nihilists wore their hair long, female Nihilists had theirs cropped short, while both sexes flaunted and cultivated sexual freedom. They preached feminism, materialism, atheism and socialism—all doctrines which were soon to become anathema to Dostoyevsky. Within a few years 'Nihilist' was to be one of his strongest terms of condemnation, and he was to apply it to virtually all those whose views were to the left of his own: a fairly large section of the educated Russian public. Nihilists of one kind or another were to figure in all his great novels from *Crime and Punishment* onwards.

Meanwhile events of early 1862 were already conspiring to mobilize Dostoyevsky's fear and detestation of the opposition movement even as it was in process of being christened Nihilist by Turgenev. Anonymous proclamations calling for revolutionary massacres were being distributed in the capital, while a series of mysterious fires, caused by arsonists whose identity has never been established, devastated large areas of the city. They were blamed by many, without evidence, on students and revolutionaries, and though *Vremya* rejected this imputation, Dostoyevsky himself inclined to accept it. Even as the holocausts raged in the streets around him, he chanced to come into possession of a particularly blood-curdling revolutionary pamphlet, metaphorically caught fire himself, and naïvely rushed off to beard the radical leader Nikolay Chernyshevsky in person with an appeal to him to call off the fire-raising campaign. Chernyshevsky was indeed the main ideological torch-bearer of Russian radicalism, but was surprised to find himself identified as a mere fire-raiser in the literal sense. He concluded that Dostoyevsky had gone mad, but humoured him by pretending to fall in with his wishes. Meanwhile the fires, however originated, continued to break out.[9]

Such is the version of the interview given by Chernyshevsky, who was soon to become established as Dostoyevsky's main ideological enemy. His account differs from Dostoyevsky's, as published eleven years later in *The Diary of a Writer*, which makes no mention of the fires, but only of the anonymous pamphlets. Having found one of these outside his door, Dostoyevsky had (says he) sought out Chernyshevsky, and had appealed for the latter to use his influence to halt the flow of subversive propaganda emanating from his presumed converts. As described by Dostoyevsky, this was a low-key meeting at which Chernyshevsky politely denied knowing the authors of the pamphlets and professed his inability to help.[10]

Two months later, in July 1862, Chernyshevsky was arrested as a political suspect, the prelude to a long martyrdom by *katorga* in the depths of Siberia. Meanwhile Dostoyevsky, who had been through that phase, was preparing his first fictional denunciation of Russian left-wing politics—*A Nasty Story*. This is only a minor work, but is significant as the first essay in didactic fiction by one whose later masterpieces were all to be inspired by a zeal for purveying instruction, incidentally providing many a variant on the specific theme of *A Nasty Story*. Published in the November 1862 issue of *Vremya*, it is a superficially trivial anecdote about a senior civil servant—an outright 'progressive' infected by the liberal ideas of his age. In keeping with these beliefs, he decides to favour an insignificant subordinate by attending the man's wedding unannounced, thus demonstrating his egalitarian and democratic sentiments. But the result is disastrous: the intruding bureaucrat causes general embarrassment, eventually becoming so drunk that he falls face forward into a plate of blancmange and has to be put to bed in the only available place, the nuptial couch. Here is a parable directed against the liberals of the age, not against its Nihilists, left-wing radicals and revolutionaries. But as Dostoyevsky's hatred of the left developed it was soon to become clear that he barely differentiated between mild and virulent carriers of the disease.

Shortly after publishing this, the first of many satires on Russia's 'progressives', Dostoyevsky reverted to the deficiencies of foreigners with his *Winter Notes on Summer Impressions*. It appeared in *Vremya* in early 1863, and it records an event of crucial importance in his life, his first visit to western Europe. The excursion had occupied two months of the previous summer, taking him to Germany, Switzerland and Italy, as well as to the countries which are his main targets in *Winter Notes*: France and England. More like an Old Testament prophet than a conventional tourist, he was appalled by his week in London, and vividly describes this modern Nineveh with its garish gin palaces, soot-impregnated air and massed prostitutes swarming beneath the Haymarket's gas jets. Disliking the city's newly erected Crystal Palace, he was later to invoke it as the symbol for what he most deplored in life: all claims and attempts to organize human beings for their own good. In London, Dostoyevsky also called on one who, as a socialist, was to become an ideological enemy, but whose views on the decadence of the doomed and materialist West he yet fully shared—Aleksandr Herzen, nineteenth-century Russia's most illustrious political émigré. Herzen found Dostoyevsky 'naïve and somewhat obscure', but also 'very charming and an enthusiastic believer in the Russian people.'[11]

Dostoyevsky left London for Paris, but was even more exasperated by France than by England. The French were a nation of shopkeepers and hypocrites with an insufferable air of moral superiority. 'By God, the French do make me sick.'[12]

It would be misleading to claim Dostoyevsky's attitude to western Europeans, or to any of his other numerous enemies, as rejection pure and simple. Denying that western Europe would or should influence Russia's future, he yet acknowledged that 'practically all existing Russian progress, learning, art and civic virtue' stemmed from Europe, 'that land of holy miracles.'[13] As this indicates, though he was close to the Slavophile view of Russia's prospects, his interpretation of his country's past could reveal an occasional Westernist streak.

Dostoyevsky's xenophobic urges were further inflamed when, even as *Winter Notes* was being published in *Vremya*, the second of the two great nineteenth-century Polish revolts against Russian rule broke out in January 1863. Eventually suppressed after a year's fighting, the rebellion accidentally brought his career as a journalist and unofficial editor to an abrupt halt when an article by Strakhov ('The Fateful Problem') in the April issue of *Vremya* was misinterpreted by authority as asserting the superiority of Polish over Russian culture. Poles the superiors of Russians! Nothing could conceivably have been further from Strakhov's, or from Dostoyevsky's, view of the world. But the journal, Dostoyevsky's main source of income during the two-and-a-half years of its existence, was permanently and irrevocably banned before the misunderstanding could be cleared up.

Now suddenly destitute, Dostoyevsky borrowed fifteen hundred roubles from the Society for Assisting Needy Authors and Scholars, and set off for the despised city of Paris to join his mistress Apollinariya Suslova.

Apollinariya soon emerged as a purveyor of anguish more adept, and far more deliberately malicious, than Dostoyevsky's ailing wife.

A strikingly attractive woman in her early twenties, she had contributed a story to *Vremya*—the occasion for her first meeting with the journal's unofficial co-editor. Having embarked on a liaison, probably in the winter of 1862–3, they had arranged to continue it in Paris in the following summer. But Dostoyevsky, delayed by the winding-up of *Vremya*, appeared at the rendezvous 'too late' in more senses than one, as Apollinariya was quick to inform him on his arrival in August. In the interim she had fallen in love with a young Spaniard, to whom (she announced) she had immediately 'given herself.' A seeker as well as a purveyor of anguish, she had evidently selected her paramour with both urges in view, for he had quickly abandoned her, thus enabling her to relish the delights of sexual frustration while simultaneously inflicting them on Dostoyevsky. Denying herself to him as emotionally committed to her faithless Spaniard, she yet agreed to a joint tour of Europe on a 'brother and sister' basis. They accordingly stayed in separate hotel rooms, but varied the relationship in that the 'brother' made sexual advances, to which the 'sister' responded in an ambiguous manner consciously designed to keep his desires inflamed but unsatisfied—as is recorded in her laconic but revealing diary.[14] Apollinariya was behaving as an accomplished tease, especially in view of Dostoyevsky's strong but rarely satisfied sexual appetites. Fortunately he remained an addict of powerful emotions who preferred intense frustration to mild satisfaction; and he must, in part of his mind, have savoured the acutely tantalizing aspects of a situation that a more 'normal' man would have solved by requiring the young woman to disentangle herself from his life without delay.

Dostoyevsky's reaction to Apollinariya's unkindness was (again according to her diary) to accuse her of avenging herself for having originally yielded to him—a trait that may be noted as foreshadowing Nastasya Filippovna in his novel *The Idiot*. Another verdict on his mistress, given in his letter of 19 April 1865 to her sister, is that 'Apollinariya is a great egoist. Her selfishness and conceit are colossal. She demands *everything* of people, all perfections, never forgiving a single flaw in consideration of good qualities, while exempting herself from the slightest obligation.'[15]

Not content with courting sexual frustration, Dostoyevsky was also feeding a still more destructive addiction, to reckless gambling at the casinos of German spas. Hazarding his scanty funds at the roulette table, an amenity not available in Russia, he had discovered an exquisite new form of self-torment. In August 1863, while on his way to Paris, he won five thousand francs at Wiesbaden, having hit upon an infallible 'system': it consisted of 'keeping oneself constantly under control.' Soon afterwards he is at Baden-Baden with Apollinariya, having lost both his self-control and his money, but contrives to borrow enough, by post from his sister-in-law Varvara Constant, to tide him over. After pawning a watch in Geneva, Fyodor and his ex-mistress appear in Turin, once more destitute and fearing police proceedings because they cannot pay their hotel bill; but Mikhail Dostoyevsky luckily sends 1,450 francs. Such are the recurrent themes of a holiday that also took Dostoyevsky and his partner to Rome, Naples and Leghorn. In early October Apollinariya left him and returned to Paris, only to receive a desperate letter from Bad Homburg, where her former lover had once again lost all his money. Fortunately she was able to send three hundred and fifty francs borrowed on his behalf, and he could return to St Petersburg later in the month.[16]

Mistress — The dual anguish, sexual and financial, of his 1863 travels was to serve as admirable copy when, three years later, he came to write his short novel *The Gambler*.

By the end of 1863 Dostoyevsky seemed almost to have abandoned fiction: a five-year hiatus in the writing of full-length novels separates *Insulted and Injured* (1861) from *Crime and Punishment* (1866). Since *Winter Notes on Summer Impressions* his journalistic productivity had also begun to dwindle. But then Mikhail Dostoyevsky obtained permission to launch a new journal *Epokha* ('The Epoch'), and Fyodor was encouraged to resume work. In March 1864, when *Epokha* made its début, subscribers were rewarded with the first instalment of his *Memoirs from Underground*.

This long story or short novel (about a hundred pages) was perhaps the most disturbing work yet to have come from a Russian pen. It sums up and brings to fruition much of what its author had already been expressing during the previous two decades. It also points to his future, for it is his first work of philosophical fiction, and as such forms a prelude to the five mature novels from *Crime and Punishment* to *The Brothers Karamazov.* Established by his early forties as a writer notable and original indeed, yet still of the second rank, Dostoyevsky pivoted on *Memoirs from Underground* to become the supreme master that we know.

The work consists of the reminiscences of an unnamed narrator, the 'Underground Man', and falls into two sections. The first is a long theoretical tirade, while the remainder is narrative designed to illustrate the theory.

The opening analytical section itself falls into two parts. Of these the first looks to Dostoyevsky's past, for his hero or anti-hero characterizes himself as one of the distorted self-portraits that go back to the twin Golyadkins of *The Double*. Here is another St Petersburg introvert, a lonely poverty-stricken 'outsider', unstable and hypersensitive. Like his predecessors in Dostoyevsky's work, he is obsessed with the humiliation that he both courts and seeks to inflict. But he is even more addicted than any forerunner to violent sensations, explicitly preferring intense suffering to mild contentment. He asks which is better: 'cheap happiness or lofty sufferings?' A true image of his creator, he chooses the sufferings, and they need not necessarily be 'lofty' if only they are sufficiently severe or degrading. He even relishes acute toothache, for example, and the prospect of having his face slapped. He also gloats over certain unspecified evil deeds committed by him on some 'excessively foul St Petersburg night.'

So far the Underground Man has merely given more potent expression to material already familiar, but in the second part of his analytical tirade he proceeds to break new ground. Here through his narrator, Dostoyevsky at last proclaims a thesis that was to dominate his later thinking and much of his greatest fiction: man is unpredictable, irrational, inconsistent, wayward and capricious. This was not a new discovery in itself, but its expression is highly original. It owes little to the positive stimulus of literary models, and everything to a violent negative impulse of philosophical hatred such as tended, for Dostoyevsky, to be the most fruitful literary influence of all.

His new, supreme hate-object was the Russian socialist movement, especially as inspired by Chernyshevsky. We have seen how that outstanding leader of radical thought had briefly clashed with Dostoyevsky in 1862 over the St Petersburg fires or pamphlets. But it was Chernyshevsky's novel *What is to be Done?* (written in the Petropavlovsky Fortress in the following year) that raised him to the eminence of Dostoyevsky's chief ideological bogyman. Through an oversight of the censorship, and to the fury of the government, this thinly disguised revolutionary sermon was immediately serialized in *Sovremennik*. It is widely considered to be the worst novel ever written, yet it influenced nineteenth-century Russians more than any of their greatest works of fiction. It was Chernyshevsky's ideas, not his technical shortcomings as a novelist, that impressed his disciples, also arousing Dostoyevsky's fury as conveyed in *Memoirs from Underground*. Here, though Chernyshevsky's name is not invoked, his theory of 'rational egoism' is bombarded with indignant rhetoric.

According to Chernyshevsky's theory, human affairs can proceed in perfect harmony if only men will perceive and follow their own true interests. A working model of the doctrine is provided in *What is to be Done?* as the characters, rationally motivated near-automata, are manipulated into predetermined postures designed to project the author's views on marriage, female emancipation, industrial co-operatives and the like. Learn to discern where your true advantage lies, pursue it intelligently, and society will become a paradise on earth—here, in Chernyshevsky's thesis, was the powerful negative thrust for which Dostoyevsky had been waiting all his life. So obnoxious was the doctrine to his deepest instincts that it provoked the spasms of splendidly articulate rage expressed, in greater or lesser degree, by all the novels of his maturity.

It was, then, partly through his loathing for a bad novelist that Dostoyevsky became a great novelist. As we are reminded, antipathy can be an even more powerful spur to literary creativity than sympathy.

As the Underground Man inveighs against enlightened self-seekers' utopias, we hear his creator's authentic voice. 'When oh when, in all the millennia, has man ever acted solely in his own interests? What shall we do with millions of facts showing that men have, *knowingly* and well aware of their true interests, neglected them to rush down a different road—one of risks and who knows what? They have clearly made a point of rejecting the obvious course, while not being in the least forced to do so, and have stubbornly and wilfully pioneered a new, difficult, meaningless track, seeking it out in near darkness.' Even if a heaven on earth should be achieved men would reject it. 'Now, I shan't be in the least surprised if, for instance, some joker with an ignoble—nay, reactionary and sneering—countenance should suddenly pop up without warning in this universal future paradise. .... "Well, gentlemen," he'll say to us. "How about kicking the hell out of all this harmony? Let's send the logarithms to blazes so that we can live by our own silly impulses again." '[17]

In the narrative section of the story Dostoyevsky shows the Underground Man's theories in action as he first courts and then purveys humiliation. He clashes with extrovert 'men of action', his envied opposites, and he viciously insults a young woman who pities and befriends him, forcefully demonstrating at every turn that he is not to be regimented for his own good. Whatever enlightened egoists may say about heaven on earth, he damn well means to go to hell his own way. Unenlightened self-destruction—that, not enlightened self-interest, is the Underground Man's goal, in which he faithfully follows the real-life procedures of his creator.

The composition of *Memoirs from Underground* was closely followed by a threefold tragedy in Dostoyevsky's life: the loss of his wife, of his brother Mikhail and of *Epokha.*

Progressively succumbing to tuberculosis, Mariya Dmitriyevna spent her last months in Moscow, comforted by her husband, who stayed with her there from January 1864 until her death on 15 April. Thus ended a marriage on which the husband has provided his own epitaph in a letter to Vrangel. 'She and I were decidedly unhappy together owing to her weird, pernickety and pathologically fantastic character. But we could not stop loving each other. The unhappier we were, actually, the more attached we became to each other.'[18]

Three months later Mikhail Dostoyevsky suddenly fell ill, from an affliction of the spleen, and died on 10 July 1864 aged forty-three. Fyodor was deeply grieved to lose the man who had been closer to him than any other, besides which Mikhail's death added greatly to his burdens. The widow, Emiliya Fyodorovna, and her four children had been left without resources, and Dostoyevsky, who already had his feckless stepson Pasha on his hands, at once assumed responsibility for his brother's family as well. He incidentally took over Mikhail's large debts, of between twenty and forty thousand roubles—differing figures occur in the sources.

Some of these debts were contingent on the management of *Epokha*, and Dostoyevsky's chief mistake was to carry on that publication. Never, even during the brief period when Mikhail managed it, had the new journal looked like repeating the success of *Vremya*. The momentum established by the earlier publication had fallen off, former subscribers had had to be wooed again, the delay in publishing in-dividual numbers had exceeded even the norm for Russian periodicals of the era, and there had been difficulties over delivering copies to subscribers. Mikhail's death naturally made matters worse, and Fyodor was heroically imprudent to take over the moribund enterprise.

As a former political prisoner he was still ineligible for the editor-ship, and so a nominal editor was appointed, while Dostoyevsky took responsibility behind the scenes. His efforts were impressive, but deployed in vain: *Epokha* collapsed under its debts in June 1865. For his continuing lull in literary productivity in 1865 the labour of sustaining the review was largely to blame. 'I was sole editor', he wrote to Vrangel. 'I read proofs, dealt with authors and censors, corrected articles, obtained funds, sat up till six a.m., slept five hours out of twenty-four, and though I did put the journal into shape it was then too late.'[19]

In keeping with the shift in Dostoyevsky's views, *Epokha* had abandoned *Vremya*'s policy of reconciling progressives and tradition-alists. The new periodical adhered to the latter school, and Dostoyevsky seemed to signalize this move to the right by publishing in the journal a new short fantasy of his own, *The Crocodile*. It describes a man who has been swallowed by a crocodile; but who proceeds, unabashed, to enlighten mankind with long instructional harangues delivered from the creature's belly. As was inevitable, these messages issued from a crocodile were taken as a sneer at Chernyshevsky's widely admired utterances—including his novel *What is to be Done?*—issued from the belly of the Petropavlovsky Fortress. Dostoyevsky was later to deny the charge of mocking Chernyshevsky in *The Crocodile*,[20] but this was perhaps one of the occasions on which his conscious mind imperfectly sensed the full purport of his creative promptings.

Though Dostoyevsky had not fully severed his traumatic association with Apollinariya Suslova, he had acquired a new mistress or probable mistress in the winter of 1864–5. She was a Martha Brown, and she was Russian despite a surname acquired through a lapsed marriage with a Baltimore sailor. After an adventurous life and a succession of lovers, she had obtained work on *Epokha* as a translator from English. That she was, or was about to be, Dostoyevsky's paramour on New Year's Day 1865 is clear from her letter to him of that date, where she discusses their liaison in language more appropriate to an official memorandum than to communion between lovers. 'Whether I do or do not succeed in satisfying you physically, and whether we do or do not attain the degree of spiritual harmony on which the continuance of our relationship will depend, believe that I shall always be grateful to you for finding me worthy, albeit only for a fleeting moment, of your friendship and sympathy.'[21] Shortly after meeting Dostoyevsky, Martha was admitted to hospital, and their association, of which we know nothing beyond the few surviving letters from her to him, was brief.

Soon afterwards Dostoyevsky met a twenty-one-year-old woman, Anna Korvin-Krukovskaya—like Apollinariya Suslova before her a contributor of fiction to his journal. To vivacity and beauty Anna added the piquancy of ideological inacceptability, for she was in process of becoming a militant revolutionary and feminist. She was, in other words, what Dostoyevsky called a Nihilist, and as such an enemy. But then he had always been fascinated by enemies, and he fell in love with Anna and proposed marriage. But though she regarded her suitor highly she did not return his passion, also finding the prospect of this union incompatible with her political crusade.[22]

Our information on Dostoyevsky's visits to the Korvin-Krukovskys comes from Anna's younger sister Sofya, later to become a well-known mathematician under her married name, Sofya Kovalevskaya. Aged fifteen at the time of Dostoyevsky's visits, she contracted a schoolgirl 'crush' on him, and has left a sensitive account of his appearance in her home. The famous author was nervous at first, continually twitching, plucking his beard and biting his moustache, but became more assured when he realized that he was among friends. His preferred form of conversation was still the long monologue, and there were also occasions, Sofya notes, when the old soldier employed expressions unsuitable for the ears of young ladies.[23] Dostoyevsky was later to use the Korvin-Krukovsky household as a model for that of the Yepanchins in *The Idiot*. The charming, wilful, teasing Anna was to inspire Aglaya Yepanchina; and the socially inept, harangue-addicted 'Prince Myshkin' was to be, in these respects at least, yet another self-portrait by the author.

7

Emerging Genius

Crime and Punishment; The Gambler

By mid-1865 Dostoyevsky's fortunes and morale were at their lowest
ebb since his return from Siberia. He was writing nothing, he was
exhausted by the unsuccessful struggle to save *Epokha*, and he was in
worse financial straits than ever. Tailors' bills, printers' bills, demands
for fees from contributors to his defunct journal, summonses to
redeem promissory notes recklessly signed on his own and his brother's
behalf, threats to distrain on his property, the prospect of indefinite
imprisonment for debt—how were these menaces to be met? By
signing yet more IOUs, obviously; by begging yet more loans from
his friends; by applying yet again to the Society for Assisting Needy
Authors and Scholars. There was also the possibility of foreign travel.
It would temporarily rid him of his Russian creditors, and might even
solve all his financial problems at a stroke through a spectacular coup
at roulette. But he could not even think of going abroad in the absence
of ready cash.

This dilemma was cruelly exploited by an unscrupulous publisher,
F. T. Stellovsky, who had been quietly buying up Dostoyevsky's
promissory notes at well below their face value. One day Dostoyevsky
was confronted at his door by a policeman with a summons taken out
by Stellovsky's lawyer.[1] The policeman proved friendly, and was
fobbed off for the time being, but Dostoyevsky knew that he had been
trapped into signing a grotesquely disadvantageous contract presented
by the publisher. Its stipulations are barely credible. In return for three
thousand roubles, much of which was immediately swallowed up to
redeem promissory notes held by Stellovsky, Dostoyevsky not only
made over to him the copyright of all his existing works, to be brought
out in a three-volume complete edition, but also agreed to provide
for that edition a new item of fiction of at least ten signatures (a hundred
and sixty pages) by 1 November 1866. The penalty for failure to
deliver was that his entire writings, past, present and future, would
be forfeit to Stellovsky, and might be published without payment over
a period of nine years.

Dostoyevsky had thus been manipulated into mortgaging virtually his whole literary future as well as his past.

Travelling to Wiesbaden on the remnants of Stellovsky's advance, he was by no means relieved of financial torment; he had merely changed the pattern, for his surviving funds had soon vanished at the local casino. When, after a brief visit from Apollinariya, he could not meet his hotel bill, the 'fat German proprietor' gave orders that he was not to be served meals, while the staff brewed him atrocious tea, refused to clean his boots, starved him of candles and treated him with open contempt; 'to a German there's no greater crime than having no money.'[2] Meanwhile letters urgently requesting loans were of course going out to his friends. One even went to an old enemy— Turgenev, who was living in Baden-Baden. Dostoyevsky wrote in August asking for a hundred thalers, which was worth roughly a hundred roubles at the time, and Turgenev sent fifty. This small debt Dostoyevsky was to leave unpaid for eleven years until it developed into a major irritant; and may even, one suspects, have been carefully cultivated as such by one who so 'wanted to suffer.' In September a less traumatic loan, of a hundred thalers, was extracted from Baron Vrangel, Dostoyevsky's old ally from his Siberian period, who was now in Copenhagen. Dostoyevsky visited the Baron, spending a pleasant week with him and his family in early October.

Loans, from whatever source, could only shift and increase the burden of debts that must be paid in the end through the practice of Dostoyevsky's profession. Before leaving St Petersburg he had asked two editors for an advance against a projected longish novel to be called *The Drunkards*, a study of alcoholism and its effects on family life. But his proposals were turned down, and by September the topic had been shelved for another idea: a short story to be based on a murderer's confession of his crime. He was ready to sell the notion to any journal which would put up a three-hundred-rouble advance, and soon obtained that sum from M. N. Katkov, publisher of the Moscow monthly *Russky vestnik* ('The Russian Herald'). None of Dostoyevsky's work had previously appeared there, but it was a leading conservative organ, and as such a suitable vehicle for an author who had adopted extreme traditionalist views. *Russky vestnik* was eventually to bring out four of the five long novels of his maturity.

His contribution to *Russky vestnik* was, he told Katkov, to be 'the psychological account of a crime' committed under the influence of 'certain strange, half-baked ideas that are floating in the air.'[3] Here was the embryo of *Crime and Punishment*, which was to grow from the story originally conceived into his longest novel to date, incidentally incorporating his earlier project for a novel, *The Drunkards*, as a sub-plot. In mid-October 1865 he returned to St Petersburg and settled down to work, harassed by reactivated Russian creditors, by epilepsy and by his still smouldering passion for Apollinariya. Her diary records a meeting between them on 2 November at which he told her: 'If you ever marry you'll hate your husband and leave him two days later'; yet she also claims that Dostoyevsky had 'long been offering me his hand and heart.'[4]

By the end of November he had a sizeable draft of *Crime and Punishment* on paper. But then 'a new form, a new plan' swam into his head. He burnt the draft and started again, to such effect that he had dispatched the first chapters to *Russky vestnik* by mid-December. They appeared in the January 1866 number, after which serialization continued throughout the year.

Meanwhile, on 4 April, St Petersburg had been shaken by news of an unsuccessful assassination attempt. As the Tsar was mounting his carriage in the capital's Summer Garden the student terrorist Dmitry Karakozov fired a revolver at him, but missed. News of the episode put Dostoyevsky into a state of 'great excitement', one of his acquaintances has reported. The attempt on the Emperor inflamed his growing hatred of Nihilism and associated left-wing terrorism. It also induced his publisher Katkov to hold back the current instalment of *Crime and Punishment* for a month, since this was no time to sponsor accounts, however fictional, of murderous students.[5]

Karakozov was sentenced and executed in September 1866. His was the first of several attempts on Alexander II's life, and it encouraged the adoption of more oppressive domestic policies in the later years of the reign.

In summer 1866 Dostoyevsky was at last able to enjoy comparative peace and calm when, still at work on his new novel, he occupied a country cottage at Lyublino near Moscow. Here he enjoyed the company of his sister Vera, who was married to a Dr Ivanov, and of their nine children. The eldest, the nineteen-year-old Sonya, was Dostoyevsky's favourite niece, and the Ivanov family circle was to supply the background for an episode in his future short novel *The Eternal Husband*.

Crime and Punishment is the first of the five long novels of Dostoyevsky's maturity, the others being *The Idiot*, *Devils*, *A Raw Youth* and *The Brothers Karamazov*. It is on these five works that his reputation chiefly rests—with the minor qualification that one item in the great Quintet (*A Raw Youth*) falls somewhat below the level of the others, as will be argued below.

Complex and subtle in so many ways, *Crime and Punishment* yet has a central plot of extreme simplicity. A former student, Rodion Raskolnikov, kills an aged female pawnbroker and her sister with an axe, after which he is psychologically impelled to betray himself and confess the crime, being sentenced to imprisonment in Siberia. In the tracing of these developments skilled use is made of suspense. Raskolnikov's mysterious and sinister intentions tantalize the reader in Part One. Then, in Parts Two to Six, more prolonged and agonizing tension takes over: will he be detected?

The work's novelty lay less in the use of suspense, already successfully exploited in Dostoyevsky's earlier fiction, than in the yoking of suspense to a theme hitherto neglected: murder. Violent crime had not yet figured in his fiction, though it occupies a prominent place in the largely factual *House of the Dead*. But from 1866 onwards murder becomes thoroughly integrated into his imaginative work too. *Crime and Punishment* is, on one level, a 'thriller' or detective story, as is *The Brothers Karamazov*, while spectacular slayings are also to be found in *The Idiot* and *Devils*.

The product of a profoundly creative imagination, *Crime and Punishment* is yet surprisingly deep-rooted in details drawn from life. The setting is St Petersburg's Haymarket (*Sennaya ploshchad*) with its stifling dust, sordid taverns, thronging drunks and prostitutes—a district in which Dostoyevsky himself had lived both in the 1840s and the 1860s. He wrote with particular buildings in mind, and three are still standing. 'Raskolnikov's house', 'Sonya's house', 'Alyona Ivanovna's [the pawnbroker's] house' all look out on streets that still retain, in the city now called Leningrad, their nineteenth-century character. I have inspected all three from the outside, shadowed by cars of—presumably—the KGB: a touch of local colour that Dostoyevsky himself would have appreciated.

Then again, it seems likely (though it is not certain) that an early inspirational stimulus came from the widely publicized trial of an actual axe-murderer, the twenty-seven-year-old Gerasim Chistov, in Moscow in August 1865. He had killed two elderly women, a cook and a laundress, while committing a robbery in the previous January; and he happened to belong to the religious denomination known as the Old Belief. The word for Old Believer, *raskolnik*, possibly put the name 'Raskolnikov' into Dostoyevsky's mind, for he was a keen reader of trial reports. His defunct journal *Vremya* had published articles on famous crimes of the past: yet another of the many possible influences on the new novel's conception.[6]

As for the originals of its characters, we have already noted the odious Luzhin as probably modelled on Dostoyevsky's pompous brother-in-law Karepin, while the Marmeladovs, husband and wife, were distantly inspired by the author's deceased wife Mariya and her drunken first husband. But when we seek a distorted portrait of the author, such as had been so common in his early work, a significant deviation emerges. If there is any such figure in the novel it can only be Raskolnikov himself. As an impoverished ex-student in debt to his landlady in a St Petersburg slum, and as a prey to intense introspection, he has some of the credentials of a 'St Petersburg dreamer' or 'Underground Man', resembling those obsessive sufferers from, and would-be inflicters of, humiliation who litter Dostoyevsky's early work, and with whom he seems to identify himself so closely. But Raskolnikov is nothing of the sort, as his creator serves notice in the novel's first pages, where he explicitly calls his hero the very opposite of cowardly and downtrodden. When we learn that the young man is also tall and remarkably good-looking, we can no longer suspect Dostoyevsky of once again describing himself. And when, soon afterwards, Raskolnikov explodes into action—albeit brief, frenzied, regrettable and ultimately sterile—he further distinguishes him from the 'self-portrait' predecessors, all of them outstandingly passive.

This raises a still more significant point: *Crime and Punishment* is more objective than its predecessors. Not that it has rejected introspective inspiration; rather has Dostoyevsky balanced that inspiration with closer observation of the outside world. This more objective approach was facilitated by a crucial decision in the early planning of the novel. He had begun writing it in the first person, with a prototype of Raskolnikov as his narrator, but then switched to third-person narrative. The change marks his rejection of the excessive author's narcissism from which he had greatly profited in the past, but which may yet have delayed the full flowering of his talents. By contrast, *Insulted and Injured* and *Memoirs from Underground* are both written in the first person, and in the name of what we have termed self-portrait characters.

Such are some superficial externals of a psychological study that probes deep into Raskolnikov's reasons for resorting to homicide. His motives are revealed piecemeal, and in two distinct strata. It first seems that the crime was prompted by philanthropic urges. The proceeds are to enable the criminal to return to the university, embark on a useful career, and redeem with a hundred good deeds his solitary lapse—the killing of an ugly, nasty, parasitical hag depicted as almost comically ripe for murder. Besides helping humanity as a whole with the proceeds of his crime, Raskolnikov also plans to save his poverty-stricken mother and to rescue his sister Dunya from a fate worse than death—marriage to Luzhin.

So much for the philanthropic motive. Only at a later stage does it gradually turn out that other, more sinister, entirely contrary urges have been at work. By committing a monstrous crime without remorse, Raskolnikov has sought to show himself a 'Napoleon' or superman. Alternatively, he wanted to turn himself into a superman by the act of murder; or else, yet another variant, he needed to find out whether he was or was not such a person. Did he possess, could he acquire, the necessary strength to ignore the conventional taboos that hold lesser beings in thrall? Was he, to put it differently, a 'strong personality' worthy to take his place beside the casual psychopathic killers of *The House of the Dead*?

Neither of these two opposing motive-streams, the unselfish-philanthropic and the selfish-Napoleonic, excludes the other; for Raskolnikov is a split or oscillating personality swinging between alienation from his fellows and a desire to identify with them. But though he may veer from one pole to the other, it makes no difference in the end since both drives, the philanthropic and the Napoleonic, are equally based on rationality. They derive from 'logic' and 'rational egoism' as previously denounced by the Underground Man. Both as a would-be superman and as a would-be benefactor, Raskolnikov has been driven to kill by the exercise of his analytical powers. Therein lies the novel's central message, to which all its other ramifications are incidental.

Raskolnikov's crime has not been to bash out the brains of an old woman, but to place too much reliance on his own.

Another of *Crime and Punishment*'s innovations lies in harmony of structure. Here Dostoyevsky surpasses his previous works. Depending (as noted above) on a central plot simple in the extreme, despite elaborate psychological embellishment, the novel also has two important sub-plots. Each balances the other, each invokes a network of emotional and financial involvements, and yet each lacks the weight of analysis borne by the central plot. One of these intrigues concerns the Marmeladov family; carried over from the projected but shelved *Drunkards*, they resemble in spirit the 'poor folk' of Dostoyevsky's first novel. The second sub-plot revolves round Raskolnikov's sister Dunya and the pursuit of her by the scoundrels Luzhin and Svidrigaylov. This last-mentioned figure echoes and much develops the type of Prince Valkovsky in *Insulted and Injured*, while also foreshadowing Dostoyevsky's most famous villain—Stavrogin in *Devils*. A representative of casual criminality, Svidrigaylov stands at the opposite pole to the virtuous Sonya Marmeladova. Like a devil and an angel they struggle for the soul of Everyman-Raskolnikov, thus presenting the first major ideological conflict in Dostoyevsky's fiction. The clash is eventually won by Sonya after Svidrigaylov has demonstrated his moral bankruptcy by suicide and Raskolnikov has confessed his crime.

Despite the eventual triumph of virtue, the novel is typically more compelling when it portrays evil than when it preaches virtue, Sonya being a less memorable character than Raskolnikov and Svidrigaylov. But she represents yet another significant landmark. Never before had Dostoyevsky introduced into fiction a figure seemingly designed to edify, and even to be imitated by, his readers. This saintly young woman, driven to prostitution by her family's poverty, is a fervent Christian believer. She offers Raskolnikov a way out, urging him to abandon the treacherous intellect, to act on the dictates of the heart, to accept the teachings of Christ, to confess his crime and to expiate it through Siberian sufferings. Here Dostoyevsky first introduces implied Christian apologetics into his fiction, though there is evidence that he had already attempted to do so in *Memoirs from Underground*. In a passage of that work—banned by 'those bastard censors', said Dostoyevsky, and since lost—he had deduced from the negative circumstances surrounding his hero a need for the positive balance of Christ's teaching.[7]

Now adding Orthodox Christianity to the ingredients of Russian nationalism, folk worship, Pushkinolatry and socialist-baiting, Dostoyevsky had already assembled much of the great structure of dogma that he was to preach until the end of his days. It is tempting to see in the near completion of this crystallization process, as in his choice of murder as a fictional theme, yet another of those prerequisites for the attainment of artistic maturity that had been lacking in his first two decades of authorship. To depth of analysis, symmetry of structure and the heat of metaphysical battle must be added many other features that also contribute towards making *Crime and Punishment* Dostoyevsky's finest novel to date. There is the superb characterization, of minor as well as major figures; there is the humour that surrounds Dunya's suitor Razumikhin and her mother Pulkheriya Aleksandrovna. A superb *skandal* scene, occurring at the wake following Marmeladov's funeral, shows comedy and poignancy cunningly blended.

The appearance of the novel's first chapters in *Russky vestnik* had been closely preceded by a second Moscow homicide remarkably similar to Raskolnikov's crime. It took place on 12 January 1866, soon after Dostoyevsky's copy had been delivered to the journal, and the murderer was a student, A. M. Danilov; his victims, whom he also robbed, were a (male) pawnbroker and his maidservant. The timing shows that this killing cannot have inspired *Crime and Punishment*, as the earlier Chistov murder (mentioned above) may have done. Nor, conversely, can *Crime and Punishment* have inspired Danilov's crime; it was not in any case 'ideological', having been committed purely for

St Petersburg in the 1850s:
Below Nevsky Prospekt
Bottom Easter celebrations

Above left Dostoyevsky in 1863
Above right Dostoyevsky's second wife
Anna Grigoryevna (née Snitkina)
Left The house in Kaznacheysky Street
in which *Crime and Punishment* was
written

ПРЕСТУПЛЕНІЕ

И

НАКАЗАНІЕ

РОМАНЪ

ВЪ ШЕСТИ ЧАСТЯХЪ СЪ ЭПИЛОГОМЪ

Ѳ. М. ДОСТОЕВСКАГО

ИЗДАНІЕ ИСПРАВЛЕННОЕ

ТОМЪ I

ПЕТЕРБУРГЪ
Изданіе А. Базунова, Э. Праца и Н. Вейденштрауха
1867.

gain. But the murder seemed no mere coincidence to Dostoyevsky; rather did it convince him that he had his finger on the pulse of his epoch. He was proud to have anticipated an actual event, and contrasted his own literary method, that of the novel of ideas, with the pedestrian fact-grubbing of certain unnamed contemporary writers whom he called 'realists'. 'Their realism can't explain a single real event in a hundred. But I, basing myself on ideas [*idealizmom*], have even predicted events.' Coinciding almost exactly with the first instalment of *Crime and Punishment*, the Danilov murder and trial helped to publicize the novel.

'A novel is a poetical activity requiring peace for the mind and imagination', Dostoyevsky had written to Vrangel in February 1866. Such peace had eluded him during his relative inactivity of the previous year, and seemed no closer now that his creative energies were fully deployed. To ordeal by creditors, epilepsy and Apollinariya was added the anguish of acute haemorrhoids, which had taken to afflicting him every February and March; this year one attack immobilized him on his sofa for a fortnight. Another irritant was *Russky vestnik*. Its editors were 'frightful misers', said Dostoyevsky; they found his novel too long and therefore too expensive, even though they were only paying a miserable 125 roubles a signature. Soon his publisher Katkov was tinkering with the text, and insisted on pruning Sonya Marmeladova's exegesis of the Gospels despite the author's request that no alterations should be made.[8]

As the months went by another threat loomed closer, the new novel to be written under the crippling contract to Stellovsky. That 'speculator and rather foul individual', as Dostoyevsky described him, would hear of no postponement or monetary indemnity, forcing his victim (as the latter wrote to Anna Korvin-Krukovskaya) 'to do something unheard-of, something eccentric: write thirty signatures in four months and in two different novels.' Yet, as Dostoyevsky now for once admitted, he positively relished such eccentric and extraordinary situations. 'I'm not one of your solid, respectable citizens. . . . None of our writers past or present has ever written in the conditions I write under *all the time*. Turgenev would perish at the thought.'[9]

How well Dostoyevsky could stand pressure was soon to be demonstrated. At the beginning of October 1866 a substantial part of *Crime and Punishment* was still unwritten, while not one word of the new novel contracted for delivery to Stellovsky by 1 November was yet on paper. The only hope was to enlist the aid of shorthand, a craft not yet widely practised. He hastened to hire a stenographer, and on the morning of 4 October an Anna Grigoryevna Snitkina duly appeared at his flat on the third floor of a large lodging house in Stolyarny Street. She had been engaged from a secretarial school where she had still to complete her course.

It was with awe and trembling that the twenty-year-old girl reported for this, her virgin stenographical assignment, to the famous author whose work she admired: she had wept over *The House of the Dead*, and was now deep in *Crime and Punishment*. Demure in black, with a specially purchased briefcase, she concealed her nervousness behind the cool, businesslike style of a professional woman. Dostoyevsky liked her grave demeanour, she later discovered, for he had feared to meet yet another self-important, crop-haired, feminism-obsessed lady Nihilist. Meanwhile Anna had 'taken a strong dislike' to her employer at first sight; as was fully revealed only in 1973, when a long, hitherto unavailable section of her diary, transcribed at last out of the curlicues of Gabelsberg's Shorthand, was given to the world. By collating the new diary material with her previously published memoirs we can piece together the first impression that she had of Dostoyevsky. She found his manner odd; he looked like a bad-tempered schoolmaster; he wore an old, stained jacket, but at least his linen seemed clean. Producing a 'weird, shattered, battered, exhausted, sick' impression, he at once announced himself a sufferer from epilepsy. He tested her shorthand, remarked that she was too slow, and 'very rudely' pointed out that she had omitted two prepositions.[10]

Though he explained that he had an urgent deadline to meet, he seemed in no hurry to start work, and was soon retailing the story of his mock execution of 1849. He accused Turgenev of having rejected his motherland, and he denounced Nekrasov for cheating at cards and pontificating on humanity's sufferings from the comfort of a luxurious carriage.[11]

It was all most unnerving, especially as Dostoyevsky kept forgetting her name. But it meant of course that he had immediately responded to this woman twenty-five years his junior, and he plunged straight into spontaneous speech while ignoring, as was his custom, the canons of polite discourse between strangers. His behaviour was again anticipating that of Prince Myshkin in his future novel *The Idiot*; as it already had, we remember, when he visited Anna Korvin-Krukovskaya and her family. Within two days he was confiding details of that unsuccessful courtship in Miss Snitkina, and he also showed her a photograph of his deceased wife Mariya. He said that he had been happy with Mariya despite her jealousy, but further embarrassed his new secretary by telling her details (which she unfortunately did not record) of his extra-marital affairs.[12]

For all the difference in age, station and experience of life, Fyodor Mikhaylovich soon captivated Anna Grigoryevna with his childlike directness, a quality that she shared. What matter if he did not conform to any conceivable manual of deportment? Whether he was spouting profundities or babbling trivialities, whether he appeared with egg on his face or denounced Peter the Great—and he did all these things —she soon sensed the man behind the somewhat comic façade: his loneliness, his desperate need to be looked after, cared for, loved. Younger men, some of them her suitors, seemed empty and trivial by comparison.[13]

Meanwhile, between badinage and confidences, dictation proceeded and Dostoyevsky's short novel *The Gambler* rapidly took shape. It drew heavily on one of those love affairs which the author had so embarrassingly revealed to his secretary, that with Apollinariya Suslova. Polina, *The Gambler*'s heroine, is just such an imperious, strong-minded disrupter of male calm and sadistic sexual tease; she even bears the same first name, Polina being a more intimate variant of Apollinariya. And Polina's main victim is, appropriately, yet another self-portrait of the author, a young tutor called Aleksey who is autobiographically inspired in his introspectiveness, his extreme touchiness, and above all in his addiction to gambling at the roulette tables of Europe. In him Dostoyevsky vividly depicts his own obsession, recording the intense excitement—part of his future as well as his past—of staking his last florin at the tables 'alone in a foreign country, far from one's homeland and friends . . . without knowing what one is going to eat that day.'[14]

The Gambler is one of Dostoyevsky's finest short works, and emphasizes yet again the beneficent influence of acute tension on his creative mind. Here is a study of severe financial and emotional strain, written by a man himself suffering severe financial and emotional strain, to an impossible deadline itself encapsulated within the equally impossible deadline for a longer work, *Crime and Punishment*. Moreover, not only did Dostoyevsky contrive to complete *The Gambler* on time, thus fulfilling his contract with Stellovsky, but he also managed to fall in love with the stenographer with whom he had established a daily work routine. She would arrive at noon, hand over a transcript of the previous day's dictation and then take down the new material on which he would have been working, as was his habit, well into the small hours of the morning. Closeted so long and so regularly with an eccentric genius, Anna began to fear for her reputation with her employer's neighbours: might they attribute her frequent visits to some purpose other than stenography?[15]

On 30 October, his forty-fifth birthday, Dostoyevsky finished dictating, and on the morrow Miss Snitkina delivered her last transcript. In place of the black dress in which she had so far discharged her functions she now wore a confection in lilac silk so becoming that she brought a blush to Fyodor Mikhaylovich's cheek.[16] A few days later he was invited to her home and met her recently widowed mother, who was Swedish by birth.

On 8 November his proposal of marriage was accepted.

When not taking dictation Anna was a vivacious creature, much given to laughter and tears; her family (which included her married sister Mariya and her brother Ivan, a student) had nicknamed her Netochka Nezvanova after Dostoyevsky's early heroine. Her company delighted him, and he could be heard singing 'Anna Grigoryevna' in a pleasing tenor to the metrically equivalent tune of Verdi's aria *La donna è mobile*, from *Rigoletto*. The prospective mother-in-law found him charming.[17]

With the Snitkin family the engaged couple's relations seem to have been uniformly amicable, but unfortunately the same cannot be said of their involvements with the Dostoyevsky tribe. To read Anna's account of these is to become painfully aware of the ugly pressures, psychological as well as economic, under which her fiancé had laboured since his brother's death. His stepson Pasha, a year older than herself, was especially disconcerting. Idle, graceless, seemingly unemployable, with a rare vocation for scrounging, Pasha lived off Dostoyevsky in the belief that 'the old man' had only one function—to provide for his most important parasite's material needs. The youth openly treated Anna as an interloper. Nor was he the only hanger-on. There was also Dostoyevsky's destitute and alcoholic youngest brother Nikolay. Above all there was Mikhail Dostoyevsky's relict, the disdainful Emiliya Fyodorovna, together with her four children now aged between fifteen and twenty-four. Here was a clan of dependants poised to plunder Dostoyevsky's assets, though at least four of the seven claimants were in a position to earn their own living. Combined with his own congenital improvidence these human encumbrances seemed to remove all hope of solvency, and so Anna offered him her own modest resources to help pay his debts. But he wisely refused, knowing that her funds would only disappear into the bottomless pit.

While Dostoyevsky had been wooing and dictating to Anna, the serialization of *Crime and Punishment* had perforce been suspended, and at the end of November a reminder came from *Russky vestnik* that the ending (Part Six and the Epilogue) was overdue. Not a word of it had been written, but at least a plan existed. In December Anna settled him into a second dictating marathon, and a second miracle of productivity followed as the novel's climax took shape in her elegant squiggles. Completed in four weeks, this represents a creative *tour de force* even greater than the composition of *The Gambler*.[18]

That working to a deadline imposed by serialization, or rather to a series of such deadlines, need not prove fatal to the novelist's craft the examples of Balzac, Dickens and others had already shown. But the method has one serious disadvantage: it commits the author in advance, preventing him from revising the material as a whole—preventing him, at least, until the usual next stage when, serialization being completed, he can issue his work as a self-contained book. Dostoyevsky indeed was to bring out *Crime and Punishment* in two volumes in 1867, revising it for that edition. Yet he found no need for extensive changes. In its serialized form the novel was already a well-integrated work of art, thanks to care taken in the planning stage, and to the author's insistence on rewriting unsatisfactory material again and again. It is the first of his works for which extensive rejected drafts have survived, covering three early strata of the novel: a foretaste of the still more extensive preparatory material bearing on his later long novels.

In the case of *Crime and Punishment* these intensive efforts stimulated a particularly lively response from readers and critics. The reading public could talk of nothing else, Strakhov has recorded. Reviews and articles—polarized on political lines in a manner characteristic of the age and country—began to appear immediately after the publication of Part One in January 1866. By February the leading left-wing journal *Sovremennik* was already denouncing Dostoyevsky for libelling 'progressive' university students in the person of Raskolnikov. A more considered left-wing review, which appeared after publication of the novel was complete, came from the radical critic Pisarev. The root cause of Raskolnikov's crime was social injustice, Pisarev claimed; and he came near to assessing *Crime and Punishment* as a protest against poor housing conditions in contemporary St Petersburg. Only one among the novel's many critics had understood it correctly, according to Dostoyevsky himself. This was his old colleague and fellow-conservative Strakhov, who stressed that Raskolnikov's crime was the outcome of carrying a theory to its ultimate conclusion with traditional Russian excess of zeal. The interpretation is considerably closer than Pisarev's to that adopted here.[19]

As the critical reception of *Crime and Punishment* indicates, Dostoyevsky was now firmly identified as a representative of the political right wing. As such he could and did expect that his writings would be abused by the left-wing and liberal opposition, which had mobilized unprecedented momentum, militancy and self-confidence since the death of Nicholas I. Though hampered by continuing censorship, and by governmental oppressions which became more severe from 1866 onwards, adherents of the left yet contrived to continue publishing their journals and to make their views plain—though still in oblique and disguised form. In doing so they acquired a collective authority of their own, developing into an oppositionist 'establishment' imbued with an absolute conviction of its own moral rectitude. Terrorizing the craven-hearted, of whom of course Dostoyevsky was never one, with the appalling threat of being considered inadequately liberal, the Men of the Sixties (as these newly emerged oppositionists came to be known) imposed a considerable degree of subservience to their own taboos and dogmas. 'The Press was able for some time to exercise a "Liberal" tyranny scarcely less severe than the "Conservative" tyranny of the censors in the preceding reign.' Such is the verdict on conditions in the 1860s of the Scottish journalist Donald Mackenzie Wallace, a visitor from a slightly later period. A Russian contemporary, Aleksandr Nikitenko, who also happened to be a censor, put the same point as follows. 'In their intolerance they [the new opposition] are becoming representatives of a new and almost greater despotism than the previous one.'[20]

The less strong-minded among Russian intellectuals accordingly found themselves in a quandary. On the one hand they could not speak out openly against the state for fear of the Third Section and ultimately even of the *katorga*. Nor, on the other hand, did they dare speak out against the now-imprisoned Chernyshevsky or other prophets of the left, for fear of being considered *retrogrady*, 'reactionaries'—to some, an even worse fate.

Though the Men of the Sixties might frighten hesitant or undecided fellow-intellectuals, they could not frighten Dostoyevsky, who continued to call them Nihilists and to denounce them in his fiction and journalism until the end of his days. Anti-left polemics are an ingredient in all his later novels, each of which contains its mocked and derided Nihilists, from Lebezyatnikov in *Crime and Punishment* onwards. Only in *Devils*, as will be described, does this element come near to dominating an entire novel, but it is present in all. Nor was Dostoyevsky the only novelist to engage in these polemics. So far was the leftist literary 'establishment' of the 1860s from establishing a monopoly that a whole school of 'anti-Nihilist' novelists arose in that decade. Though Dostoyevsky himself transcends and dwarfs the genre, some of its other practitioners—not least Leskov and Pisemsky—are artists of considerable stature.

As for the manner of Dostoyevsky's writing—that, now that he had long ceased to display the cruder symptoms of Gogol's influence, was all his own. Here is dynamic fiction admirably adapted to the basic theme which had remained the author's broadest and most persistent from the days of *Poor Folk* onwards: humanity under strain. In *Crime and Punishment* his newly perfected narrative torrent whirls the reader through dozens of crises, great and small, while time almost seems to have stood still; for calculation will often show that the action has lasted only a few hours or days, yet here are hundreds of pages to cover so brief a span.

In the increased cultivation of pace and urgency the mature novels from *Crime and Punishment* onwards form a strong contrast with the earliest work, as they also do in the prevalence of direct speech. An astonishingly high proportion of Dostoyevsky's mature texts consists of dialogue; and, moreover, of dialogue constructed with uncanny sensitivity to the rhythms of individual Russian speakers. All the great novels have, consequently, proved easily adaptable for stage and screen, with minimum need for alteration in the wording of the original. This is the natural outcome of the special method of constructing fiction devised by this great playwright who never wrote a play.

Dostoyevsky's tense and urgent atmosphere is further enhanced by what are, in effect, his stage directions: all the frothing, the seething, the spluttering, the guffawing, the 'vicious hissing', the 'gloating sniggers' of characters who blench, blush and even turn green, yellow and purple at less than the drop of a hat. Such are the dramatic postures which they rapidly don and doff as they switch from love to hate, kill themselves or each other, are thrown or throw each other downstairs, lurch simultaneously or by turns into spasms of treachery, mental derangement, philanthropy, mockery, compassion, jealousy, sycophancy, paedophiliac lust, self-abasement and self-assertion. At times, perhaps, saved from melodrama only by their own and their creator's intense involvement with philosophical and religious profundities, these frantic figures are rarely presented, as are Tolstoy's, in course of development from one character type to another. For the stately 'epic sweep' of Tolstoy, as for the leisurely investigations of a Goncharov or a Turgenev, the hyper-concentrated Dostoyevsky and his brain-children simply have no time. We also note that Dostoyevsky had now irrevocably established himself—by contrast with these famous contemporaries, all noted for their rural scenes—as an incorrigibly urban novelist.

Such was the pattern of creativity, elaborated by trial and error over two decades, which Dostoyevsky brought to maturity with *Crime and Punishment*, there linking it for the first time to the supremely profitable theme of murder. And such the technique was essentially to remain in the four long novels, as also in certain minor works of fiction, which were to succeed *Crime and Punishment*. Yet that technique, far from imparting uniformity, was almost always to be harnessed to the creative strivings that prevented Dostoyevsky from repeating situations, characters, themes and ideas in any dull or mechanical fashion. Having once evolved the basic approach, he already stood poised to evolve it further, within the general framework here indicated, in a myriad new variations.

Anna and Fyodor faced many problems after celebrating their wedding on 15 February 1867. Of some the bride was already aware: her husband's irritability, his allegedly advanced age, his incurable disease. Living on his nerves and easily roused, he often shouted at the maid; and he would yell at the loutish Pasha, for whom he yet had great affection, often ordering the young man out of his study. There were also stormy scenes between Fyodor and Anna herself; one was provoked by his habit of risking his health in St Petersburg's freezing winter without his overcoat, which he frequently had to pawn. But such tiffs were soon forgotten, for there was no viciousness in his domestic nature, as there could be in his attitude to intellectual opponents.

Though Fyodor was more than twice Anna's age, he was only in his middle forties. Yet his stepson, his brother Mikhail's family, and even he himself spoke as if he were tottering on the verge of senility. Anna too claims to have accepted this view of him. She loved her husband 'without limit', she tells us in her memoirs, but goes on to invoke a limit significant indeed. 'It was not physical love, not a passion such as is possible between persons of equal age. My love was entirely cerebral and intellectual. It was more like adoration and reverence for a man so gifted and noble-spirited.' It was, says she, a love based on pity, and on distress at the unkind treatment of Dostoyevsky by his nearest relatives.[21] This version of their marital relations must be respected as coming from one with inside knowledge of the subject, yet it seems contradicted by much of her own and her husband's testimony as found in her memoirs and diaries, and in his correspondence. I believe her talk of an entirely cerebral love to have been partly delusionary, and to some extent inspired by a wish to present her marriage to posterity as more decorously sexless, and thus more 'respectable' (in the Victorian sense) than it actually was.

Anna knew that her husband was grotesquely jealous—she had only to exchange a word with a younger man for him to suffer agonies.

And so she shielded him by dressing and behaving in as prim and sedate a manner as she could contrive.

Though she had been informed of his epilepsy at their first meeting she did not witness an attack before she married him. A day or two later that omission was repaired when the wedding celebrations, including an excess of champagne, brought on a violent double seizure. Speechless, racked by convulsions, Fyodor screamed for two hours, uttering 'inhuman howls', his eyes staring wildly, his face unrecognizable and twisted with pain. It was more frightening than his bride had foreseen; but she held his head during the attack and comforted him through the week of black depression that followed in conformity with the normal pattern of his affliction.[22]

That Dostoyevsky had found a mate with resilience comparable and complementary to his own was not at once obvious to either partner. Anna could tolerate his irritability, his fits of jealousy, his alleged senility and even his epilepsy, yet she felt helpless when confronted by his infuriating family. They were, collectively, a most confounded nuisance, and they also brought out the worst in him. For all his moral robustness and intellectual force, he was the feeblest of creatures in any domestic context. Tears, shouts, screams, accusations—these could always be marshalled to control him, to extract more money from him, even to alienate him from his beloved young wife.

Somehow the relatives created an assumption that Anna, being so young, must need the constant presence of other young people. While she yearned to be alone with her middle-aged husband, the relatives accordingly insisted on inviting relays of youthful guests to their flat; and they did so, says she, expressly to show up her deficiencies as a hostess. Then the domestically experienced Emiliya Fyodorovna would criticize Anna's inadequate housekeeping to the unprotesting Dostoyevsky, while the hobbledehoy Pasha waged a campaign of outright nerve warfare. Deliberately disrupting the household, he would send the maid away on useless errands, hide the matches and gobble up the cream, all in order to inconvenience his stepfather and thus convince him that the young bride could not manage her home. Such is Anna's version. We do not have Pasha's, but his selfishness and ungraciousness are firmly established in his stepfather's correspondence.

In the end Anna was reduced to such despair that she accidentally hit on the only possible solution, a torrent of tears so violent as to outbid even the tantrums of the parasites. Sublimely unaware, hitherto, of his bride's sufferings, as of the domestic crisis brewing around him —and no doubt deep in contemplating the misdemeanours of a Peter the Great or a Chernyshevsky—Dostoyevsky quickly responded to a tempest of protest more impassioned than he could have expected from the gentle Anna. Deafened by her sobs, he quickly agreed that they must detach themselves from his obstreperous relatives at all costs, and that they could only do so by going abroad. He agreed with all the more alacrity owing to yet another threat of arrest for debt, on a writ taken out by a certain Pechatkin, one of his most persistent creditors.[23] Fyodor and Anna accordingly informed their hangers-on that they were immediately leaving for foreign parts.

The announcement naturally provoked a new sequence of financial demands which at once seemed to render their foreign journey impossible by claiming all the funds needed to finance it. But Anna, whose gentleness concealed a formidable will, now proved victorious on the practical as well as the emotional level. She pawned or sold the jewellery, furniture and other trappings of her dowry. Thus, in one way and another, sufficient cash was raised for man and wife to travel abroad while allaying the relatives' most insistent demands.[24]

On 14 April 1867 the Dostoyevskys took the train from St Petersburg for Berlin, leaving creditors and relatives behind. They intended to spend only three months abroad, but over four years were to elapse before their return to Russia.

8

Reluctant European

The Idiot

When Dostoyevsky left St Petersburg with his bride in April 1867 he was at the height of his literary powers, and was to write *The Idiot*, *The Eternal Husband* and much of *Devils* during a period of foreign residence extending until July 1871. In the course of this exile 'worse than Siberia' he and his wife spent an initial four months in Germany, over a year in Switzerland, nearly a year in Italy, and a final two years back in Germany; their chief cities of residence were Dresden, Geneva and Florence, and then Dresden again.

It was a life of discomfort and sufferings in a succession of furnished rooms. For the sufferings Dostoyevsky's three afflictions—his epilepsy, his financial helplessness, his gambling—were responsible, as also were the pangs of literary creation and the death of their first child. The minor irritations came from landladies, creditors, pawnbrokers, waiters; from the noisy plasterers working alongside their Dresden flat; from the even noisier blacksmiths beneath their rooms in Baden-Baden; from the aggravating wind, the *bise*, in Geneva; from the furnace of the Tuscan summer and a myriad other nuisances among which obtuse, dishonest foreigners loomed large.

Compensation was amply provided by the joys of creativity, which was by no means all suffering, and above all by Anna. Their marriage was developing more happily than had seemed likely to her husband, who had left Russia 'with death in my soul', as he wrote to Maykov from Geneva in August. This 'young creature naïvely and joyously eager to share my nomad existence' would be bound, he had felt, to become bored and homesick. In fact, though, 'Anna Grigoryevna has turned out stronger and more profound than I had realized or anticipated. In many ways she has been a real guardian angel.'[1]

Of Anna's response to married life we learn from her detailed diaries, kept in shorthand. They have been transcribed and published, and they cover, in some six hundred pages of close print, the period from April to December 1867. The entries from 14 April to 12 August 1867 have long been available in English translation, but those beginning on 24 August 1867 and ending in December of that year were not available even in Russian until 1973, when they were brought out in Moscow. This newly released material also includes entries, on which we have already drawn, for October and November 1866. The value of the whole is as an immediate record, intended for the diarist's eyes only, and it forms a corrective to Anna Grigoryevna's *Reminiscences* (first published in 1925, seven years after her death). Though these are based on the diaries, and though they remain an indispensable major source, they are marred by the widow's natural wish to impart an aura of reverential decorum to her husband's memory. There is no trace of such a cult in the diaries, where 'poor Fedya' appears just as he seemed to his wife at the time: pathetic, infuriating, impossible, wonderful, grand, petty, lovable.

Neither the wife's diaries nor her memoirs tell us much of his intellectual and spiritual life. We see him overwhelmed in the Dresden Picture Gallery by Raphael's *Sistine Madonna*, and even standing on a chair to examine the masterpiece at close quarters. We also learn what a shattering effect Holbein's *Christ in the Tomb* had on both Dostoyevskys when they passed through Basle on their way to Geneva. And we find him eagerly reading Russian and other material from local libraries and bookshops; they included works banned in Russia as politically obnoxious, among them being Herzen's memoirs, *My Past and Thoughts*, and the Russian-language periodicals published by Herzen in London.

Poor Fedya's own literary activities were largely in abeyance during the first months covered by the diary. We learn of a long, irksome article on Belinsky which he rewrote five times over a period of six months, but which has unfortunately disappeared. We also hear a little about his next novel, *The Idiot*, of which he discerned the first dim outlines in Geneva in August 1867. The inquisitive Anna did not hesitate to read any jottings that her husband might leave lying around their rooms, besides which she was still professionally involved in his work by taking his dictation. But though she regarded his mental processes with awe and respect, she yet had little understanding of them; nor did she claim insights into the recesses of his mind, but meekly accepted him, his ideas and his writings as far above her head.

Anna was an educated woman who visited art galleries and museums, and who could read her husband's and Balzac's novels with pleasure, but her supreme passion was for the minutiae of everyday life. She was fascinated by local price levels. A pair of shoes costing three thalers, five silver groschen; a tie bought for five silver groschen; another, with blue spots chosen in preference to a crimson one with bars, purchased for three gulden fifteen kreutzer. Such, indefinitely extended, is the core material of the diary. It is difficult to conceive of a work more riveting to a reader obsessed with the cost of mid-nineteenth-century European consumer goods and services. The price of chocolate, beer, scent, soap, pears, laundering, furnished rooms and the like, whether these items were cheap or expensive, the financial implications of being served coffee with too much sugar in it—these are typical themes of the banal saga. Occasionally the dramatic level rises, as when Fedya burns a hole in a sheet with a cigarette and they co-operate to conceal the crime from their landlady.

Despite Dostoyevsky's intellectual passions he too was capable of brooding on the price of soap and gooseberries, and there is no evidence that he was bored by Anna's obsession with such matters. On the contrary, her nature delighted him, and he grew more and more devoted to her. Rarely meeting anyone (apart from innumerable briefly encountered foreign landladies, flower-sellers, shopkeepers, laundresses, waiters, ticket collectors, librarians and pawnbrokers), man and wife were almost exclusively dependent on each other for companionship. That they spent much of their time bickering we know, for these clashes are also minutely chronicled by Anna Grigoryevna. Irascible, highly-strung, living on his nerves and with a very low flash-point, Dostoyevsky was often unreasonable and unkind. So too was his wife. She was not a tempestuous prima donna like Apollinariya Suslova, but she was no mild, submissive, mouse-like creature either. Each partner, then, was poised to make some fancied slight the basis for accusing the other of ruining his or her life. But then a delicious loving reconciliation would follow, and tears of rage would yield to uproarious laughter. Anna could never hold Fyodor's bad temper against him for long; she put it down to his illness, and however badly he might behave she found him basically sweet-natured and adorable. He had many of the qualities, good and bad, of a child—enough to arouse the maternal instincts of a male biographer, let alone of a loving wife.

His bad temper was vented on others besides Anna. He would threaten to box the ears of some restaurant *habitué* for giving him 'an inquisitive look'; he had a noisy quarrel with a Russian consular official who adopted a 'patronizing tone' when asking to see his passport; he was permanently braced to rebuke foreigners for assuming, as he tended to suppose they must, that all Russians were barbarians and savages. In summer 1867 his touchiness with those who 'jostled' or 'insulted' him became such a byword at the Baden-Baden casino that Anna discerned hopes of his being banned from the premises.

Throughout four years of foreign residence his addiction to gambling repeatedly arose to torment them both. It could only be a sporadic affliction; casinos were not available in their main places of residence, and so it was necessary for him to make a special journey whenever the lust for roulette became irresistible. This first happened less than three weeks after their original arrival in Dresden, when he abandoned his bride, took the train to Bad Homburg and embarked on a familiar routine. Convinced that he had an infallible 'system' which would make his fortune, he had soon lost all the money he had taken with him. He wrote to Anna demanding more cash by post; lost that; caught a cold; pawned his watch; contracted toothache; wrote for more money to pay for his journey back to Dresden: 'Don't think I'll go and lose that too, my angel.' Surprisingly he did not, and returned safely to his wife after twelve days' absence, about a thousand francs (three hundred and fifty roubles) the poorer.[2]

He was back at the tables again in June, having broken what was to be his normal gambling pattern by taking his wife with him. Baden-Baden was now the scene. Here she spent seven miserable weeks watching him in the grip of his addiction. Periodically refloated by sporadic loans and literary earnings; visiting the casino several times a day to hazard sums wheedled out of his wife, who usually held their money; making occasional triumphant minor coups as a prelude to 'losing everything' for the nth time; pawning, redeeming, repawning in bewildering succession his overcoat, his wife's brooches, ear-rings, wedding ring, fur coat, lace shawl, and even the lilac dress that had so impressed him on the day following his forty-fifth birthday—Dostoyevsky nevertheless endeared himself to her by his kindness. Whenever he had winnings in his pocket he would buy her flowers and fruit. On one joyful occasion he brought back all her favourite foods—caviare, bilberries, French mustard and even the edible fungi known as *ryzhiki* (saffron milk-caps): a Russian delicacy which, she claimed, no other husband in the world could have unearthed in this benighted German spa.[3]

What woman could have resisted him?

Constantly bemoaning his losses, Dostoyevsky yet knew that gambling eased his inner tensions if only by providing different tensions. 'My state is excited and alarmed, but that's what my nature sometimes demands.' Even when he was losing, a strange elation would come over him. Acutely conscious of his follies as he committed them, which was of course the best of the fun, he wrote to Maykov deploring his 'base and excessively impetuous nature. Everywhere and in all things I go to the limit. All my life I've overstepped the mark.'[4]

Hating and fearing her husband's addiction, Anna yet encouraged him to gamble on occasion. She has claimed that she 'never reproached' him for it,[5] but that is manifestly untrue on her own showing.

Of course she reproached him; she did so again and again. But she also knew that she was as powerless to stop him as he was powerless to stop himself. The folly of Bad Homburg and Baden-Baden was later to be repeated at Saxon-les-Bains near Geneva, and also at his old haunt Wiesbaden. But his craving for roulette was fortunately weaker, in the last resort, than his craving for Anna, and so these disastrous trips tended to be brief.

Before going on to Geneva we must briefly dwell on Baden-Baden, where Dostoyevsky's seven weeks of 'sheer hell', in summer 1867, included an experience yet more wounding than being broken on the roulette wheel. This was his visit of 28 June to his old rival Turgenev, now a local resident. Two years previously, we remember, Dostoyevsky had borrowed fifty thalers from Turgenev. The small sum had naturally not been repaid, and so the refined conventions governing relations between Russian borrower and Russian lender now came into operation. These obliged the debtor to pay his respects, however unwillingly, to the creditor, since the former might otherwise be suspected of indelicately suspecting the latter capable of the supreme indelicacy of asking for his money back.[6]

Arriving at noon, the caller found Turgenev at lunch. 'Frankly, I never liked the man personally', Dostoyevsky later explained to Maykov. 'I also dislike the aristocratic buffoonery of his embrace, whereby he makes as if to kiss *your* cheek, but then proffers his own. What appalling self-importance. But what most irked me was his book *Smoke*.'[7] The keynote of this recently published and generally ill-received novel had, Turgenev now explained to Dostoyevsky, been that 'it would be no loss if Russia perished from the face of the earth, nor would mankind be in the least affected.' Perhaps Turgenev was reviving his old habit from St Petersburg of the 1840s, of deliberately baiting Dostoyevsky, for he also boasted of having become an incorrigible atheist. In face of these provocations the militant Russophile and Christian Dostoyevsky remained cool, according to his own account. For once the plebeian contrived to 'needle' his aristocratic opponent: it was Turgenev, not Dostoyevsky, who first burst into heated discourse, pillorying all attempts to develop Russia's national spirit and cultural independence as 'bestial idiocy', and adding that he was even now composing a long diatribe against all Russophiles and Slavophiles.

Meanwhile the Russophile and Slavophile guest was waiting patiently to insert his poisoned darts. He calmly advised Turgenev, by now a confirmed expatriate, to order himself a telescope from Paris so that he could observe his motherland from his distant German retreat. Then, as Turgenev fell into a 'terrible rage', Dostoyevsky artfully feigned sympathy for his distress. 'I really had no idea that the failure of *Smoke* and all the hostile criticism would upset you so', he remarked with what he later called, when relating the incident, 'a brilliantly successful display of *naïveté*.' The disingenuous imputation caused Turgenev to flush and protest that he wasn't upset at all, but Dostoyevsky cut this short by picking up his hat and denouncing Germans as so many rogues and scoundrels; their common people were more dishonest and most certainly stupider than the Russian. Turgenev retorted that he considered himself a German, and no longer a Russian, and that Dostoyevsky's remarks were therefore personally offensive. Dostoyevsky then took his leave, both parties displaying the excessive politeness of the grievously insulted. Meanwhile Dostoyevsky was secretly vowing never to darken Turgenev's door again. 'He has insulted me . . . *by his beliefs*', he told Maykov,[8] and the phrase that I italicize is significant. To hold convictions on matters theoretical differing from those of Dostoyevsky was to offend him more grievously than would be possible by merely abusing him, stealing his wallet or spitting in his face.

The above version of the quarrel is Dostoyevsky's, as related in a long letter from him to Maykov of 16 August 1867, and also as recorded at second hand in his wife's diary.[9] Soon afterwards a copy of the relevant passage in the letter to Maykov was anonymously sent to the Moscow historical journal *Russky arkhiv* ('The Russian Archive') together with the request that it should be kept 'for posterity', but not published before the year 1890. When Turgenev learnt of this development (from a correspondent who had it from the editor of *Russky arkhiv*), he assumed the journal's anonymous informant to have been Dostoyevsky, of which there is no evidence, and replied giving his own very different version of the original interview. According to this, he himself had maintained the dignified reserve appropriate to one confronted by a raving lunatic, while his unhinged visitor launched an unprovoked stream of abuse against Germans, the ill-fated novel *Smoke* and its author. Turgenev wrote that he would have considered it most improper to express his heartfelt convictions to 'Mr Dostoyevsky', if only because 'I regard him as one who, through his nervous seizures and other causes, is not wholly in control of his mental faculties . . . I treated him as a sick man.'[10]

We do not know which version of the clash is nearer to the truth, but the episode brings out one important feature in Dostoyevsky's development: increased contact with foreign countries had further inflamed his impassioned patriotism. The same is true of other items in his system of beliefs: xenophobia, Christianity, monarchism, anti-socialism. The strength of these convictions was growing, and his letters from abroad express commitment to them more intense than is found in his preceding correspondence. 'Here, abroad, I have irrevocably become an out-and-out Russian monarchist.' He also asserted, and many a historian would agree, that the reigning Emperor Alexander II had done almost as much for Russia as all his predecessors put together. When, on 25 May 1867, the same reforming Tsar became the target for a second unsuccessful assassination attempt, during a visit to Paris and by an émigré Pole, Berezowski, Dostoyevsky was 'horribly shaken', and he accompanied his wife to the Russian consulate in Dresden, where they signed the visitors' book as a gesture of loyalty.[11]

Ultra-loyalist as he now was, Dostoyevsky was angry to learn from an anonymous letter what has later been confirmed from official records: that he was still on the books of the Russian police as a political suspect under surveillance, and that strict instructions had been given to search him with particular care on his return. He also believed that his mail was being intercepted by the St Petersburg authorities, and that a certain Russian priest in Geneva was spying on him on their behalf.[12] Dostoyevsky was furious. Did they take one of the Tsar's most devoted subjects for a Nihilist after all these years?

Love of Russia in the abstract coexisted for the Dostoyevskys with fairly extensive dislike of the few Russians that they met on their travels. There were casual encounters with insignificant travellers and brief meetings with the famous, among whom Goncharov figured as well as Turgenev. Accidentally running into Herzen in a Geneva street, Dostoyevsky took part in an exchange less cordial than they had had in London in 1862; they parted after a brief duel by 'politely-hostile' sneers. Recalling the episode soon afterwards in a letter to Maykov, Dostoyevsky embarked on a denunciation of 'our *intellectuals*. What wretched insignificant scum puffed up with vanity! What shit!'[13]

As for non-Russians, both Dostoyevskys heartily despised them Germany was depressingly full of Germans, as was Switzerland with Swiss. 'I hate having foreigners about the place', Anna confided to her diary on one occasion; she seems not to have realized that she and Fyodor, not the Dresdeners, Badenese or Genevans who jostled them in the streets, were the foreigners in these parts. The Germans were unbelievably stupid, deceitful and grasping, the Swiss were little better. As for Jews, connoisseurs of Russian anti-Semitism may note Anna's ludicrous account of the occasion when her husband, desperately anxious to pawn or repawn the famous lilac frock, was compelled to wait at the house of a Herr Weissmann. 'He sat there for over an hour—my poor, poor Fedya! So sweet, and so brilliant and so altogether fine, and there he has to sit and wait among a lot of Jews.'[14]

Distasteful or comic though the Dostoyevskys' xenophobia must seem, their yearning for Russia calls for sympathy. To Fyodor direct contact with the motherland was a professional as well as an emotional necessity. To write while living abroad was an impossibility, he felt, and though he devoured Russian periodicals in foreign libraries and cafés, they could be no substitute. Meanwhile, having few or no Russians to love, with the important exception of his half-Swedish wife, he had to make do with hating foreigners, and tackled this with the genial gusto that he habitually brought to the expression of hostility.

Another of Dostoyevsky's hatreds, the most fruitful of all, was boosted by the 'Congress of Peace and Freedom' which took place in Geneva in August 1867. It was attended by the Italian patriot Garibaldi, and also by an assortment of leading international socialists and anarchists, including followers of Bakunin. It was, according to Dostoyevsky, his first encounter with flesh-and-blood socialists and revolutionaries; so far he had met them only in books. And 'these gentry' turned out yet more nauseating than he could ever have anticipated. 'The lies they told from the platform to an audience of five thousand: fantastic, they beggar description. Absurdity, feebleness, muddleheadedness, contradictions, inconsistencies! It's grotesque. And this is the filth that tries to stir up the wretched workers! How sad! Their premiss was that to achieve peace on earth it was first necessary to destroy the Christian faith!'[15] Thus Dostoyevsky fulminated from Geneva to his favourite niece Sonya. Never previously had he given such forthright expression to his growing anti-leftist views which, together with many of his other major dogmas, were approaching their most extreme form during the years of his foreign wanderings.

Difficult though it was for Dostoyevsky to settle down to serious work on foreign soil, he began planning *The Idiot* at Geneva in the late summer of 1867. It was to develop in a very different way from *Crime and Punishment*. Whereas the evolution of that work had been clearly conceived at an early stage, the new novel was to prove tantalizingly elusive long after much of it had been committed to print. The first of its four parts was published in *Russky vestnik* for January and February 1868, but only after a long and complex process; no less than eight plans, covering with their attendant variations only the first quarter of the novel, can be traced in the extant Notebook material. Once again, as with *Crime and Punishment*, Dostoyevsky destroyed an ex-

Below Postcard showing the house in
Vevey where the Dostoyevskys lived in
1868; the writing is Anna's
Bottom The house in Dresden in which
the Dostoyevskys occupied a flat in 1870

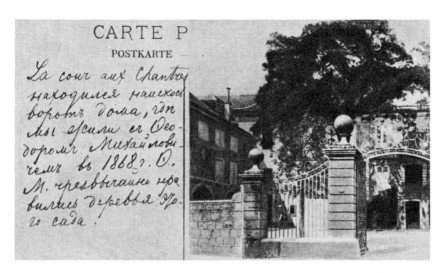

Rouge et Noir at Baden-Baden in the
early 1870s

Left The political terrorist S. G.
Nechayev, whose name Pyotr
Verkhovensky (*Devils*) bears in
Dostoyevsky's Notebooks
Below left Nikolay Chernyshevsky,
Russia's leading radical thinker of the
1860s
Below Page from Dostoyevsky's
Notebooks containing preparatory
material for *Devils*

tensive draft almost in its entirety, and then wrote the final version at tremendous pace. With the aid of stenography the first six signatures (over ninety pages) were composed in twenty-three days. It was the third such *tour de force* accomplished by himself and Anna.

Part One was enthusiastically received. But what form was the sequel to take? The author had only the vaguest idea, and there were distractions to keep him from concentrating on the matter, for Anna was in the last stages of pregnancy. The birth of their first child, on 22 February 1868, was a frenzied and chaotic affair characteristic of so disorderly a *ménage*. Labour pangs began at an hour when the prospective father lay prostrated by a fit; and the midwife, eventually summoned after delays and difficulties, failed to display the extreme degree of emotional involvement required by the birth of a Dostoyevsky. Muttering '*Oh, ces russes, ces russes!*' she claimed, once their little girl had been born, that she had never in many years of practice witnessed a newly delivered father so distraught and frantic. Alas, the child, named Sonya after Dostoyevsky's favourite niece, suddenly and unexpectedly perished of pneumonia before attaining the age of three months. Both Dostoyevskys were shattered by the tragedy. Fyodor sobbed bitterly, Anna has recorded, adding that she had never seen such paroxysms of grief. He covered the baby's tiny white face and hands with burning kisses, after which he and his wife dressed Sonya for her small, white-satin-upholstered coffin, weeping uncontrollably. Inconsolable, Dostoyevsky railed against his fate more bitterly than he had, to Anna's knowledge, at any other time in his life, while she herself was equally desolated. Dostoyevsky wrote some moving lines on the bereavement to Maykov. 'People try to comfort me by saying I'll have other children. But where is Sonya? Where is the tiny creature? To restore her to life I'd accept the torments of crucifixion.'[16]

The child's death made Geneva's associations intolerable, and the Dostoyevskys moved to the small lakeside resort of Vevey. But this too proved disappointing. Dostoyevsky has described it as a filthy little town of four thousand inhabitants with one of the finest views in Europe and nothing else.[17] Meanwhile he was still battling with Part Two of *The Idiot*, which was published in four relatively small instalments between April and July inclusive. Then, after the Vevey summer, the most wretched of their married life, the Dostoyevskys crossed the Simplon Pass by carriage in early September. They stayed a few weeks in Milan, where they admired the Cathedral. They then settled in Florence, valued for a variety of cultural amenities which included, besides the famous art galleries, a library containing Russian periodicals. Here *The Idiot* was completed in January 1869 after seventeen months' work.

The Idiot is, like *Crime and Punishment*, a one-hero novel—a single character dominates, being present on almost every page. But how sharply contrasted those dominant figures are. *Crime and Punishment* portrays a man who, if not irredeemably bad, is at least grievously mistaken. It is indeed an effective moral tale, but it is so largely in a negative sense, for most of it demonstrates how, according to Dostoyevsky, human beings ought not to behave. Now, with *The Idiot*, he had decided to think positively. 'A positively good man'—the formula is several times applied, in letters to his friends, to the central figure of his new novel who is also the 'idiot' of its title, Prince Myshkin. To realize this conception was the most difficult thing in the world, Dostoyevsky asserted, for the task of effectively portraying virtuous heroes had defeated all authors, Russian and non-Russian, who had attempted it. The sole exceptions were Cervantes's Don Quixote and Dickens's Pickwick. But those characters are presented as figures of fun, says Dostoyevsky; they are humorously described, and are therefore sympathetic to the reader. 'Now, I have nothing like this, absolutely nothing, and so I'm terribly afraid of being an out-and-out failure.'[18]

Besides helping to inspire *The Idiot*, this determination to develop a 'positive' hero was to haunt Dostoyevsky throughout the rest of his life. Nor is the fixation by any means unique to him among Russian authors. It had begun with Gogol in the 1840s, it became epidemic in the 1860s, and it has outlived the imperial state, surviving into the present day. Here is an abiding Russian literary obsession from which, despite Dostoyevsky's above-mentioned references to Cervantes and Dickens, western literatures have remained comparatively immune. 'Less content than foreigners to portray life as it is, Russian authors have long profited or suffered, as they still do, from an itch to portray life as it ought to be.'

Fired by this national obsession to create a positively good man, Dostoyevsky modelled certain aspects of his idiot on Jesus Christ, 'Prince Christ' being the name under which Myshkin occasionally figures in the Notebooks. Myshkin is given certain features of the Saviour as depicted in Russian icons—hollow cheeks, blond hair, a thin, pale, pointed beard. Christ-like, he 'turns the other cheek' when mocked and insulted by the novel's equivalent of publicans and sinners. There is also his habit of 'not judging' others, however sinful, criminal or indecorous their behaviour may be; as when conspiring Nihilists try to extort money from him on false pretences, but are won over by his refusal to take offence. By contrast with Raskolnikov, so reliant on the mind, Myshkin—being an 'idiot'—*has* no mind. He is all self-abasement, love, heart.

Neither feeling nor provoking resentment, the Prince lacks irritability, self-importance and consciousness of status; in which respects he is the very opposite of his creator. But in other ways he closely resembles Dostoyevsky, as has been noted above. He suffers from epilepsy and does not hesitate to inform total strangers of this affliction. While he is waiting to be received by the influential General Yepanchin and his family, he engages the butler with a harangue on the horrors of capital punishment. Such was the conversational style of his creator, whom we remember surprising his stenographer and future wife with similar embarrassing disclosures at their first meeting.

Christ-like or Dostoyevsky-like, these unconventional touches impart an endearingly comic flavour to Myshkin; and also, surely, to his creator. But two qualifications must be added. First, we know, as is mentioned above, that Dostoyevsky did not consciously conceive Myshkin in a humorous light; still less, of course, did he so regard himself. And, secondly, where phenomena as elusive as humour and Dostoyevsky coincide, much latitude must be left for competing interpretations. Neither seriousness nor humour unalloyed, but an unresolvable tension between the two, is perhaps the key to Myshkin.

Since a reconstituted nineteenth-century Russian Christ was doomed to fail by the standards of 'this world', it is no surprise to find Myshkin crucified by a series of harassing ordeals until he eventually relapses into idiocy, and has to be freighted back to his Swiss lunatic asylum. But this symbolic Calvary is followed by no symbolic Resurrection; and so *The Idiot* seems to preach hopelessness, by contrast with Christianity's message of hope. The novel therefore represents a confession of failure by Dostoyevsky the moralist, whose positively good man had turned out a mere negatively good man. Aesthetically speaking, however, the comic Myshkin's tragic failure makes a more powerful impact than a more 'positive' figure might have contrived.

Structurally too the novel may seem to fail, being as diffuse as *Crime and Punishment* is taut and controlled. Here is a web of amatory and financial relationships well qualified to entertain the reader, but also to baffle him. Even at the moment when he puts the novel down he might be unable to summarize its intrigues as a whole, unforgettable though many individual episodes are.

One reason for the confusion may be that Dostoyevsky began projecting *The Idiot* without any Myshkin in mind. Only at a late stage of the planning did that tantalizing figure assume his final dominant and saintly form after a bewildering variety of earlier concepts—even including a satanic, self-willed Prince—had been discarded. An entirely different figure had obsessed Dostoyevsky from the beginning: a tempestuous woman with a huge sense of grievance, the eventual

Nastasya Filippovna. Somehow this image arose out of a real-life court case involving a teen-age Moscow girl, Olga Umetskaya, who had four times set fire to her family home after being savagely misused by her neglectful and sadistic parents. But there is little of Miss Umetskaya and far more of Miss Suslova in the finished Nastasya Filippovna. Seduced in youth by an elderly roué, she has decided to capitalize on the emotional hurt of being a 'fallen woman', as she chooses to regard herself. Much of the narrative concerns her oscillating amatory and emotional involvements: with Myshkin himself, with her original seducer Totsky, with the imperfectly realized Ganya, with the demoniac Rogozhin who eventually murders her. Some details of that murder were inspired by newspaper reports of an actual murder trial of November 1867, that of the Moscow merchant V. F. Mazurin who had killed a jeweller with a razor.[19]

To invoke these details is to realize that *The Idiot* does ultimately conform, for all its apparent shapelessness, to a simple structural principle. Throughout it runs a fundamental contrast between Myshkin and all the other characters. Serene, except during his epileptic fits and occasional impassioned harangues, he is a figure 'not of this world': one who can feel intense pity, yet remains personally uninvolved in the frantic activities cultivated by everyone else. Lying, cheating, stealing, fornicating, getting, spending, they lay waste their powers on pursuits more futile than the blissful inactivity of their saintly foil. We may accordingly contrast the two-part scheme of *The Idiot* with the three-part scheme of *Crime and Punishment*, as represented by Sonya, Raskolnikov and Svidrigaylov. Taking over the mantle of Sonya as representative of Dostoyevskian virtue, Myshkin faces unregenerate humanity, and is defeated by it.

Nowhere is *The Idiot* more creatively tantalizing, nowhere does it more eloquently present the gulf between the hero and his associates, than in the Chinese vase incident: ripest of all the many fictional *skandaly* that Dostoyevsky had so far created. The scene is a reception at the home of General Yepanchin, whose daughter Aglaya (modelled on Anna Korvin-Krukovskaya) is thought likely to become affianced to the blundering Myshkin. Here is a test of the Prince's social eligibility. Can he appear in polite society and behave in accordance with normal conventions? His chances are compromised by the bossy Aglaya, who visits him on the eve of his ordeal to warn him against committing three particular gaffes. He is not to deliver a philosophical tirade. He is not to have an epileptic fit. And he is not to knock over and break Madame Yepanchina's Chinese vase; as, Aglaya fears, he inevitably must.

Myshkin is not, in brief, to behave like a Dostoyevsky.

In the event he of course commits all three solecisms in succession. His first offence is to embark on a heated discourse, unacceptable in a civilized drawing room, by developing an exuberant onslaught on Roman Catholicism, and he ends with an appeal for the regeneration of humanity by the Russian idea, the Russian God and the Russian Christ. This oration not only breaks the social conventions, but does so in a significant and puzzling form. For Myshkin's sentiments, Myshkin's words, Myshkin's whole style are precisely those of Dostoyevsky expressing his cherished beliefs in his letters and articles. And yet here is that very creed ingeniously exploited as a device for increasing the comic, if painfully comic, pressures of a superb farcical scene. It is a Myshkin still babbling Dostoyevskian revealed truths who, with a careless wave of the arm, sends the Chinese vase crashing to the ground before crashing to the ground himself in an epileptic seizure similar to many that accompanied the writing of the novel.

The Chinese vase scene reveals certain key features in the mature Dostoyevsky's brain. Having embraced certain dogmatic views, he was yet subject, even while expressing those views, to diametrically contrary tugs. It is as if he could not believe without wanting to discredit his own faith. Creating Myshkin in his own and Jesus Christ's combined image, he could not help mocking his own creation even as he sought to worship it. Such ambivalence is found in much of his later fiction, where he often creates idols only to hold them up to implied ridicule.

Eight years earlier, in 1861, Dostoyevsky had evoked the elusive phenomenon of belief in a fascinating passage of his *Series of Essays on Russian Literature*. Here, though he discusses the matter with others ostensibly in mind, his observations seem especially applicable to himself. Perhaps no other words of the master, either in his fiction or his philosophical essays, so much help to chart the caverns and pot-holes of his brain.

'There's a sort of believer who doesn't believe in his own beliefs. "You don't really mean it, do you, old boy?" So he keeps telling himself, even as he tries to convert others. Meanwhile he has worked himself into white-hot fury over his faith, but not necessarily out of a wish to deceive. I once knew an individual, a believer, who actually admitted this. He belonged to the category of unquestionably intelligent persons who spend all their lives behaving idiotically; and, by the way, how is it that limited, dull spirits act far less obtusely than clever men? "Why preach what you don't believe?" we asked the individual who had made the disclosures. "Whence all this raging, blazing conviction in one who doubts his own assertions?" The reason for this impetuosity was, he replied, a persistent urge to convert himself. . . . Perhaps there really are men who never stop frenziedly and frothily proselytizing; and who do this with the sole aim of converting themselves, while yet remaining unconverted till their dying day.'[20]

If one bears this 'individual' in mind Dostoyevsky's beliefs, and their part in his later fiction, acquire a new resonance. How subtly didactic, yet at the same time tension-provokingly anti-didactic, these works can be *The Idiot* well illustrates with its hero who expresses his creator's ideas yet also seems to discredit them.

The reception of *The Idiot* was almost as disappointing as that of *Crime and Punishment* had been encouraging. Though Part One of the new novel was ecstatically welcomed by the public, and received some favourable reviews, this early enthusiasm faded as the three remaining parts appeared. For two years the completed work did not inspire a single article or review. In view of this, and also of mixed comments from readers, Dostoyevsky several times referred to *The Idiot* as a 'failure', in his letters. But he later concluded that the public as a whole liked the novel, even if the critics had ignored it. He might have derived further consolation could he have been aware of Tolstoy's high opinion of Prince Myshkin, whom he once described as 'a gem'.[21]

Inclining to Tolstoy's view of Dostoyevsky's hero, posterity has tended to admire *The Idiot* as an even profounder achievement than *Crime and Punishment*, inferior though the later work must be judged by any conventional criterion of what a novel should be. *The Idiot* was, moreover, the author's own favourite among his works; but with the possible exception of *The Brothers Karamazov*, since he expressed his preference at a time (in 1877) when that, the last of his great novels, was still to be written.[22]

9
Scourge of Socialism

The Eternal Husband; Devils

After the last instalment of *The Idiot* had been sent off, in January 1869, the Dostoyevskys hung on in Florence for a further six months while it became increasingly necessary, yet increasingly difficult, for them to leave Italy. Anna was pregnant again; and Fyodor, speaking no Italian, felt unable to make even such unsatisfactory arrangements for her accouchement as had been contrived in Geneva. Meanwhile they were marooned by debts and destitution in a city where the summer's heat-wave made their rooms seem like a Russian steam-bath, even at night. But then at last another advance from Katkov, of seven hundred roubles, floated them out of Tuscany in July. They headed north through Bologna, Venice, Trieste and Vienna to Prague, where they intended to stay. But lodgings suitable for a family proved unobtainable, and so they went to Dresden, which they had quitted over two years earlier, and which was at least a known quantity. Here in September a second daughter was born: Lyubov (Lyuba), who was to write one of the many biographies of her father.

In Dresden, where the Dostoyevskys were to reside for two years until July 1871, the pattern of foreign exile was varied by the pleasures of parenthood and by the arrival of Anna's mother, who lived with them for a while. In other respects life was much the same as ever. There was still the same poverty, sporadically eased as loans and advances became available. They were still pawning their possessions, including for the first time poor Fedya's very trousers. Among other financial projects was his encouragement of Anna's younger brother Ivan to elope with an heiress, and an attempt to sue the scoundrelly publisher Stellovsky, through proxies in Russia, for a large overdue fee.

Dostoyevsky's routine was little disturbed when, in July 1870, Dresden and Saxony became involved in the Franco-Prussian war. But the distant hostilities, and the signs of military activity in the city, did evoke from him some generalizations on the beneficent nature of war, a theme later to be taken up in his *Diary of a Writer*. 'Without war', he wrote to his niece in August, 'man ossifies in comfort and wealth, completely losing the capacity for generous thoughts and feelings, while unobtrusively becoming embittered and sinking into barbarism.'[1]

In war, as in peace, Dresden continued to offer the Dostoyevskys little scope for social communion outside the home. Still irritated by the few Russians that they encountered, and still hyper-irritated by the many foreigners, both pined for their motherland more than ever. With mounting despair Dostoyevsky again and again claimed that he simply must go home if he was to preserve his vocation as a Russian novelist. But despite all his efforts substantial Russian debts remained unpaid, and he still feared that his creditors would have him arrested if he were foolish enough to cross the frontier.

Fortunately opportunities for gambling remained restricted, and I find no trace of the roulette wheel on record between Dostoyevsky's last visit to Saxon-les-Bains in April 1868 and a trip that he made from Dresden to Bad Homburg exactly two years later. In the April after that he went to Wiesbaden, quickly squandered all his cash at the tables and wrote asking Anna for thirty thalers to pay his return fare. Promising as usual not to hazard *that* money when it arrived, he also undertook for the *n*th time to give up gambling for good. His father had (he explained) appeared to him in a dream, 'boding dire doom and in a dread aspect that he had only twice presented to me in life.' Swayed by the grim apparition thus described in one of his exceedingly rare references to the deceased doctor, Dostoyevsky added that he at last felt released from his 'vile fantasy' of acquiring sudden wealth at the tables, a delusion that had plagued him for nearly ten years. 'Now I'm yours, yours, yours indivisibly, all of me', he told his wife. 'So far I'd *half belonged* to that blasted fantasy.'[2] Anna had heard this kind of thing before. Still, her husband had always been unpredictable, and was supremely so on this occasion by doing exactly as he said: he never did gamble again.

Here, in the renunciation of a major destructive habit, is the second milestone in his slow evolution, under his wife's influence, towards a somewhat less chaotic and distraught existence. The first step had been the renunciation of anguish-purveying female associates, though not of sexual torment in another of its aspects: the spasms of unreasoning jealousy that were always to trouble him, even in the haven of a secure marriage.

Though marital jealousy was a curse it could also be an inspiration, as Dostoyevsky shows in his short novel written in Dresden in the last three months of 1869, *The Eternal Husband*. It presents a psychological duel between two rivals in love, the widower Trusotsky and his wife's one-time lover Velchaninov. The erring Mme Trusotskaya has conveniently died nine years before the action commences, and so the two men are free to concentrate on their fascinating mutual relations, unhampered by feminine tantrums or demands. Meeting after so long an interval, they savour the torments of having betrayed and having been betrayed; and with all the more relish when the paternity of a charming little girl, Liza, born to the Trusotskys shortly before Madame's death, comes into play as a major counter. The childless Velchaninov learns that he is—well, probably is, since doubt is of the essence when Dostoyevsky deploys such situations—Liza's father, and he conceives a strong paternal affection for her. But she, knowing nothing of this, continues to believe Trusotsky (whom she adores) to be her father, a situation that the latter craftily exploits by uttering suicide threats in her presence. He thus terrorizes the little girl with the prospect of her darling daddy's death and thereby, through her, exquisitely tortures his hated rival Velchaninov who, supposing himself to be the child's father, suffers correspondingly. Eventually, after exhausting the possibilities of psychological torment, Trusotsky tries to murder Velchaninov by stabbing—but fails. Such is the climax of a tautly constructed tale quintessentially Dostoyevskian in its ingenious perversities.

While writing this account of betrayal, Dostoyevsky was himself simultaneously indulging in a betrayal of his own, for he had failed to offer this latest work to Katkov's *Russky vestnik* despite a definite, albeit non-contractual, undertaking to supply the journal with a new novel to be serialized from January 1870 onwards. *The Eternal Husband* appeared instead in the January and February numbers of a new review, *Zarya* ('Dawn'), which shared with *Russky vestnik* a nationalist flavour congenial to so patriotic a contributor. Having received many sizeable and still undischarged advances from Katkov, Dostoyevsky committed a breach of faith in sending *The Eternal Husband* to another editor. Still forgetful of his obligation to *Russky vestnik*, he was soon extracting from *Zarya* advances for further work, which was never to be written; nor, for at least three years, were those advances repaid.

While performing these manœuvres, Dostoyevsky was, like a very General Ivolgin, simultaneously congratulating himself on his professional integrity. 'I have always fulfilled my literary obligations most scrupulously, I've never let anyone down', he boasted. Never had he accepted an advance unless he already had a 'ripe' and detailed plan waiting to be realized. So he said. But some of his editors would probably have considered the following comments (from his letter to Anna of 21 May 1867) a more accurate reflection of his business methods. 'I'll write . . . and ask *Katkov* to send me . . . another five hundred roubles. He'll frown no end, of course, but he'll send it. Having given me so much already (three thousand roubles), he won't refuse this. In fact he's hardly in a position to, for how am I to finish the thing without money?'[3] As for never taking an advance except when a 'ripe' plan had been worked out, he had done so for *The Idiot* again and again. We may also remember his strenuous efforts to extract three thousand roubles against the never-to-be written *Drunkards*, for which no more than the sketchiest of plans ever existed.

So much for Dostoyevsky the publisher's pest, at his worst. It would be ridiculous and unjust to condemn him for professional malpractice, especially as helplessness, innocence and despair played so large a role. On the other hand it would be equally naïve to claim that no element of calculation whatever lay behind these shifts. His was a broad nature: sublimely petty, often enough, when it was not sublimely magnificent. Those capable of the major intellectual effort of absorbing his great novels can, surely, contrive to respect both the author himself and the standards of professional integrity that he so often ignored or flouted.

What motives inspired these immortal creations? Like many a lesser man, Dostoyevsky found himself baffled by the relations between his career and the material benefits that it produced. 'I've worked for money all my life', he wrote to Strakhov in February 1870. Yet, in a sense, he had never written for money at all. Never, he claimed, had he chosen his subjects on the basis of financial calculation; never, at least, had he written 'for money alone'.[4] And despite all evidence of his failure to meet specific undertakings, the integrity of his artistic conscience does indeed remain unassailable. He might take money for work that was never written, fail to repay advances, miss urgent deadlines. But he was temperamentally incapable of submitting material that fell below his best potential, as witness his practice of destroying extensive drafts and rewriting them until they satisfied his severest critic, himself.

Yet how rarely was he satisfied with his achievements when he saw them in print. Again and again he confessed his shortcomings with a natural modesty such as is implicit in a letter to his niece Sonya of August 1870. Here he bewails his situation with much humility towards his literary rivals, of whom the first-mentioned was a personal enemy. 'Oh, Sonechka, if you only knew how hard it is being a writer, that burdensome fate. I'm quite sure, believe it or not, that if I had two or three years' financial security for my novel, like Turgenev, Goncharov, and Tolstoy, then I too would write something that would be spoken of a hundred years later.'[5] Whether greater security would indeed have enabled him to achieve even more we can never know. He who wrote *Crime and Punishment* and *The Idiot*, he who was now writing *Devils*, while racked by epilepsy, tormented by domestic cares, hounded by creditors, persecuted by his addiction to gambling—would he really, granted the ease and serenity for which he craved, have surpassed those masterpieces? Possibly, for a considerable palliation of domestic chaos and discomfort was not to prevent him from writing *The Brothers Karamazov* towards the end of his life. But it is also possible that a Dostoyevsky wholly purged of anxiety might not have put pen to paper at all.

Devils (also known in English as *The Possessed*) was the product of three years' agonizing labour from its initial conception, at the beginning of 1870, to the completion of serialization in *Russky vestnik* for December 1872. Chronologically the creation of the novel was bisected almost exactly by the Dostoyevskys' return to Russia in July 1871, by which time about a third of the text was in print. But though the remaining two-thirds was to receive its final form on Russian soil, the main planning effort belongs to Dresden and the year 1870. *Devils* took almost as long to plan and create as did *Crime and Punishment* and *The Idiot* combined, and the Notebooks in which Dostoyevsky recorded his evolving intentions are correspondingly more extensive than the preparatory material bearing on any of his other works. More extensive too are the successive radical transformations which the Notebooks record as taking place in his developing plans. 'No work ever cost me more toil', he told Strakhov in October 1870, by which month a sizeable section of Part One (the first third of the novel) was ready for the printer after the initial plan had been changed again and again. Part One had been redone and rewritten 'a score of times, if not more', Dostoyevsky informed his niece Sonya in the following January; but, he added, it was still the merest 'rubbish'.[6]

In one crucial respect *Devils* all along remained true to Dostoyevsky's initial conception: that of a polemical novel directed against the Russian left wing. He intended to 'have it out with the [violently radical] younger generation in total frankness and with no fooling.' The work was to be deliberately provocative, a 'tendentious' study, a political 'pamphlet'. It would, said he, cause both Nihilists and Westernists to label him a reactionary. But no matter, for these same Nihilists and Westernists needed, in his view, 'a good spanking'.[7]

Specific impetus for this jeremiad against the left was provided by a sensational political murder of which Dostoyevsky was able to read in the Russian and foreign press in late 1869. On 21 November a student, the memorably named Ivan Ivanovich Ivanov, at the Petrovsky Agricultural Academy in Moscow was lured to a deserted part of that institution's grounds on the pretext of helping to dig up an illicit printing press; and was then beaten, strangled, shot in the back of the neck, weighted with bricks, and thrown into a pond by four fellow-conspirators who were members, together with their victim, of the same revolutionary cell. The group's head and founder was Sergey Nechayev, apostle and implementer of revolutionary destruction for its own sake, and he had persuaded his pathetic associates that their small unit was part of a world-wide conspiratorial network which did not in fact exist. The motive for Ivanov's execution was that he had challenged Nechayev's authority within the cell.

The murder of Shatov in *Devils* reproduces many features of the Ivanov murder: the theme of a printing press, echoing Dostoyevsky's involvement with such an apparatus as an active member of the Petrashevsky group in 1849; the dumping of the body in a pond, where it is soon discovered; the apprehension and confession of the accomplices; the temporary escape of the chief murderer. But the scene has been changed to the unnamed provincial 'our town' which is the setting for the novel as a whole, and which is unavowedly modelled on Tver—Dostoyevsky's place of residence in late 1859, and incidentally the only European Russian provincial town that he knew well. The names of the participants have naturally been changed; and their characters are substantially those of Dostoyevsky's imagination, further stimulated by certain real-life figures who had nothing to do with the Ivanov murder. The victim, for instance, bears more resemblance to Dostoyevsky himself than to Ivan Ivanovich Ivanov. But the chief murderer, Pyotr Verkhovensky, is in some ways a recognizable Nechayev, though far from a replica, and is regularly called Nechayev in the Notebooks.

Occurring towards the end of the novel, Shatov's murder is the climax to the campaign whereby Pyotr Verkhovensky and his attendant Nihilists accomplish the demoralization of 'our town'. Some of their earlier intrigues are less harrowing. For instance, they comically disrupt a literary recital organized for charity purposes, thus participating in the most memorable *skandal* scene in all Dostoyevsky's works. It veers from cruel laughter to tragedy later in the day when the fiasco of the evening's charity ball coincides with the outbreak of a disastrous fire in the working-class quarter of the city and the murder of two of the characters.

Such are the main activities of Dostoyevsky's political villains, the Nihilists or revolutionary socialists. They are far from obsessed with political ideas, and Pyotr Verkhovensky on one occasion remarks: 'I am a scoundrel, not a socialist.' Rather are they trivial, busy, officious, silly little mediocrities. One, Virginsky, is so obsessed with fashionably exaggerated feminism that he welcomes his wife's adultery: 'My dear, hitherto I had only loved you. Now I respect you.' Another, Lyamshin, specializes in tasteless practical jokes that include placing a live mouse in the case containing a holy icon, and introducing pornographic pictures into the stock-in-trade of an itinerant Bible-seller. Yet another, Shigalyov, is at least politically engaged to the extent of having written a treatise on revolutionary theory; but his offer to spend ten evenings reading it out to his fellow-Nihilists evokes hoots of laughter.

Trivial, pathetic, mediocre, yet somehow thoroughly nasty—these Nihilists are to Dostoyevsky the Gadarene swine of St Luke's Gospel into which the metaphorical devils of his title have entered, sending them plunging over a cliff into the sea. In a letter of October 1870 he explains to Maykov that 'the devils have left the Russians and entered a herd of swine—the Nechayevs, that is. . . . They have drowned or certainly will drown, while the healed Russian from whom the devils have departed, sits at Christ's feet. It was bound to happen. Russia has spewed out this filth on which she has been fed, and of course there's nothing Russian left in these spewed-out bastards.'[8]

By the time when the novel was completed the accent was more on the filth than on the feet of Christ, for here is a message of doom with hardly a gleam of hope. Dostoyevsky does not confine his political denunciation to the notoriously violent and radical younger generation, the 'children' of Turgenev's novel *Fathers and Children*; he also extends his strictures to their elders, Turgenev's 'fathers'. Mild, sentimental and easy-going though these might be, liberals rather than terrorists, they are in effect 'fellow-travellers' of their extremist offspring, and are presented as tainted with the same guilt. To Dostoyevsky all Russian oppositionist thinking of the centre or the left—be it liberal or reformist, socialist or revolutionary—was by now part of a heresy so monstrous that there was no point in distinguishing degrees of culpability. Hence the ridicule that he pours on the older as well as the younger generation.

These fellow travellers, without whose connivance the Nihilists might have been powerless, include Pyotr Verkhovensky's father and the mother of a still more important hero to be discussed later (Stavrogin), together with the Governor of the Province and his lady. All are pilloried as guilty. Yet they are treated in a comparatively gentle spirit, with the solitary exception of the 'great writer' Karmazinov. Here is Dostoyevsky's old enemy Turgenev viciously caricatured. Turgenev's tendency to emotional self-indulgence, his insultingly condescending social manner, his complacency, his indecisiveness, his tendency to truckle to the young, his timorousness, even his prose style—all are lampooned with the loving vindictiveness that Dostoyevsky could lavish on a hate-victim. Thus did he have his revenge on Turgenev for the crimes of lending him the still unreturned fifty thalers in 1865 and of proclaiming himself an adoptive German in 1867. As for Turgenev's reaction to the lampoon of himself in *Devils*, we discover this in a letter of 15 December 1872. Still claiming to regard Dostoyevsky as a lunatic, Turgenev also points out that the one work of his own selected for parody in *Devils* (the short story *Phantoms*) was 'the only story that I published in a periodical he had edited [*Epokha*], and for which he had showered grateful and appreciative letters on me.' Turgenev added that he had kept those letters, and that it would be amusing to publish them. 'But he knows I would not do so.'[9]

Karmazinov is a relatively minor figure, and the most memorable 'fellow-traveller' in *Devils* is Stepan Trofimovich Verkhovensky, father of the villainous Pyotr. Dostoyevsky based this, one of his most successful character studies, on T. N. Granovsky, a half-forgotten liberal of the 1840s, and he lavished great skill on making his vain, idle, elderly hypochondriac both ridiculous and sympathetic. So sympathetic is Stepan Trofimovich to his creator that he is eventually portrayed as renouncing his political heresies shortly before expiring at the end of the novel.

The gentle treatment of Stepan Trofimovich accords with Dostoyevsky's handling of the older generation, always excluding Karmazinov. But it contrasts with some of the savage remarks that Dostoyevsky was now making in his correspondence about Russia's premier political dissident of the same generation, his own original 'discoverer' of 1845 —Belinsky. To this period belongs, for example, Dostoyevsky's reference to 'mangy liberalism as preached by the dung-beetle Belinsky and shits of that ilk.' Describing Belinsky as 'the most stinking, stupid and shameful phenomenon in Russian life', Dostoyevsky also recalls that the critic had used obscene language about Christ in his presence. Such, he said, were the heretics who, going back to the original arch-heretic Rousseau, had dreamed of 'recreating the world on the basis of reason and experience, i.e. positivism.'[10]

Once again we see Dostoyevsky, in this passage from his letters, equating evil with the assumption that society can be organized rationally and 'by the mind alone'. It seems an inescapable inference that he attributed such heretical super-rationality to the Nihilists of *Devils*. Interpreters have accordingly claimed that these conspirators are pilloried as guilty, on a collective and political basis, of the same crime—excess of logic—that Raskolnikov had committed on an in-dividual basis.[11] There is, however, the difference that Raskolnikov is eventually redeemed, whereas the Nihilists of the later, more tragic novel are not. It must also be added that Dostoyevsky does not, in *Devils*, explicitly attribute the heresy of excessive rationality to his villains, with the exception of their comic philosopher Shigalyov. Rather are they portrayed as empty and muddle-headed. And their leading drive is not logic, but an instinct for mischief-making.

Mischief-making, self-importance, complacency, meddlesomeness and the pleasure of belonging to a group of unpunished naughty children—here, in Dostoyevsky's conception, are prime ingredients in the mentality of those who choose to dedicate themselves to left-wing politics. He was, of course, strongly partisan in confining his strictures to the left, which has never held a monopoly in cruelty, buffoonery and silliness. But it had never been his aim to provide a judicious, balanced assessment such as we find in Turgenev's *Fathers and Children*; and so there is no need to join issue with those who, Karmazinov-like, complain that *Devils* is 'unfair' to the Russian revolutionary movement. The novel is a work of art, not the report of a Commission of Inquiry, and Dostoyevsky was rarely visited by a vision more luminescent than this conception of *homo politicus*. Here are no tribunes of the people, but—in effect—so many nasty fat boys giggling with jam-smeared cheeks over a successfully raided larder, while also tittering at their cleverness in strangling the cat.

But what of any counter-currents? Is *Devils* all denunciation of the left? Has Dostoyevsky no paladins of traditionalist virtue to set against the forces of evil, no successor to Sonya Marmeladova and Prince Myshkin? Indeed he has—the murder victim Shatov. Here is yet another recognizable author's self-portrait, another Dostoyevsky even in his physical appearance: fair colouring, broad shoulders and frowning forehead. Shatov has the same social awkwardness, the same inability or unwillingness to assume drawing-room manners. He has also undergone, Dostoyevsky-like, the evolution from juvenile socialism to mature traditionalism. Like Myshkin on the point of shattering the Chinese vase, Shatov voices Dostoyevsky's own views on the Orthodox Church and Russia's special mission to save humanity. And yet he also makes the puzzling admission, indirect but clear enough, that he does not believe in God. And since Shatov seems expressly designed to be equated with his creator, this is one of the points at which Dostoyevsky the fervent believer seems to permit the other Dostoyevsky, the furtive unbeliever, to peep through his lines. Nor does Shatov function as an effective counter-balance to the Nihilists, for his squalid death shows the forces of good yet more devastatingly defeated than they had been even in *The Idiot*. Against this may be set the complementary defeat of the Nihilists, dispersed or arrested at the end of the novel; the conversion of Stepan Verkhovensky to anti-liberalism on the eve of his death; and such comfort as might be derived from Dostoyevsky's vision of Nihilists as swine who will carry the plague of left-wing ideas into the depths of the sea, leaving Russia to face the future unpolluted by their prejudices and malpractices. But these redeeming features do little to brighten the sombre perspectives of *Devils*. Not only is it Dostoyevsky's most tragic novel, but it is also the work in which violent crime (including four murders and two suicides) is more prevalent than elsewhere in his fiction.

The first of the two suicides in *Devils* is that of Kirillov, who (like Svidrigaylov in *Crime and Punishment*) carries the principle of self-assertion to the ultimate point of destroying himself. While killing himself he also serves the Nihilist cause by leaving a confession falsely claiming responsibility for the murder of Shatov. And yet Kirillov somehow remains untainted by the political and moral pollution so characteristic of his fellow-Nihilists. With his unidiomatic speech, addiction to tea-drinking and general air of eccentricity, he is a particularly puzzling character. So too, in even greater degree, is the second self-destroyer in the novel—Nikolay Stavrogin, whose suicide makes its last pages so memorable.

It is a measure of the complexity and elusiveness of *Devils* that many of its basic aspects have been discussed without reference to this, the novel's most important character.

Stavrogin is good-looking, wealthy, a natural leader. He has great charm, prestige, intelligence and strength of will. On one level his origins may be sought in the works of Byron and Lermontov; in Dostoyevsky's own earlier villains, Valkovsky of *Insulted and Injured* and Svidrigaylov of *Crime and Punishment*; in at least two early Russian revolutionaries—the dare-devil Decembrist Mikhail Lunin and the author's one-time associate in the Petrashevsky group, Nikolay Speshnev. Combining characteristics derived from these and other sources, Dostoyevsky has created a blasé superman who has spent all his life vainly seeking a way of deploying his strength. We learn of vague crimes and acts of debauchery committed by Stavrogin in the period before the action begins, and he emerges as a bullying eccentric who propels his associates into painful situations as a means of experimenting with them and himself. He has killed a duelling opponent, married a crippled imbecile, pulled the nose of an inoffensive provincial worthy. He has even fastened his teeth in the ear of the provincial Governor and held on to it for several paragraphs. By the time when the narrative begins he has gone beyond even these futile displays, having sunk to behaving in a fairly decent and conventional manner, but always with the suggestion that he is a wild beast about to use his claws. In the end he turns them on himself, committing suicide after leaving a note expressing his ultimate sterility. 'Nothing has come from me but negation, without magnanimity and strength. Even negation has not come.'

Stavrogin's links with the plot of *Devils* are multiple. He seduces, fascinates, marries or betrays in various combinations four of its women; he consorts with the infamous Pyotr Verkhovensky, allowing his name and prestige to be exploited for political purposes. Yet these, like all other purposes, mean nothing to him, his connection with the fundamental political theme being tenuous indeed. Rather is it in his detachment from political issues that his main function may be discerned. Stavrogin helps to make *Devils* much more than a novel about left-wing politics—an activity too trivial in Dostoyevsky's eyes, despite his hatred for it, to sustain a major work unaided. Here is a parable about Man without God, or, to phrase it more irreverently, about Man bereft of Dostoyevskian doctrine. While exploring the implications of the deprivation in a political context, that of the Nihilists and their 'fellow-travellers', Dostoyevsky deepens his message by simultaneously extending it to the non-political context of Stavrogin. Whether political-minded or not, whether engaged in collective action (as Pyotr Verkhovensky) or operating as an isolated cynic (as Stavrogin), Man-without-Dostoyevsky is demonstrated as equally doomed to moral bankruptcy, sterility, mindless violence, emptiness, frivolity and despair.

Yet *Devils* had been partly conceived in affirmative terms, for though it first arose from Dostoyevsky's preoccupation with left-wing wickedness as personified by Nechayev, it also owed much to a competing urge that long delayed and complicated its progress. Originally intending the novel, in early 1870, as a short, light-weight political satire to be completed in a month or two, Dostoyevsky had then been mainly concerned to clear the decks for a very different, truly major work on the planning of which he was engaged. This never-to-be-written masterpiece, for which preliminary notes exist and which is frequently discussed in the author's correspondence, assumed various guises. It emerged in early 1869 as a projected novel, to be entitled *Atheism*. Then the title changed to *The Life of a Great Sinner*; of which the central theme was to be the problem 'by which I have been consciously or unconsciously tormented all my life, the existence of God.' The hero was to veer between atheism and religious fanaticism through a cycle of three or five novels before eventually attaining redemption. The first novel was to be set in Russia of the 1840s, and the second would take place in a monastery to be entered by the hero after he had committed a violent crime at the age of thirteen. Here he was to meet Tikhon of the Don; or, presumably, since that historical pious figure had died in the late eighteenth century, a contemporary figure modelled

155

on Tikhon. 'Let's hope I shall produce a grandiose, *positive*, saintly figure', Dostoyevsky continues his discussion of *The Life of a Great Sinner*, using terms implying confirmation of what he many times indicated: that his Prince Myshkin, similarly conceived as 'positive', was a failure in his creator's eyes.[12]

In view of Dostoyevsky's strong moralistic urges, and of his abiding concern with man's destiny, one may easily understand this continuing determination to cultivate an affirmative approach and to write a novel that might prove a more effective force for good than any of his previous works. Such was his wish. But when writing *Devils* he was driven by some perverse urge in the opposite direction. It is the least hopeful, the least affirmative, the most deeply tragic of all his works; as it is also, in effect, the most hate-inspired, for the finished novel retains few traces of the edifying urges behind the Great Sinner conception. And yet that conception may ultimately have been the most fruitful of all if, as seems likely, it was responsible for detaching him from his original scheme for a short political satire, and for leading to a longer, more complex work which, while embracing politics, also goes far beyond politics.

Above all, the Great Sinner complex of ideas forced upon Dostoyevsky's attentions the concept of the 'new hero', who insisted on forcing his way into the plot of *Devils* when the programme for a short, exclusively political novel already seemed settled. This new character, at first called 'the Prince' but eventually to emerge as Stavrogin, functions in the early Notebook material as the mouthpiece of Dostoyevsky's own most cherished ideas, later to be ascribed to Shatov. He champions Russia against the West, defends the Orthodox Church against atheism. A 'gigantic idea' is arising in the East, says the Prince, and will 'regenerate the world. . . . We are bringing the world the first paradise of the millennium.' So far so good. But the words immediately following in the Notebooks emphasize Dostoyevsky's capacity for switching from positive to negative in the twinkling of an eye: '*Leaves for St Petersburg and hangs himself.*'[13]

So much for the regeneration of the world and the first paradise of the millennium!

Since Stavrogin was expressly designed as a mystery, and since the Notebooks show that he always remained an enigma to his creator, we shall not explore him further except in his relations to the notorious 'banned chapter' entitled 'At Tikhon's'. This aroused Katkov's objections as too obscene for the journal's censors or readers. But Dostoyevsky was determined that it should go in, and paid a special visit to Moscow to argue his case for including it. Failing to gain his point, he then wrote a second, toned-down version to 'satisfy the prudishness of the editorial office.'[14] But he was again unsuccessful. Nor, when publishing the novel in book form in 1873, did he take the opportunity to insert 'At Tikhon's', with which he had intended to begin Part Three of *Devils*. In it Stavrogin confesses to what is presumably the most evil deed that his creator could imagine: the rape of an eleven-year-old girl who later commits suicide while her violator, aware of her intentions, makes no attempt to save her. Stavrogin's strength and criminality are revealed by his ability to commit so vile an act without any qualms of conscience, and later by his admission of the crime, an account of which he even proposes to publish in printed form.

Is *Devils* better with or without this unsavoury material? The problem has been repeatedly debated, one critic calling the passage 'Dostoyevsky's loftiest artistic creation'. Another, more recent suggestion is that 'At Tikhon's' spoils the elusive Stavrogin by making him too comprehensible.[15]

Unaware of the existence of the 'banned chapter', contemporary readers of *Devils* found their sensibilities adequately titillated by the novel's provocative political features. As was only to be expected, conservative periodicals reviewed it favourably, while left-wing organs tended to disparage it. Among the latter was *Otechestvennyye zapiski*, where the leading critic Mikhaylovsky denounced Dostoyevsky for building *Devils* round the Nechayev affair, 'in all respects too great a monstrosity to form the theme of a novel of fairly broad scope.' The Nechayev theme was fit only for the plot of a trivial 'thriller', Mikhaylovsky added.[16]

A particularly bizarre sequel to *Devils* was provided by a rumour attributing to Dostoyevsky a crime analogous to that of Stavrogin in the 'banned chapter'. The story gained currency in various versions, none very convincing, and the account least lacking in substance comes from his old friend and travelling companion in Europe, that fellow-journalist and fellow Slavophile Nikolay Strakhov. For reasons that still remain obscure, Strakhov conceived a violent antipathy for Dostoyevsky about two years after the latter's death, and wrote to Tolstoy on 28 November 1883 to express the disgust now aroused in him by memories of his former friend. Strakhov portrays Dostoyevsky as 'vicious and debauched', adding that he prided himself on possessing 'obnoxious proclivities'. One Viskovatov (an acquaintance of Dostoyevsky's) had 'begun telling' Strakhov that Dostoyevsky had once bragged of having had intercourse 'with a little girl brought to him in a bath-house by her governess.' Strakhov's account gives no indication of date or location, and it names neither the child nor the governess. Nor does it even purport to be first-hand. Yet it gained sufficient currency to be indignantly refuted by Dostoyevsky's widow when she learnt of it many years after his death. She insists that such a debauch would have been beyond his limited means; but that particular argument is unconvincing since he is known to have squandered hundreds of roubles in a day in the 1840s. As for infant female prostitutes—they were, alas, available at a remarkably low tariff in St Petersburg. Yet can we wonder that Anna Grigoryevna dismissed the charge as a calumny? Or dispute her right to do so? Unfounded, too, in all likelihood was another version of the same story that has Dostoyevsky volunteering a confession of sexual relations with a minor to Turgenev, of all people.[17]

And yet, flimsy though Strakhov's evidence is, his ugly accusations could seem to acquire a hint of plausibility from the pederastic urges to which Dostoyevsky, on the evidence of his fiction alone, was inferentially prone. His works abound, from the start, in elderly lechers who conceive lust for immature females, the most notable example before Stravrogin being Svidrigaylov—described as having violated a fourteen-year-old nymphet who later committed suicide. However, Svidrigaylov was not Dostoyevsky, and to feel sexual desire is not inevitably to implement it; otherwise the world might be richer by many a multiple rapist. It must also be stressed that there is no shred of serious evidence, such as could stand up in a court of law, to connect Fyodor Mikhaylovich with such a tasteless outrage. I therefore cannot accept that he ever ravished, seduced or purchased an infant sex-object, especially as he was so civilized, sensitive, decent and kindly a man, despite the many aberrations of his nature and the appalling crimes that he could commit in his imagination.

Such is the verdict of instinct. But Dostoyevsky's was a dark and ultimately mysterious character, and I am intellectually unwilling to dogmatize without qualification on what his conduct might have been under all conceivable circumstances. Indeed, his supreme unpredictability is, outside the ugly context under review, a part of his charm.

What, to return briefly to *Devils*, of the rating to be assigned to that tantalizing novel, with or without its rape theme? It is perhaps worth repeating the opinion which is expressed in my previous, critical, study of Dostoyevsky (1962), and to which I still adhere: that here is the finest of all the works. Dostoyevsky's is above all a creatively destructive talent; and he is, however paradoxically, most effectively creative when—in *Devils*—he is most devastatingly destructive. Without seeking converts to *Devils*-worship, and above all without the remotest wish to disparage *The Brothers Karamazov* or any of the master's other works, I regard his greatest onslaught on Nihilism as one of humanity's most impressive achievements—perhaps, even, its supreme achievement—in the art of prose fiction.

The novel also constitutes an awesome, prophetic warning which humanity, no less possessed of collective and individual devilry in the 1970s than in the 1870s, shows alarmingly few signs of heeding.

10

Uneasy Compromiser

A Raw Youth

Returning from abroad in mid-1871, Dostoyevsky was a more established figure than the man who had left St Petersburg with his bride
four years earlier. With two major novels, and a substantial part of a
third, behind him he could at last feel that his literary reputation was
secure. He had been mellowed by fame and marriage, and he was
milder, kinder, more tolerant and more easy-going than before, though
he was still irritable and quarrelsome on occasion. He had also become
more devout, had acquired an interest in church history, and would
harp on religious themes in conversation.[1]

His wife too had changed. 'I had developed from a timid, bashful
girl into a woman of decisive character.'[2] Arriving in St Petersburg
with her husband at an advanced stage of her third pregnancy, she
was successfully delivered of their first son—another Fyodor (Fedya)—
eight days later. Soon afterwards she arose from child-bed to face
creditors who had waited four years to pounce on the returned exiles.
She has calculated Fyodor Mikhaylovich's debts at twenty-five
thousand roubles, owed to a wide variety of claimants. Some were
strangers who had bought up his promissory notes for a pittance as a
speculation. Others, as she only now fully realized, had obtained his
IOUs by fraud, falsely claiming to have been owed money by his
brother Mikhail. Faced by their tears and lies, he had signed whatever
was put in front of him. Now these tricksters, and creditors more
genuine, were again threatening to attach his possessions, and to have
him confined in the debtors' prison; as would probably have happened
before long had Anna been a less shrewd and flexible businesswoman.
She persuaded the creditors that prosecution would be to their disadvantage. It would give them their revenge, certainly, but never
would they see the colour of their money; besides which they would
also have to pay for his keep in gaol. And so Anna was able to persuade
them to accept payment by instalments.

Anna also rented their apartment in her own name; they were to
occupy a succession of five in St Petersburg during the ten years of life
remaining to Dostoyevsky after his return. And she obtained furniture,

of which they had none owing to their failure to keep up interest payments on the numerous articles pawned before they had left St Petersburg in 1867. Here too she showed her resourcefulness, buying new furniture on an instalment plan proposed by herself: it remained the vendor's property until fully paid for, and so could not be attached by creditors. And yet, despite all her persistence, their debts were not to be finally liquidated until the year of Dostoyevsky's death.

Fortunately Dostoyevsky was no longer burdened by his sister-in-law Emiliya Fyodorovna, whose children were grown up and self-supporting at last. But he still helped to maintain his alcoholic younger brother Nikolay, who now suffered from cancer. Nor had adult years and marriage palliated the worst irritant of all, his stepson. During his absence abroad the ridiculous Pasha had sold Dostoyevsky's treasured library and pocketed the proceeds, and he presented 'the old man' with peremptory demands for cash after his return. A specialist in extortion, Pasha would make his approach through Anna, knowing that she preferred to buy him off rather than permit her husband's peace of mind to be disrupted. Dostoyevsky was still fond of Pasha, and several more years passed before that atrocious parasite was finally prised loose.

In May 1872 the Dostoyevskys embarked on a new routine by renting a cottage at Staraya Russa, about a hundred and fifty miles south of St Petersburg and reached by train to Novgorod, followed by a steamer crossing of Lake Ilmen. Here they spent a peaceful summer away from the sultry capital where, Anna noted, food cost three times as much. But the beginning of their first visit was marred shortly after their arrival by a domestic calamity. After the two-year-old Lyuba had fallen and injured herself, her broken arm was wrongly set by local doctors, and so she had to be taken back to the capital for an operation. While this was in progress the anguished parents were on their knees praying fervently for their child's recovery, and fortunately not in vain.

As the episode reminds us, Dostoyevsky was devoted to his children. He loved decking the annual Christmas tree, he adored buying them presents, he sat up with them when they were ill, and he greatly missed them during his absences from home, when he could not learn enough of their antics and sayings. They also figured in his nightmares, during one of which the new baby was seen falling out of a fifth-floor window as his father woke up desperately shrieking 'Farewell Fedya!'[3] Such visions alarmed the superstitious Dostoyevsky, who took them for omens of disaster.

In late 1872 the Dostoyevskys were back in St Petersburg, badly needing to restore an income curtailed by the completion of *Devils*. By now Anna Grigoryevna had taken the momentous decision to publish her husband's works herself. For a novelist's books to be brought out, and even sold, from his home was unheard-of, and many experienced advisers said that she was sure to fail. But they reckoned without her flair and persistence. She had a handsome three-volume edition of *Devils* printed, bound and advertised for about four thousand roubles, and on 22 January she was ready to do business. Booksellers arrived at the Dostoyevskys' flat and began haggling over their discount on the retail price of three roubles fifty copecks, only to find themselves dealing with a woman of affairs who had investigated their trade and knew exactly what terms to fix. Awaking towards lunch-time, as he usually did after working into the small hours, Dostoyevsky was typically uncommunicative until he had drunk two cups of hot coffee. But he was delighted when his wife showed him a wad of banknotes, having sold a hundred and fifteen copies of his novel that morning. Meanwhile their superstitious old nanny, hearing so many references to 'devils', had deduced that they were breeding imps of darkness in their flat; no wonder (she concluded) that baby Fedya was sleeping badly.[4]

All three and a half thousand copies of *Devils* were eventually sold, yielding a profit of about four thousand roubles. Many of Dostoyevsky's other works were also to be published by his wife, and later widow, over the next thirty-eight years.

Having no new creative project on hand and needing a change of occupation, Dostoyevsky accepted an invitation to edit a newly founded weekly, *Grazhdanin* ('The Citizen') in January 1873. It was regarded as the most reactionary organ in St Petersburg, and as such was widely unpopular. So too was its proprietor, Prince Meshchersky, who wished to halt or undo the governmental reforms of the period. Even the arch-traditionalist Dostoyevsky, himself now widely execrated for his attacks on the left in *Devils*, found the paper's political line excessively deferential to the government. On one occasion he flatly refused to print a suggestion by Meshchersky that the authorities should set up university hostels designed to keep students under political surveillance.[5] As the episode illustrates, the new editor did not hesitate to speak his mind to his titled employer, and there were several occasions for doing so. The Prince interfered in editorial matters, and he submitted an article, on the death of the poet Tyutchev, so incompetently written that Dostoyevsky had to revise it extensively.

A conscientious editor in the 1870s, as he had been in the 1860s,

Dostoyevsky read all contributions, negotiated with authors, vetted proofs, and carried out many other chores, often sitting at his desk all night to do so. His duties also included conciliating the censors, for which exercise in caution his impetuous temperament was ill adapted. After infringing one minor regulation he was sentenced to a fine of twenty-five roubles, followed by two days' compulsory incarceration in a military guardhouse—the traditional means of disciplining errant editors.

Though he had once discharged similar tasks for *Vremya* and *Epokha*, they had never been his *métier*, and were less so now that he was no longer his own master. But there were compensations in association with like-minded contributors to *Grazhdanin* whom he knew from the past, including Maykov and the still friendly Strakhov. There was also the satisfaction of secret collaboration with a highly influential figure, Konstantin Pobedonostsev, a tutor to the Heir to the Throne and destined to become, in 1880, Procurator of the Holy Synod (in effect Minister for Church Affairs). Pobedonostsev, nineteenth-century Russia's most notorious political reactionary, published anonymous articles in *Grazhdanin*, and conferred from time to time with Dostoyevsky, who availed himself of this august intermediary to present a copy of *Devils* to the future Emperor Alexander III.

Dostoyevsky was now earning a fixed income, and for the first time in his life if we exclude his army pay. His salary from *Grazhdanin* was three thousand roubles a year, which increased to about five thousand through additional fees for articles from his own pen. Having again acquired a vehicle for his philosophical journalism, as previously practised in the early 1860s, he now published the first section of his most important non-imaginative work: the series of articles entitled *The Diary of a Writer*. Only about a fifth of this extensive monument, sixteen items in all, was published in *Grazhdanin*, all of it in 1873. The bulk was to follow in 1876-7, when it was to be brought out by Anna Grigoryevna as an independent periodical of which it was the sole item. Dostoyevsky also wrote a dozen articles on foreign affairs for *Grazhdanin*.

The Diary of a Writer will be considered as a whole at a later stage. Meanwhile we shall merely note one significant feature of the 1873 items: a tendency for the new, more serene Dostoyevsky to discuss representatives of the left in a tone less harsh than that of *Devils* and his correspondence from abroad. Now, in the *Diary*, Belinsky is no longer the 'shit' or 'stinking dung-beetle' of the letters, but a man of impressive if misdirected intellectual force. Nekrasov, another political enemy of the 1840s, is also singled out in the *Diary*, where lines from his poem of 1854, *Vlas*, are quoted as 'a miracle of excellence'. There is a tolerant reconstruction of Dostoyevsky's own relations with the Petrashevsky group in the late 1840s. There is also a friendly reference to Herzen, whom the diarist had last met while exchanging polite sneers in a Geneva street in 1868. But the kindest, the most surprising comments are on his supreme bugbear, Chernyshevsky. It is here that he rejects the accusation, noted above, that he had designed his sketch *The Crocodile* as a lampoon on Chernyshevsky, who was now in his eleventh year as a political prisoner in Siberia. Among other sympathetic remarks, Dostoyevsky states that 'Chernyshevsky never offended me by his convictions. One may respect a man greatly while differing radically from his views.' One may indeed, but to find Dostoyevsky admitting it is surprising and an indication that he was indeed undergoing a character change. Yet he was still implacably opposed to liberal and left-wing doctrines, for it was his manner rather than his matter that was new. As this evolution indicates, even a Christian may, despite much historical evidence to the contrary, permit himself the occasional indulgence of forgiving his enemies.

Dostoyevsky's new tolerance of ideological heretics reflects the peace of mind that he now simulated, cultivated and in part genuinely acquired from professional success, a happy marriage, an increasingly fervent religious faith and advancing years. As for his traditional biliousness, irritability, touchiness and so on—we have already noted that they had declined, not disappeared. And to his present biographer at least those very faults help to make him more sympathetic than the saintly paragon that he sought, fortunately with limited success, to become.

More easily reconciled to his distant enemy Chernyshevsky than to Prince Meshchersky, that all-too-present ally, Dostoyevsky gave up his editorship in April 1874. In the same month he received an unexpected visit from Nekrasov—now editor of *Otechestvennyye zapiski*, in which Dostoyevsky had published much of his early work and which had since become Russia's premier radical left-wing review in succession to *Sovremennik*, banned in 1866.

Nekrasov had come to solicit a new novel, and offered two hundred and fifty roubles a signature. Both as a working author (whose previous best rate had been a hundred and fifty roubles) and as one newly tolerant of human error, Dostoyevsky was glad to accept subject to consultation with *Russky vestnik*. He felt that he owed them first refusal, but Katkov did not match Nekrasov's terms. And so Dostoyevsky consented to contribute to Russia's leading left-wing journal at a time when his authorship of *Devils* and editorship of *Grazhdanin* had made him intensely unpopular with the left.

Shortly after accepting Nekrasov's offer Dostoyevsky left St Petersburg for Germany to take the waters at Bad Ems for a few weeks. The excursion was to be repeated in the two following summers and also in 1879, his life at Ems being documented in the many long letters that he wrote to his wife while undergoing the cure. He persevered with this, on medical advice, as treatment for emphysema, from which affliction of the lungs he now suffered in addition to his epilepsy.

The letters from Ems consist largely of complaints, also frequently listing the number of glasses of Kränchen and Kesselbrunnen waters that he drank. In order to consume these fluids, with their whiff of rotten eggs, he was forced to rise at six in the morning to queue for his prescribed dose. Again and again he curses Ems: the exorbitant prices, the grasping landladies, the excruciating boredom, the intolerably vulgar and rude Germans, the no less intolerable Russians of whom some persecuted the touring notability with literary conversations. If they were not snobs and aristocrats, these travelling fellow-countrymen, then they were something worse: merchants, Nihilists or Jews. Among them were two 'filthy little wishy-washy liberals' who sought his company while making it clear that they looked down on him as a *retrograd*. 'Conceited creatures ... these two creepy shits think to instruct a man such as myself.'[6] Easily irritated when jostled in the queues for the waters, Dostoyevsky tended to take offenders 'down a peg'; according to his wife he was fluent in German only when quarrelling.

Anna was constantly in his thoughts. He was lonely without her, and felt extreme sexual frustration. 'I kiss *you all over in a way that you can't even imagine*', he tells her. He dreams about her 'in a seductive form', once recording that this vision has occasioned 'nocturnal consequences'.[7] We note these excursions into the language of intimacy, of which not a few have been posthumously deleted by Anna Grigoryevna, as confirmation of continuing sexual vigour that years of exposure to epilepsy, Nihilists, merchants, pulmonary catarrh, liberals, socialists, Jews, Germans, creditors, literary creation, Poles and piles had not impaired. The remarks also serve as a corrective to Anna's picture of their union as more decorously non-physical than, in the light of their correspondence, it obviously must have been.

Dostoyevsky also pined for Lyuba and Fedya, who were never far from his thoughts during these spells of German exile that he called, as he called so many of his post-*katorga* experiences, 'worse than Siberia'. But he persevered with Ems because he had faith in the cure; so too, it seemed, had the crowned heads of Russia and Prussia, both of whom he occasionally observed at this same fashionable spa.

Summer visits to Staraya Russa—less fashionable than Ems, but also a spa with its own mineral waters and mud-baths—were an established part of family routine from 1872 onwards. In the following year Dostoyevsky himself managed only a brief August visit owing to his new editorial duties, but after returning in the summer of 1874 he agreed to stay on through the next autumn and winter as well. Far from the distractions of the capital, he could concentrate on writing *A Raw Youth*, while enjoying what Anna calls the most tranquil period of their life together. The villa that they now rented was pleasantly situated on the outskirts of the small town, and it had an attractive garden and a bath-hut. Remembering it in later life, their daughter Lyubov has described it as a 'house full of surprises', with concealed cupboards and spiral staircases: the model for the home where Fyodor Pavlovich lives and dies in *The Brothers Karamazov*.[8] At Staraya Russa Dostoyevsky enjoyed his children's company, telling them folk tales, reciting Krylov's fables to them and praying over them devotedly when they went to bed at nine o'clock each evening. Anna would retire at eleven, when her husband settled down to four or five hours' work. Another feature of their routine was the main meal at five o'clock in the afternoon, which always began with Dostoyevsky pouring out a tot of vodka for the children's elderly nanny. On summer evenings, husband and wife liked to take a stroll together.[9] Such was the pleasant pattern of life offered by Staraya Russa during six of his last nine summers as well as in the winter of 1874–5.

One abiding irritation of Dostoyevsky's later years was a family quarrel over the estate of his rich aunt Aleksandra Kumanina. As may be remembered, she and her merchant husband (who died in 1863) had often helped the Dostoyevskys in Fyodor's earliest youth. Aunt Kumanina had also come to the rescue in 1864, when Mikhail and Fyodor Dostoyevsky had each borrowed ten thousand roubles from her to support the ailing journal *Epokha*. Five years later Dostoyevsky received disquieting news in Dresden: the rich old lady had died, leaving forty thousand roubles to a monastery. Distressed by this intelligence, he had written letters seeking to upset the will on the grounds of the testatrix's unsound mind. The scheme had the advantage that his aunt was indeed thought to have been off her head for years, but the grave defect that she turned out, on further enquiry, to be still alive. Here life was in a sense imitating art, for Dostoyevsky's *Gambler* contains a comic character modelled on Aunt Kumanina—the rich, deranged, supposedly moribund 'Grandma'. Presumed dead, she suddenly turns up at a German casino, and ostentatiously loses a large part of her fortune at the tables in the presence of her chief heir.

In spring 1871 Aunt Kumanina did indeed die at last, but the ensuing legal tussle between numerous heirs had not been fully settled even by the time of Dostoyevsky's own death ten years later. It was of course the businesslike and determined Anna who championed their household, and eventually with some success, in this struggle.

Always ready to quarry his troubles for literary copy, Dostoyevsky adapted the affair of the Kumanina inheritance to provide his next novel, *A Raw Youth*, with an important intrigue. Here the seductive Madame Akhmakova has written a letter seeking to have her elderly father, seemingly on the point of squandering his large fortune, put under restraint on the pretext of mental derangement. Should this document come into his possession he would be certain to disinherit her; and Dostoyevsky may well have feared, in the period immediately before his aunt's death, that his own imprudent letters from Dresden might have the same effect.

In the new novel, serialized in *Otechestvennyye zapiski* between January and December 1875, Mme Akhmakova's letter falls into the hands of the 'raw youth' of the title, Arkady Dolgoruky. But he makes no effective use of it, vaguely inclined though he seems either to extort money from the young woman or to force her to yield to his embraces. Skilfully evoked, the theme of the letter is ineptly permitted to expire, as is that of a second indiscreet letter which would have enabled a blackmailer more effective than Arkady to put pressure on his natural father, the mysterious Versilov. Also permitted to fizzle out is Arkady's no less skilfully developed ambition to 'become a Rothschild' by a combination of financial speculation and extreme thrift. Yet another inelegant anti-climax is provided by the novel's Nihilists— the so-called 'Dergachov Circle', based on an actual conspiratorial group, the Dolgushin Circle, as put on trial in St Petersburg in July 1874 for disseminating revolutionary manifestos. Compared with Pyotr Verkhovensky and his fellow conspirators in *Devils*, Dergachov and company are insipid indeed. Neither annihilating his latest Nihilists, as in *Devils*, nor yet propounding any significant re-evaluation of the type, Dostoyevsky seems to have lost his way in this as in many other areas of *A Raw Youth*. The disorientation was partly due to con- sciousness of writing for a radical journal and for his ideological opponent Nekrasov. How hampering that thought was Dostoyevsky himself freely admitted; but he also said that he would not abandon his principles just because he was writing for an organ hostile to them.[10]

If *A Raw Youth* fails—as by common consent it does, at least when compared with the other four long novels of Dostoyevsky's maturity —one reason must lie in its diffuse, over-complex and elusive plot.

The above details are only a few in a confusing medley that lacks any strong central intrigue to hold it in shape. To describe briefly 'what happens' in the novel would be even more difficult than to summarize the comparably intricate *Idiot*, and it will not be attempted here. Perhaps *A Raw Youth* is less effective because it contains no murder, but only another inept anti-climax: the projected slaughter of Mme Akhmakova by Versilov, which is not carried out. We are forced to conclude that the mature Dostoyevsky could only mobilize his full powers when the ingredient of implemented homicide was present.

If there is no proper plot, or perhaps far too much plot, in *A Raw Youth*, there is at least an original and dominant character. Arkady Dolgoruky is present throughout and is made to tell his own story, being the only fully participating narrator in the long novels. He represents yet another of those 'self-portraits' in which Dostoyevsky's earlier fiction abounds. Socially inept, painfully self-conscious, withdrawn into himself, he is obsessed—like the Underground Man and so many others—with receiving and dispensing humiliation; and this is especially so where the circumstances of his birth are concerned. Technically speaking he is not illegitimate, as he constantly protests, since his mother and his legal father (Makar Dolgoruky) had been married at the time of his arrival in the world. They had then been serfs, and it had been their owner, the mysterious Versilov, who had actually fathered Arkady. This dubious parentage enables that 'raw youth' to agonize over his status as a bastard, as does Nastasya Filippovna (in *The Idiot*) over her position as a 'fallen woman'. Arkady also resembles Nastasya in exploiting his sense of injury to torment others as well as himself.

However many 'self-portraits' he created, Dostoyevsky rarely if ever repeated himself inartistically, and Arkady is not only the most extensively portrayed specimen of the type, but is also the most memorable, except possibly for the very different Underground Man. Nor is Arkady impaired, as some earlier exemplars are, by the impression that his creator has too closely identified himself with his own creation. This is no longer a portrait of the artist as he sees himself; it is a portrait of the artist as a young man observed by that same artist when well launched on his sixth decade and able to look back forgivingly from a distance on earlier follies. Arkady is accordingly portrayed with detachment, sympathy and humour, and above all with a sensitive feel for the psychology and style of the insecure young adult male.

In its philosophical implications the novel takes up yet again the conflict between evil and good: between the harmful principle of self-assertiveness—obsession with status, money, lust, et cetera—and the beneficent principles of serenity, aloofness, submissiveness. From one to the other of these two poles Arkady oscillates like Raskolnikov before him, chiefly cleaving to evil. Yet he retains his potentialities for good, as represented in the novel by his legal father Makar Dolgoruky, even as he succumbs to the allure of evil as personified by his natural father Versilov.

Versilov is a worldly, self-possessed figure in the tradition of Valkovsky, Svidrigaylov and Stavrogin. A reputed frequenter of 'low haunts', a rumoured violator of infant girls, he has also allegedly seduced one of the heroines and driven her to suicide. He speaks Russian with a French accent, and he has been a Catholic. To be more precise, he has probably committed some of these crimes, since Dostoyevsky here as elsewhere prefers to surround his chief villain with oracular hints rather than positive statements. Polite, urbane and considerate, like preceding villains, in his dealings, Versilov has a special penchant for sudden outrageous acts. They include a spectacular feat of sacrilege: suddenly smashing a holy icon to pieces on the corner of a stove. And yet, the powerful icon scene excepted, Versilov is a less potent incarnation of evil than Svidrigaylov and Stavrogin, and would be more intelligible as a preliminary sketch for those monsters than as what he is: the product of a later stage in Dostoyevsky's evolution. There is also the confusing detail that Versilov—like Myshkin, Shatov and the embryonic Stavrogin of the Notebooks— occasionally utters his creator's own pet ideas; he claims, for example, that Russians are the only true Europeans, and that Russians are truly free whereas other Europeans are not.

Versilov very largely represents the rehashing of old themes. But his opposite number, that representative of Dostoyevskian virtue Makar Dolgoruky, signals a new departure, being a former serf, a man of the people, a peasant. He belongs, in short, to the *narod*: that ignorant, illiterate, numerically overwhelming social element which Dostoyevsky had now come to idealize as the embodiment of mysterious, awe-inspiring merits defying description and beyond the attainment of educated men. But however much he might idealize the *narod*, he was remarkably reluctant to describe it in fiction; and so Makar Dolgoruky remains the only full-scale specimen in his work. Perhaps it is as well that there are no others, for this saintly, white-bearded, benevolent mouther of rustic saws, edifying maxims, soothing platitudes and hedgerow philosophy is, for the most part, an intolerable bore. But his disquisitions are at least significant in stressing yet again the primacy of instinctual over cerebral reactions. Designed, it seems, to encourage readers to live by the dictates of the heart rather than 'by the mind alone', Makar cannot have inspired many conversions.

But his legal son Arkady is to some extent his acolyte: he regards the old man as a spiritual anchor and as the one psychologically stable person in his orbit. Arkady has chosen to model himself on Makar, we infer, but no such transformation is portrayed in the novel, where the author characteristically prefers—as he had in *Crime and Punishment*—to concentrate on his hero's unregenerate phase.

Inferior though *A Raw Youth* is generally judged to be, at least when compared to the other long novels of Dostoyevsky's maturity, it provoked remarkably lively discussion in the contemporary press, Dostoyevsky's new and somewhat ambivalent political stance being reflected by a complementary change of emphasis. Conservative periodicals, especially the recently abandoned *Russky vestnik*, tended to abuse this work by one who seemed to be deserting their cause. Meanwhile left-wing critics, disarmed by Dostoyevsky's apparent change of posture, were inclining to guarded approval. One of these, that advocate of the revolutionary *coup d'état* Pyotr Tkachov, even claimed to prefer the new novel to *Crime and Punishment*. With this assessment few other readers have concurred—certainly not Turgenev, who (in 1877) wrote to Saltykov-Shchedrin describing *A Raw Youth* as sheer 'chaos': a mish-mash combining 'sloppy sentimentality, the stink of the lazaret, superfluous verbiage and psychological nitpicking.'[11]

Though Turgenev's judgement is grossly unfair, enough has been said above to indicate why *A Raw Youth* cannot stand comparison with Dostoyevsky's major novels. It resurrects in half-hearted form too many themes that had previously been realized with full-blooded vigour, while the most original figure, the greatest departure from the norm—Makar Dolgoruky—is a mere absurdity. Perhaps the main fault lies in the new serenity which Dostoyevsky embodied in Makar and which he himself was beginning to acquire. Most effective, hitherto, when metaphorically battering his ideological enemies into an insensate pulp, he was less so now that he felt obliged to treat them with tolerance, especially as his one 'positive' character is so ill-conceived. The war against evil had contributed his greatest triumphs so far, and it was left to *The Brothers Karamazov* to challenge that position.

II

Arbiter of Destiny

The Diary of a Writer

The years 1876–7 were chiefly devoted to *The Diary of a Writer*, being otherwise remarkable only for domestic events. There were the joys of looking after a new infant, for the Dostoyevskys' second son Aleksey (Alyosha) had been born in August 1875. Other domestic episodes of the period included the purchase of the house that they had hitherto been renting at Staraya Russa.

In summer 1877 they failed to visit Staraya Russa for once, and went instead to an estate in Kursk Province (south of Moscow) belonging to Anna's brother Ivan. While travelling in this area Dostoyevsky made a lone expedition to the villages of Darovoye and Cheremoshna, now occupied by his sister Vera. He strolled through fields and copses, spoke to former playmates and aged peasants who remembered him as a child, and drank tea with them in their huts. No doubt he also brooded on his father's sudden death—by murder as we know him to have believed, but we unfortunately have no information on the son's thoughts of 1877 about this occurrence of 1839, or on any of his other reactions to the visit.

Despite the sombre elements in Dostoyevsky's make-up, much of his family life was light-hearted. There were practical jokes, as when the master of the house had his wife ransacking his bed for a non-existent mouse—on April Fool's Day. Anna too was playfully inclined, on one occasion with unfortunate consequences. A 'prankish thought' inspired her to copy out, in disguised handwriting from an insignificant novel of the period, an anonymous letter in which a deceived husband is warned that his wife has been unfaithful to him: he can confirm this by looking inside her locket and learning whose image she carries next to her heart. Anna posted the letter to her husband, supposing that he, having read the original, would appreciate the joke. The joke! She might as well have locked a claustrophobic child in a dark cupboard for a joke. Still liable to spasms of jealousy, Dostoyevsky ripped Anna's locket from her neck, hurting her; but only to find that it contained portraits of their daughter Lyuba and himself. A passionate reconciliation naturally followed.[1]

Dare we suspect an element of uncharacteristic callousness or cruelty behind this wifely provocation? Perhaps Anna was for once behaving like an Underground Woman by launching a sudden, motiveless act proving her to be a human being, not a mere mechanism. Or perhaps she was unconsciously driven to express resentment of her role as nursemaid to a wayward genius. It was not, incidentally, the only occasion on which she unnecessarily aroused her husband's jealousy,[2] though it was her usual practice to dress and behave like a woman twice her age in order to spare his feelings. If the occasional variation of pattern was indeed inspired by latent devilment as well as a misplaced sense of fun, then of course her husband, that enemy of consistency, logic and rationality, can only have appreciated her the more; after all, he always had 'wanted to suffer.'

It is not surprising if Anna Grigoryevna occasionally yearned for a break in routine during the central years of *The Diary of a Writer*: the period 1876–7, when the core of that monumental work was first published. The series, as we saw, made its début in 1873 with sixteen articles in *Grazhdanin*. Now, in January 1876, the *Diary* became a small periodical of which it constituted the sole item. The consolidated material of 1876–7 comprises some three-quarters of the entire *Diary*, which totals—if we add the *Grazhdanin* material of 1873 and two isolated issues to be published in August 1880 and January 1881—some twelve hundred pages, and is thus Dostoyevsky's longest single work.

From January 1876 onwards the *Diary* was published and distributed by Dostoyevsky and his wife at their home with the sole aid of an errand boy. Anna accepted annual subscriptions, posted copies to subscribers, negotiated with booksellers, paid printers' bills and kept accounts. Exhausted, she gave up all social activities, while Dostoyevsky would often return home in the small hours from a dinner or literary recital to entertain his adoring wife with a detailed account of his triumphs lasting until four or five o'clock in the morning.[3]

The retail price of the *Diary* was fixed at twenty and then twenty-five copecks for a single issue, with discounts for subscribers and provisions for purchasing consolidated bound copies at the end of the year. The circulation was about four thousand copies in 1876, and six thousand in 1877.[4] Besides representing a gross yield of over twenty thousand roubles, largely profit, these sales also reflected the diarist's growing popularity. But he had weightier motives for putting out the *Diary* than courting popularity and making money. Among them was concern for his future as a novelist. An artist must,

172

said he, 'know the milieu that he describes, its past and its present, in the most minute precision.'[5] And that close knowledge would, he believed, be fruitfully extended by his return to journalism. A few years earlier the same preoccupation had driven him to pore over Russian newspapers and journals during his foreign exile. Real-life episodes, usually from the crime reports, had often inspired his pen, though it must be stressed how small a part, and in how disguised a form, such material plays in the finished novels. These are far indeed from the creations of a documentary realist. So much, indeed, does Dostoyevsky's *œuvre* owe to the creative imagination that we can easily forget how dependent he was, in the planning stages, on the stimulus afforded by contemporary events often as petty and sordid as their eventual transformation is significant and profound.

Though the new publication was originally billed as 'a diary in the literal sense of the word',[6] it was never that. Far from recording day-by-day events, either in the author's life or in that of his society, it mostly consists of sustained sermons or harangues—often, it is true, initially stimulated by some trivial item culled from the press—on social and philosophical themes. The work conveys a full and highly repetitive statement of the body of ideas that had progressively taken shape in Dostoyevsky's post-Siberian years, approaching its final form during his period of foreign residence. Taken individually, these notions are by no means all original. They owe much to other Russian thinkers, including his old associates Grigoryev and Strakhov; and also to Nikolay Danilevsky, once a fellow-Petrashevskyite but now a militant Panslavist and author of the influential *Russia and Europe* (1869). As for Dostoyevsky's worship of the *narod*, that was a common affectation among contemporary intellectual fellow-countrymen of all political persuasions. And yet, despite its many derivative elements, the consolidated structure of the *Diary* bears the stamp of marked originality. It is a formidable achievement, despite being turgid, repetitive and almost comically vehement.

Central to the *Diary*, as to most of Dostoyevsky's other journalistic writings, is an obsession with the nature and fate of his motherland. He proclaims Russia a young, vital nation, contrasting it with 'Europe' (that is, Europe outside Russia)—notionally more 'advanced', but in practice effete and moribund. Russia's strength lies in her Orthodox Church, based on the brotherhood of man. Among European religions Protestantism does not count because it is purely negative, while Catholicism, though powerful and sinister, is condemned for being based on force and self-assertion. Here Dostoyevsky polarizes the hemispheres, just as he polarizes some of the characters in his fiction, into the submissive (the East) and the assertive (the West). He also equates the West with the principles of rationality and logic—in short of the condemned Mind—with which are contrasted the instinctual dictates of the loving Russian Heart. With the concepts of rationality and Catholicism thus strangely united he further equates, by an additional feat of mental prestidigitation, the teachings of socialism. And he opposes to this unholy triple combination (logic = the Pope = the politics of the left) the Holy Trinity of Russia, her Russian Christ, her Russian Tsar. Agreeing (without collusion) with Karl Marx that a proletarian revolution will first break out in the West, he believes that Russia will save effete Europe from revolution and itself.

Europeans despise Russians (according to Dostoyevsky, repeating an idea already expressed by him in 1861) without the remotest understanding of what they mock. But the highly flexible Russian fully understands, and can adapt himself to, the peoples of Europe. In virtue of this superior comprehension Russia is about to pronounce some portentous, never-specified New Word which, whatever it is, will somehow transform human relations into a miracle of fraternity and harmony.

For all Dostoyevsky's talk of love and faith, the *Diary* is shot through with suspicion and hatred, often descending from heights of flamboyant rhetoric to expressions of petty malice. Unable to conceive Russia's relations with Europe except as those of either slave or master, he is obsessed with what the West may be supposed to be thinking of his native country. He incidentally offers a classic statement of the characteristic Russian inferiority complex about Europe, an attitude that still bedevils international contacts over a century later. Nothing, it seems from the *Diary*, could more gratify its humiliation-craving author's deeper lusts than the supreme sensual experience of being insulted by an Englishman, whether through the arrogance of some unidentified English notability who had the cheek to remain seated in the presence of a Russian Grand Duke, or through the callousness of the current British prime minister. Quadruply damned—as holder of a title, European, Englishman and Jew—Lord Beaconsfield is above all censured for his indifference to Turkish atrocities in Bulgaria, including the crucifixion of two priests of the Orthodox Church by bashibazouks.

As this reminds us, the nationalist bombast of the *Diary* was in the spirit of the epoch, for Russia was emerging as champion of the Balkan Slavs now in revolt against Turkish rule. A surge of anti-Turkish feeling, accompanied by rampant nationalism and Panslavist passions, led to Russia's declaration of war against the Porte in April 1877. The announcement caught Dostoyevsky on the streets of St Petersburg and sent him plunging into the Kazansky Cathedral to mingle his prayers with those of the massed *narod*.[7] As a fervent nationalist, Slavophile and also (provided of course that lesser Slavic breeds could be dominated by Russians) adherent or sympathizer of Panslavism, Dostoyevsky harnessed all these passions to the cause of his holy war against the infidel Turk. The natural culmination was, he gleefully predicted, the annexation of Constantinople by his mother-land. But though Russia was indeed to win the war against Turkey in 1878, she was then to find her territorial gains restricted by the other European powers through the Treaty of Berlin.

It is not only this particular war, but war in general that Dostoyevsky praises. War saves man from barbarism, we remember him asserting in a letter of 1870. Now he proclaims his faith in the destiny of the 'great nation' (there was only one in his assessment) which must by definition believe that it, and it alone, can offer the world salvation—salvation that can best come through war. 'Our *narod* doesn't want to fight . . . but by jingo [*uzh*] if it must, it will march as a hundred-million mass . . . inspired by a single impulse, in harmony and as one man.' Such was Dostoyevsky's attitude, as revealed in the *Diary*, on the eve of war with Turkey.[8]

The idealization of war, the mumbo-jumbo about a great people's destiny, the assertion of grandiose territorial designs combined with peace-loving professions, and above all the exalted, hysterical and sometimes unharmonious prose style—all these are features uniting *The Diary of a Writer* with Hitler's *Mein Kampf*. Another common element is rampant anti-Semitism. Disliking any messianic doctrine in competition with his own, Dostoyevsky denounced an alleged inter-national Jewish conspiracy, while also condemning Jews as exploiters —through usury, commerce and inn-keeping—of his humbler fellow-countrymen. When Jewish readers wrote to protest, he replied that his tirades were a model of objectivity. He was no anti-Semite. Could he help it if Jews tended to be obnoxious? 'Some of my acquaintances are Jews', he once ungenerously admitted, not even being willing to concede the proverbial 'many of my best friends'. Confirming this attitude in his correspondence, and frequently using the pejorative *zhid* ('Yid') for the neutral *yevrey* ('Jew'), he cannot be absolved from the charge of prejudice. But he was, after all, a man of prejudice; this was only one of many. He was also hostile to such other varied and often overlapping categories as Poles, Germans, Frenchmen, Britons, socialists, stockbrokers, Jesuits, aristocrats and businessmen. Indeed, what else but contempt for actual human beings was to be expected from one who so often asserted his love for humanity in the abstract?

If Dostoyevsky appears to be a 'racist' or even a 'fascist', presaging, even as he prophetically denounced them, the horrors of twentieth-century totalitarianism, we must also remember that he lived in an age preceding the emergence and systematic political exploitation of these now hyper-sensitive and much-abused terms, while adding that he was at least only a man of words. He was not an organizer of Chekas or Gestapos. Moreover, a thinker who airs so much bias against virtually the whole of humanity, including himself, cannot logically be accused of 'discrimination', as the term has since come to be used.

This consideration becomes more powerful still when we consider the treatment of Dostoyevsky's fellow-countrymen in the *Diary*. It is true that Russians there emerge as paragons of wisdom, humility and brotherliness, distinguished by 'eternal service to common human ideals', by outstanding tolerance of alien faiths—even by a more democratic structure of society and by a lack of territorial designs on any other country. But only when Russians are compared to non-Russians do they appear in this noble guise. When Dostoyevsky surveys his fellow-countrymen without reference to foreigners, they seem no better than anyone else: For Russia's intelligentsia, by which is usually meant the radical section among her educated class, he expresses utter contempt. These miserable *intelligentiki* ('egg-heads') were to him only *nigilyatina* ('Nihilist carrion') under a different name. They had abandoned their ancestral religion, cut themselves off from the *narod*, embraced alien, godless creeds. As for non-leftist Russians of the privileged classes, they had deserted their motherland for foreign resorts, where they recklessly squandered their money while dressing their children in English costumes and teaching them to speak French—both, to Dostoyevsky, crimes against the national ethos. Despising privileged Russians in general, not merely those with radical political opinions, he exempted a single individual. The adored Tsar always remained above criticism.

So much for Russia's privileged classes. But what of the *narod*? While idealizing Russia's *hoi polloi* more than ever as a matter of philosophical principle, Dostoyevsky here goes out of his way to portray them as dirty, ignorant, barbarous, given to debauchery, drunkenness and wife-beating. The Russian common man is cruel to his children and ignorant of his Orthodox prayers. One signal virtue alone argues in his favour: self-awareness. While non-Russians take pride in behaving like beasts, and do so callously, the Russian peasant always knows, even as he maims his wife in a spasm of alcoholic rage, that he is doing wrong. Of the *narod*'s superior awareness Dostoyevsky characteristically provides no evidence. Nor does he explain why consciously committed sins should be preferable to those committed unthinkingly. But at least this premiss is consistent with the view implied in much of his fiction: a person's acts do not matter, his state of mind is everything. Better commit a whole catalogue of murders,

Oil portrait of Dostoyevsky by V.
Perov, 1872

Right Members of the terrorist group 'Narodnaya Volya' ('People's Will') against a copy of their illegal periodical of the same name, dated 15 November 1879
Below Execution of political conspirators in the Petropavlovsky Fortress, November 1880

robberies and ravishments while adhering to Dostoyevskian dogma, than to be the most virtuously behaved of unbelievers. As for his failure to provide proof or evidence of his own assertions, Dostoyevsky repeatedly shows himself aware of this omission and even boasts of it. He was not offering rational arguments, since he did not believe in reason, but revealed truths not open to discussion. If this is a crime he at least has the same defence as that of his wife-beating, drunken peasants: he himself is fully conscious of what he is about.

Despite Dostoyevsky's passionate involvement with his concept of the *narod*, he did not and could not identify himself with 'the people'— any more than other, less gifted, Russian intellectuals could. To him, as to many of them, the muzhik remained a raw material to be moulded and processed. Far from sharing or expressing such deep aspirations as the *narod* may or may not have secretly cultivated, its prophet wrote as if he represented a different biological species—inevitably so, perhaps, owing to the cultural gap between uneducated and educated Russians. Regrettably, then, Dostoyevsky belonged to a type common among intellectual Russians at all points of the political spectrum from extreme right to extreme left, that of the condescending folk-fancier. Like other fanciers he praised the folk's innate sagacity as he might have praised his dog's. And though his pronouncements on the *narod* have the importance that attaches to any obsession of a man of genius, they are, of themselves—like so much else in the *Diary*—neither outstandingly wise nor outstandingly original.

Another of Dostoyevsky's abiding obsessions—crime, as reported in the press—is also a major concern of the *Diary*. He deplores the fashionable trend for Russia's new courts with trial by jury (introduced under Alexander II) to acquit guilty persons, thus unfairly robbing them of their right to suffer. Also fascinated by the theme of cruelty to children so prominent in his later fiction, he returns again and again to this ultimate manifestation of human evil. Suicide too remains a dominant concern

As these topics indicate, the *Diary* is discursive and it is not exclusively devoted to the author's central philosophy. There are also discussions of birth control, infantry tactics and the prospect of developing an electric ray-gun to supplant conventional military weapons. He also incorporates many personal reminiscences, including a celebrated chapter, 'The Peasant Marey', mentioned above as describing an old muzhik who had calmed his childhood fears of an imagined wolf.

References to contemporary belles-lettres are surprisingly few, but include a compliment to Tolstoy's *Anna Karenina* as an emanation of the Russian spirit. The allusion is typically generous, for Dostoyevsky showed no jealousy of Tolstoy the artist (as opposed to Tolstoy the earner of roubles); nor did he dissent from the general view that Tolstoy was one of Russia's and the world's greatest writers. Another literary colleague of some note is invoked in the December 1877 issue of the *Diary*; it contains an eloquent obituary tribute to the publisher of *A Raw Youth*—Nekrasov, at whose graveside Dostoyevsky had recently pronounced a brief but much admired oration.

The *Diary* also contains three short but notable items of fiction. *Bobok* describes a discussion between newly interred corpses in a graveyard. *The Dream of a Ridiculous Man* once again satirizes the concept of a perfect human society, on this occasion as it appears in a dream to a 'ridiculous' man—who, as a good Dostoyevskian brainchild, very properly proceeds to corrupt the earthly paradise in which he finds himself. Most memorable of all is the short story *A Gentle Girl*, in which a middle-aged pawnbroker, yet another cultivator of humiliation both as receiver and purveyor, perversely drives his adored young wife to suicide by his harshness.

Apart from these short stories Dostoyevsky's *Diary* and his fiction might almost be the work of different men. Restrained by his artistic conscience, he never used his novels to propagate in comparably blatant fashion the simple messages repeated again and again in his journalism, even though it had (as we have seen) long been his practice to insert occasional brief passages of *Diary*-type material into the mouths of fictional characters. But though the revealed truths of the *Diary* are not overtly preached in the fiction, they nevertheless form part of its implicit assumptions—but only a small part, for there are so many other competing tensions. Indeed, the general effect of the novels is to suggest that there is, ultimately, no such commodity as revealed truth.

Readers of Dostoyevsky's imaginative works can and often do ignore *The Diary of a Writer* and its strident message. Yet the rewards of collating the two bodies of work are great. No complete understanding of the man and his achievement is possible without considering the beliefs which, on the surface of his mind as expressed in the *Diary*, he so passionately held or so passionately sought to persuade himself that he passionately held. And however we assess the relations between the *Diary* and the novels, there is no doubt that these splendid effusions satisfied some basic urge in Dostoyevsky's nature. Though it partly arose from a vocation for instructing humanity, and for helping it to find its russocentric destiny, a more irreverent consideration also arises. Perhaps he was irresistibly impelled, before girding himself for the last of his great novels, to purge himself of as much prejudice and bile as possible, to eliminate all this constipating hatred and bombast from his system, before he could embark on a work of love and reconciliation, *The Brothers Karamazov*.

12

Man of The Hour

The Brothers Karamazov

On 16 May 1878, soon after work on *The Diary of a Writer* had been suspended, the Dostoyevskys saw their younger son, the two-year-old Alyosha, suddenly go into convulsions and die a few hours later as the result of what his parents, uncontradicted by the family doctor, believed to be an epileptic seizure. Alyosha had not previously suffered from epileptic symptoms, but if the diagnosis was correct the affliction must presumably have been inherited from his father. This would refute Freud's speculation that Dostoyevsky's own epilepsy was hysterical rather than organic in nature.

Once again, as in Geneva ten years earlier, the bereaved parents were prostrated with grief over a young child's death. On this occasion Dostoyevsky sought consolation in a pilgrimage to the celebrated fourteenth-century monastery of Optina Pustyn near Kozelsk, about a hundred and fifty miles south-west of Moscow. The foundation was renowned as having pioneered in Russia the Orthodox monastic institution whereby an Elder—an experienced monk of egregious piety—would tutor his younger colleagues in saintliness. Optina Pustyn's current Elder, Father Amvrosy, consoled Dostoyevsky for the death of his son in terms such as were later to be put into the mouth of Father Zosima, the Elder in *The Brothers Karamazov*. Dostoyevsky drew on Amvrosy as a model for Zosima, adding traits from the eighteenth-century holy man Tikhon of the Don, and he based the novel's monastery on Optina Pustyn. He is also believed to have modelled aspects of one of the principal characters, Alyosha Karamazov, on the young man who shared his pilgrimage to Optina Pustyn—the poet and philosopher Vladimir Solovyov. Nearly thirty years Dostoyevsky's junior, Solovyov was already renowned in intellectual circles. He had given a successful series of public lectures on philosophy in St Petersburg in early 1878, and these Dostoyevsky had attended. At one of them he might have met his great rival Tolstoy, also a member of the audience, but for the strict instructions given in advance by Tolstoy that he was not to be introduced to anybody.[1] Never, despite much mutual esteem expressed in comments on each other's work, were Russia's two most renowned novelists to meet face to face.

After Dostoyevsky's return from Optina Pustyn to St Petersburg he rented a new flat, the last that he and his wife were to share together, of six rooms in Kuznechny Street. Here, in late 1878, the early chapters of *The Brothers Karamazov* were written after Katkov had offered Dostoyevsky three hundred roubles a signature, the best terms that he had ever received (Tolstoy, though, sometimes received as much as five hundred). Serialization by *Russky vestnik* began in the following January, with instalments appearing throughout the year and then continuing less regularly in 1880 until they were concluded in November of that year. The novel captured the imagination of critics and readers from the start, further boosting a reputation much enhanced by *The Diary of a Writer*. During his last two years of life Dostoyevsky consequently enjoyed renown far greater than at any time in the past. No longer could he feel that his reputation lagged behind that of a Turgenev or a Goncharov. Tolstoy too seemed almost eclipsed.

Growing fame brought new obligations. Emerging as a sage with *The Diary of a Writer*, Dostoyevsky could not complain when his counsel was sought by strangers. Young women would write consulting him on their marriage prospects; unknown writers expected him to read and place unsolicited manuscripts; other correspondents sought information on the meaning of life or proofs of the existence of God. Conscientiously responding to these enquiries, Dostoyevsky concluded that hell must be a place where one had to write ten letters a day.[2]

Enhanced popularity also brought more invitations to give public readings of his own and others' works to schoolchildren, students, members of literary associations and the like. These performances were much appreciated, for he had the art of casting his somewhat hoarse voice into the far corners of a tumultuous gathering, while his bearing commanded attention, respect and even veneration—especially from young ladies. One of his most successful recitals was of Pushkin's short, solemn lyric *The Prophet*, the title of which more and more seemed to fit himself, as his audiences were not slow to realize. 'I saw the Prophet Dostoyevsky, his face transformed. His eyes flashed lightning that seared people's hearts, his face glowed with mighty inspiration from on high.' Such is the account of a reading at the St Petersburg Pedagogical Courses in 1879 by the wife of the famous physiologist, and expert on a different type of salivation, Ivan Pavlov. On these occasions Anna Grigoryevna would accompany the frock-coated Prophet, bearing the text which he was to read as well as cough lozenges, a spare handkerchief and a plaid to wrap round his throat when he had finished. Before reciting he would peer into the audience,

looking for her and suffering agonies of jealousy whenever—as frequently happened—some gallant male acquaintance kissed her hand
or otherwise made himself amiable.[3]

What was it about this ailing elderly man that so captivated and
excited his audiences? To the main ingredient of artistic genius, and
to a flair for declamation, must be added collective nationalist fervour.
Feeling that they were only on the periphery of European civilization,
educated Russians still suffered what (since there is no reason to
dismiss them as genuinely inferior) can be best described as an acute
cultural inferiority complex. Now there stood before them one who
ministered to this obsession by assuring them again and again that they
belonged to a higher, not a lower, order of creation; that it was their
country's mission to lead the world, not to follow in its wake—one
whose own stupendous artistic achievements seemed the very embodiment of the superiority of the Russian spirit even as they proclaimed it.

Here, too, was a man who patently believed himself to have unlocked
the secret of the universe. That Dostoyevsky's works can indeed contribute to the understanding of life, substantially or marginally, even
those most hostile to his philosophy might admit. But to some of his
contemporaries, fired by his nationalist fervour, inspired by his
religious zeal and excited by his sweeping philosophical claims, he
seemed to offer far more than this. Might he not turn out to have
trapped the Absolute? Might he not produce the whole transcendental
package out of his hat or vest-pocket there and then in their very
presence? His manner, his delivery, his passionate involvement in his
own ideas and images, together with the tension provided by his
hidden doubts and reservations—all combined to mesmerize and
entrance his audiences, even as the Prophet groped for his cough sweets
or peered into the body of the hall, fearful of discovering the chaste
Anna Grigoryevna deep in sinful flirtation with some rival littérateur.

During these years Dostoyevsky attended frequent literary dinners,
was lionized in the capital's salons, and was elected a corresponding
member of the Russian Academy of Sciences. His social contacts had
moved into the most exalted sphere of all. Not only did he regularly
confer with Pobedonostsev, but he was also invited to meet the
Emperor's three sons, the Grand Dukes Sergey and Pavel as well as
the Crown Prince (the future Alexander III) and the Crown Princess.
He also met the Tsar's nephew, the Grand Duke Konstantin Kon-
stantinovich, a poet.

Life was more rewarding and less unstable than ever before, but
frustration and harassment had not disappeared. Though Fyodor's
earnings and Anna's organizing efforts had rid them of debt by the
beginning of 1881, he was still worrying about money, and with good

reason. Foreseeing, all too accurately, his own imminent death, he feared to leave his wife and two young children destitute. Nor did his cultivation of serenity fully free him from the irritability that had always been a feature of his temperament. A new and embarrassing trait had also appeared: he could no longer remember names and faces, and so unintentionally antagonized many associates. But fame had not gone to his head, as it had long ago in the days of *Poor Folk*. Despite all the adulation he remained personally modest. Nor does one find any element of snobbery in his attitude towards the titled and exalted persons with whom he was now in touch.

The years remaining to Dostoyevsky after the death of his younger son were marked by no domestic events of comparable significance. On one occasion he was attacked in the street by a drunk; when his assailant was arrested he did everything possible to save the man from prosecution and, after this proved impossible, paid his sixteen-rouble fine. In summer 1879 Dostoyevsky made a last visit to Ems, where his usual boredom and sexual frustration were augmented by another nuisance—the local orchestras would play no Mozart or Beethoven, only 'that utterly dreary scoundrel Wagner'. In 1880 Anna Grigoryevna expanded the commercial activities of their home by starting a small mail-order bookselling business, and cleared 811 roubles' profit in the year.[4]

Meanwhile, outside Dostoyevsky's family circle, Russia's first sustained campaign of political assassination gathered momentum. On 24 January 1878 Lenin's later associate Vera Zasulich fired a revolver at the St Petersburg Town Captain, in effect the city's Governor-General, and wounded him. Two months later Dostoyevsky witnessed her trial before a jury which brought in a surprising verdict of not guilty. Later assassination attempts by political terrorists proved more effective, resulting in the death of a provincial Governor-General and of the Empire's chief of political police. The conspirators then made the Tsar himself their target. Among several spectacular failures was the dynamite explosion that they caused in the St Petersburg Winter Palace on 5 February 1880; it was fatal to many soldiers of the autocrat's guard, but not to himself. Discussing the event with the well-known newspaper proprietor A. S. Suvorin (another political 'reactionary', later to become a close friend of Anton Chekhov), Dostoyevsky confessed that, had he chanced to possess advance knowledge of the Winter Palace plot, he would not have denounced it to the police.[5] The admission is surprising, given his loathing of revolutionaries and strong monarchist feelings.

Shortly after taking part in this conversation Dostoyevsky made official application to be released from police surveillance. He pointed out that he had published hundreds of pages expressing his political and religious convictions; and that 'those convictions cannot, I trust, furnish grounds for suspecting my political reliability.' But in making this application he turned out to be battering at an unlocked door, for he was officially informed that police surveillance, to which he had long been subjected as a former political criminal, had in fact ceased five years earlier, in 1875.[6] It is fortunate that the authorities who conveyed this information were unaware of his recent confession to Suvorin.

Inside the Christian loyalist Dostoyevsky there was, evidently, a submerged Nihilist as well as a submerged atheist feebly and sporadically struggling to be let out.

Dostoyevsky spent nearly three years (1878–80) planning and writing *The Brothers Karamazov*, and its initial, serialized publication was spread over the last two of those years. In both respects it resembles *Devils*. But it is nearly half as long again as that, the longest of his previous novels, and it runs to nearly a thousand pages. It is also the novel on which, by his own admission, he lavished more effort than on any other. '*Never* have I regarded any of my works more seriously.'[7] In keeping with this *The Brothers Karamazov* is far more a novel of ideas than is any of his other fictional works. It is also the novel in which his ideas are most strongly obtruded upon the reader. And, though he has the reputation of a great religious novelist, this is in fact his only work of fiction in which religion is so dominant a theme.

Much concerned with factual accuracy, Dostoyevsky consulted competent authorities on the many ecclesiastical details, besides also modelling his monastery (as mentioned above) on that of Optina Pustyn. He conferred with lawyer friends over the technicalities of Dmitry Karamazov's trial, and took doctors' advice on such medical matters as Ivan Karamazov's sick hallucinations. His concern with authenticity of detail also led him to base the Karamazov house on his own villa at Staraya Russa, where much of the novel was written. Staraya Russa itself became the model for the comically named Skotoprigonyevsk ('Cattlepentown'), the small provincial centre where the action takes place, while some of the characters—the merchant Samsonov, the seductive Grushenka—were inspired by local residents.[8] For one memorable minor character, Stinking Lizaveta, Dostoyevsky delved back into his memories of the Darovoye village idiot, Agrafena, as was mentioned in Chapter One.

In what may be the first reference to *The Brothers Karamazov* in his correspondence, Dostoyevsky spoke of writing a 'long novel' in which

children would play a leading role.⁹ And children, especially Kolya
Krasotkin and Ilyusha Snegiryov, indeed do figure fairly prominently
in the work. It also reflects Dostoyevsky's interest, intensified since he
had become a father himself, in the institution of the family. This had
long been a major theme of Tolstoy's. But Tolstoy's families tend to
be united, whereas Dostoyevsky stresses elements of domestic discord.
Tolstoy's sons love their fathers, Dostoyevsky's murder theirs.

In both of Dostoyevsky's immediately preceding novels, *Devils* and
A Raw Youth, the father-son relationship had already played a significant part. But its impact was to be still greater in *The Brothers Karamazov*, partly because four sons are involved (instead of only one) and
above all because the vital ingredient of homicide has been added. By
planting murder, and patricide at that, in the very core of *The Brothers
Karamazov*, its author incidentally supplied the novel with a central
plot even stronger than that of *Crime and Punishment*. Once again the
chief intrigue can be conveyed in brief. An elderly swindling lecher,
Fyodor Pavlovich Karamazov, is killed with a cast-iron paperweight.
The evidence points to his eldest son Dmitry, who is tried and sentenced for a crime actually committed by another son, the epileptic
bastard Smerdyakov. But the true murderer is the old man's second
son Ivan who, though far removed from the scene when the fatal
blow was struck, has inculcated into his illegitimate half-brother
Smerdyakov the necessity of homicide by feeding him with atheistic,
positivist and rationalist ideas such as Dostoyevsky himself had been
denouncing during the last fifteen years. Ivan was the killer, then, and
Smerdyakov merely his instrument.

A father's murder! Never, so far as the record goes, having made a
single reference to what he must have believed to have been the
manner of his father's death, and rarely traced as having mentioned his
father in any context at all during the years since that death, Dostoyevsky had yet thought it worth revisiting the scene of the event, the
villages of Darovoye and Cheremoshna, in summer 1877. He now
introduces a village similarly named to the latter, Chermashnya, into
The Brothers Karamazov. It is by ostentatiously leaving for Chermashnya,
in order to perform an errand for his father, that Ivan in effect gives
Smerdyakov the go-ahead signal to proceed with the old man's murder.

To what extent was this novel about a father's murder inspired by
the murder of the actual father whom, whatever the manner of his
death may in fact have been, Dostoyevsky must definitely have
believed—and this is the crucial point—to have been murdered?

Though the parallel between life and fiction surely possesses profound significance, there are disappointingly few tangible details that
we can add to embellish the bald and eloquent fact that such a parallel

undoubtedly exists. It is true that old Karamazov's main characteristic, lust, suggests a comparison with Dostoyevsky's father; it does so, that is, if the tales of the father's addiction to young serf concubines are to be trusted. That the widowed Dr Dostoyevsky added alcoholism to lechery is also reported, which suggests yet another link with the debauched Karamazov *père*. On the other hand, the two fathers differ markedly in their treatment of their offspring. Fyodor Pavlovich Karamazov, who neglects and abandons his young children in the novel, is in that respect the very opposite of Mikhail Andreyevich Dostoyevsky; whose fault, if any, had been to display an excess of solicitude over his sons' education and careers. Nor is there anything in the preliminary Notebooks for *The Brothers Karamazov* to confirm the natural assumption that the fathers of Dostoyevsky's life and of his imagination, together with the manner of their death, must have been consciously linked in his mind. But then again, failure to prove a close connection does not prove that no close connection exists. That it inevitably must have existed the bare facts suggest: a highly sensitive, talented and guilt-ridden son, believing his father murdered, writes a novel forty years later about a father murdered by his son.

What, in fiction and in life, of filial guilt for the father's death? In the novel all four Karamazov sons partake of this in some degree. Smerdyakov executes the deed. Ivan, the prime heretic, inspires and prompts it. Dmitry has desired it and come near to accomplishing it. Even the saintly Alyosha is implicated, however remotely: at the crucial moment he allows himself to be distracted by a personal emotional crisis from his father's peril, which (it is implied) he might otherwise have averted.

Wholly innocent in any legal sense, Dmitry takes upon himself the guilt for his father's murder. He can accept punishment for the crime as one who had desired it even though he had not committed it, an illustration of Dostoyevsky's thesis that states of mind are important while deeds are not. 'I accept punishment, not because I killed him but because I wanted to kill him, and might actually have done so', explains Dmitry, also invoking a key formula: 'I want to suffer.' That Dmitry's creator had gone out of his way to cultivate suffering in his own life, that he had been driven to punish himself by seeking sexual and financial torment, even by risking execution, has been repeatedly suggested in preceding pages, but only as a plausible hypothesis, never as proven fact. This self-punishment seems consistent with Freud's now widely derided theory, that Dostoyevsky's need to make himself suffer arose from guilt over a strong unacknowledged hostility to his father. If he had subconsciously wished his father dead, he must also have subconsciously felt, when he learnt of the murder, that he himself had actually killed his father. Such, at any rate, is the hypothesis. If it could be accepted we should have, as has already been mentioned, a convenient explanation of Dostoyevsky's long-standing sense of guilt and consequent habit (somewhat abated in his last decade) of 'wanting to suffer', and of punishing himself by unnecessarily cultivating acute emotional and financial crises.

I neither endorse such unproven speculations, nor yet do I feel confident in dismissing them entirely. They are invoked here as ingenious suggestions that can neither be proved nor refuted. If not taken too seriously or solemnly they are potentially illuminating, at least on the surrealist or absurd level which, in the context of a Dostoyevsky, may be allowed a little scope, even by a biographer to whom concrete data and hard evidence are paramount. As Dostoyevsky himself often contended, wild imaginings are sometimes truer to the truth than the most sober of established facts.

To the above may be added a further, still wilder, speculation: that, if Freud's theories could have been known to Dostoyevsky, *The Brothers Karamazov* might never have been written at all. If, then, Freud is to be condemned, let it not be for making silly remarks about Dostoyevsky but for helping to kill off the novel as an art form.

Fifth and last in the quintet of Dostoyevsky's mature novels, *The Brothers Karamazov* is, like all its predecessors, an arena on which evil (intellectualism) clashes with good (instinctualism). The conflict deviates from preceding patterns in that the balance between the two forces is more evenly upheld. Here evil, hitherto always dominant and usually triumphant, is more effectively countered than elsewhere. Whether good or evil ultimately proves victorious in *The Brothers Karamazov* is however, as in the other novels, for individual readers to decide: it is a measure of the skill with which Dostoyevsky distributes his tensions that contradictory verdicts are possible. What will surely be admitted by most judges is that his last novel represents his most successful, or least unsuccessful, attempt to make fiction the vehicle for an affirmative confession of faith. The powerful *Devils*, by contrast, makes an impact almost exclusively negative; it annihilates the author's enemies, but offers little comfort to his friends.

During the six years (1873–8) separating the relatively negative *Devils* from the relatively positive *Brothers Karamazov* Dostoyevsky had remained prolific, as we have seen, yet had written nothing of comparable importance. The reason was, perhaps, that his impetuous temperament fitted him for denunciation, and that more constructive statements, as attempted in the conciliatory *Raw Youth*, went against the grain. With *The Brothers Karamazov* he has at last forced himself to write against the grain, at least to the extent of making a positive affirmation more impressive than any previously attempted.

The novel's chief representative of ideologically condemned intellectualism is the second Karamazov son, Ivan. He represents a break with tradition, since he lacks the 'superman' or 'bogyman' characteristics of those earlier incarnations of evil Svidrigaylov, Stavrogin and Versilov. The academically inclined Ivan has ravished no infant girls, but has done something far worse: published a rational 'defence' of the Orthodox Church so ingeniously written that it is accepted by many believers as a fervent confession of faith, though in fact a satirical burlesque. Culpable as the author of this article, Ivan nevertheless reflects his creator's philosophy by proclaiming faith in God and immortality as the only sanction that can restrain human wickedness. Take away these beliefs and 'everything is permitted'—everything, including murder. But Ivan differs from Dostoyevsky, or at least from the surface Dostoyevsky, because *he* happens to reject both God and immortality. The result is that he is driven, by his own inexorable logic, to become his father's murderer, albeit by proxy. Otherwise by far the most virtuously behaved of all Dostoyevsky's great villains, Ivan in a sense becomes the most villainous of them all, since in him the supreme evil of intellectualism appears in its most undiluted form. Thus, once again, does Dostoyevsky drive home his basic thesis: bad thoughts are worse than bad deeds. That Ivan was conceived as a socialist, though he is not explicitly so described in the novel, as well as an atheist we could infer from our knowledge of Dostoyevsky's thought. And we can confirm it from his correspondence, where Ivan is expressly termed 'my socialist'.[10]

Only in *The Brothers Karamazov*, of all Dostoyevsky's novels, does evil become involved in an extended debate with good, the latter principle being personified by the youngest Karamazov son, Alyosha. Haranguing that saintly sibling in a tavern, Ivan harrows him with tales of atrocities committed against children. There is the little girl whose parents punished her by smearing her with her own excrement, and there is the general who set a pack of hounds on an eight-year-old boy in front of his mother. These and similar horrors reported by Ivan were, according to Dostoyevsky's own claim, made in his letters, fully authenticated episodes taken from life.[11] By forcing Alyosha to admit that the murderous, boy-hunting general deserved to be shot, Ivan claims to have won the argument. Not that he also claims to have disproved the existence of God, for that is a matter of indifference to him. What matters is that he has triumphantly proved to his own satisfaction the unacceptability of 'God's world'; which, it is implied,

191

as a good socialist Ivan would wish to reconstitute on logical principles.

So much, in brief, for the claims of evil. What of the counter-claims of good? The first and most impressive is, paradoxically, expressed by Ivan himself when he goes on to recite what he puts forward as a work of his own imagination, the 'Legend of the Grand Inquisitor'. In this chapter, the most celebrated in all Dostoyevsky's works, he describes the imagined miraculous reappearance of Jesus Christ in sixteenth-century Seville. After the newly re-resurrected Saviour has immediately been arrested as a heretic on the orders of a ninety-year-old Grand Inquisitor, the latter offers his captive a long, logical statement of the irrefutable reasons that will make it necessary to burn Him at the stake on the morrow. The main argument is that Christ has caused untold harm by offering man freedom, the most unbearable of all the burdens which can be placed upon human beings. These weak creatures crave, and are only fit for, the order and regimentation that the Catholic Church—but also, it is ingeniously implied, the future socialist movement—can supply. An ideally harmonious society (Dostoyevsky's hated paradise on earth once again) will come to be administered by a small cadre of supermen whom the moronic masses will blissfully obey, delighted to be relieved of freedom and its attendant responsibilities, and overjoyed to be so expertly and benevolently organized for their own good. But now, the Grand Inquisitor maintains, this happy consummation is menaced by the newly resurrected Saviour with his offer of freedom so inimical to men's true needs and desires. Christ must therefore perish at the hands of the Inquisition as soon as possible, and in humanity's own best interests.

To these intellectual arguments Christ supplies a devastating response, the only answer that faith can, ultimately, offer to reason. He remains silent, but kisses the Grand Inquisitor on the lips.

Put forward as what Ivan Karamazov considers an unanswerable refutation of Christ's teaching, the Legend is intended by Dostoyevsky to perform a diametrically opposite function in the minds of his readers. It is designed to refute Ivan out of his own mouth, together with his Grand Inquisitor, while vindicating Christ and uniting humanity in allegiance to the true, free religion of Russian Orthodoxy and in detestation of Catholic and socialist enslavement. Whether or not the Legend has wrought many such conversions, it remains the most important symbolic statement of Dostoyevsky's philosophy. It stands at the heart of his fiction and teaching, its hidden resonances being far more profound than any summary could convey. Here is an eloquent defence of humanity at large against those dull, self-admiring, uncreative, mischief-making, self-seeking philanthropists called politicians or statesmen, who so disastrously devote their lives to imposing on others what they know to be best for them—that host of inquisitors, petty rather than grand, who have so lamentably proliferated since Dostoyevsky's death in the government and administration of his own and other countries. Advancing this and other theses so profoundly yet so subtly, he has contributed one of the supreme achievements of the human spirit. Hence the enormous contrast between the Legend and the bulk of *The Diary of a Writer*, with its emphasis on rampant nationalism and religious fanaticism, together with a bias against human beings masquerading as love of man.

The Legend forms only part of Dostoyevsky's reply to Ivan's and the Grand Inquisitor's joint heresies. It is supplemented in the immediately succeeding section of the novel, 'The Russian Monk'. Here the saintly inmates of Skotoprigonyevsk's monastery, with Father Zosima at their head, are paraded as exemplars of human behaviour far removed from the world of intellectualizing and interfering Catholics, socialists, inquisitors and Ivan Karamazovs. Zosima acts as Dostoyevsky's chief mouthpiece in the novel, and was explicitly conceived as such. He preaches serenity and joy accompanied by the seemingly conflicting thesis that all men are guilty for all other men's misdeeds. He also attacks the theoretical position of Ivan and the Grand Inquisitor: that man 'can arrange his affairs justly by his mind alone, without Christ.' This heresy—the point is made again and again —leads logically to violence: to bloodshed and massacre on the political plane of the Grand Inquisitor; to individual murder on the personal plane of Ivan Karamazov.

While Zosima preaches and teaches at some length, Dostoyevsky's main representative of Good in the novel, Alyosha Karamazov, is free from such addictions. Trustful, cheerful, wholly unaffected by humiliation-craving, humiliation-imposing and other forms of status-obsession and assertiveness, this rosy-cheeked, handsome nineteen-year-old novice is Dostoyevsky's embodiment of love in action, and comes nearer than any of his other fictional characters to furnishing a model on which some readers might conceivably wish to base their own behaviour. But there is more to Alyosha than this. As Dostoyevsky must have realized, such a paragon could easily become irritating, and it is a relief to encounter Alyosha's occasional fallibility. He shows it in his selfish reaction to the novel's major *skandal*, the odour of corruption emanating from the saintly Zosima's corpse; for this is the shock to his emotions that prevents him (as noted above) from considering means of protecting his threatened father. We are also told that Alyosha is a true Karamazov in his lustfulness, which is so far merely latent. This and other sinful potentialities Dostoyevsky proposed to realize in a sequel, never to be written, in which Alyosha would have been the principal character. According to one of these schemes the young man was even to become involved in a crime rivalling in its heinousness the rape of infant girls, if not the writing of ingenious pamphlets ridiculing the Orthodox—a plot to assassinate the Tsar.[12]

If the novel as it stands has a principal hero, he is neither the evil Ivan nor the saintly Alyosha, but the intermediate Dmitry. Violent, impetuous, hot-blooded, warm-hearted, Dmitry corresponds closely to the ideal image in which many Russians like to see themselves. He quarrels bitterly with his father, a conflict in which the long-familiar themes of sexual and financial rivalry are intricately interwoven. Oscillating, like Raskolnikov before him, between the opposing ideological poles of self-assertion and self-abasement, Dmitry is finally vindicated by his acceptance of Dostoyevsky's ideals. His longing to undergo punishment and purification by suffering causes him to welcome the sentence of Siberian hard labour imposed on him for a crime he has not committed.

Fortunately for the demands of art, if not of morality, Dostoyevsky has left no unrelievedly edifying picture of his monastery, for that notionally ideal and harmonious community breeds numerous squabbles and absurdities. A memorable *skandal* occurs when the vigil over Father Zosima's prematurely malodorous corpse is disrupted by a fanatical rival, Father Ferapont, who denounces the dead Elder for not having kept the fasts, while asserting that devils have been breeding in his cell like spiders. Such episodes once again suggest that, in matters of faith, Dostoyevsky's mind was curiously split. He could not, perhaps, fervently believe without, in the recesses of his creative being, also mocking his belief. Was he not himself as much of an Ivan, a Smerdyakov and a Grand Inquisitor at heart as he was an Alyosha, a Zosima or a Russian Christ?

We must also stress that Dostoyevsky's strong moralizing drive repeatedly came into conflict with his creative instincts, and that a tension between these two elements contributes not a little to the success of all the great novels of his maturity. That he himself was, if only on one occasion, fully aware of this tension is shown by his letter of 24 August 1879 to Pobedonostsev. Here Dostoyevsky expresses the fear that his Father Zosima may prove either incomprehensible or an ineffective champion of his creator's philosophy. 'My task', he continues, 'has been to present a figure both modest and sublime. But life is such a ridiculous business—sublime only in its inner significance. And so I have been forced by artistic considerations to invoke its most trivial aspects, reluctantly and for the sake of artistic truth, in my sage's biography. Then again, some of his teachings are expressed with such

excess of vehemence that they will be scouted as downright preposterous. Preposterous they of course are, on a mundane level. But
on a different and deeper level they are, I think, valid.'[13]

How accurately Dostoyevsky happens to have defined, in these
comments on his Father Zosima, the task facing any serious biographer
of himself: that is, if 'scholarly' is substituted for 'artistic' in the above
quotation.

In *The Brothers Karamazov*, as in Dostoyevsky's earlier masterpiece,
the tension between artistry and didacticism, and also that between
belief and disbelief, combine to impart profundity to work which would
be magnificently imposing even without these special ingredients. The
strength of the plot, the masterly deployment of suspense, and above
all the richness of the characterization—of Fyodor Pavlovich Karamazov especially, of his four sons, of a dozen lesser figures—these are
among the features reinforcing whatever the last novel's message
may ultimately seem to be. It is not surprising that many readers place
The Brothers Karamazov above all Dostoyevsky's other works. That
they began to do so at the earliest possible moment is evident from the
ecstatic reactions provoked by the serialized novel from the appearance
of its first instalment onwards.

No other work by Dostoyevsky, not even *Crime and Punishment*, was
received with as much enthusiasm as *The Brothers Karamazov*. 'Never
have I enjoyed such success', wrote the delighted author in December
1879. Even before serialization had been completed, a year later, *The
Brothers Karamazov* had 'generated an enormous critical literature'
which included no less than thirty notices in the metropolitan press in
the year 1879 alone. By no means all were favourable, for the general
effect of so controversial a novel was to polarize readers and critics
along earlier (pre-*Raw-Youth*) lines. Admiring conservatives became
more admiring, hostile left-wingers became more hostile. Among the
less easily categorized admirers was, once again, Tolstoy. After at first
professing himself unable to finish *The Brothers Karamazov*, he later
came to prize it, and especially the figure of Father Zosima, in whom
he no doubt discerned a fellow-sage of comparable stature to the
author's and his own.[14]

As for the hostile camp, a particularly stimulating response came
from Mikhaylovsky: the general survey of Dostoyevsky's work contained in his article 'A Cruel Talent'. Quoted above in the discussion
of Dostoyevsky's first novel *Poor Folk*, this accuses the great novelist
of perversely tormenting his readers and his characters. 'A Cruel
Talent' appeared in 1882, the year following Dostoyevsky's death,
and provoked an approving reaction from Turgenev. Mikhaylovsky
had accurately identified an essential trait in Dostoyevsky, Turgenev

wrote. And Mikhaylovsky 'might have noted that French literature also contains a comparable manifestation—the notorious Marquis de Sade.' Thus, again in a letter to Saltykov-Shchedrin, was Turgenev to carry his feud with Dostoyevsky beyond the grave by endorsing the charge of literary sadism.[15] It is, however, pleasant to record that the two warring novelists did at least become briefly reconciled in the last year of Dostoyevsky's life, as will shortly be recounted.

From its first publication onwards *The Brothers Karamazov* has chiefly owed its vogue to its qualities as a novel, but the prominence of the religious issue also contributed no little to the particularly widespread interest which it immediately evoked in its country of origin. In Russia the nature and existence of God tended to be an especially lively concern—no less to the country's many unbelievers than to its many believers. Here was a people whose very atheist revolutionaries made a religion out of their revolutionary atheism. The Russian—one is tempted to suggest, greatly exaggerating—can accept any attitude (to religion or to anything else) other than indifference. Hence the special appeal, to Dostoyevsky's fellow-countrymen, of this novel by one who, far from coming to terms with his own religious strivings, struggled with them in public on the pages of his fiction, clothing them in images fascinating to the perfervidly sceptical no less than to the perfervidly devout. As for those dull spirits—and there were not a few, even in Russia—to whom the existence or non-existence of God was no matter of passionate concern, or not even a matter of concern at all, the force and creative vigour of *The Brothers Karamazov* was enough to galvanize even them into the willing if temporary suspension of apathy.

The most spectacular event of Dostoyevsky's last years was his oration delivered in Moscow on 8 June 1880 during celebrations attending the unveiling of a statue of Russia's national poet Aleksandr Pushkin, who had died in 1837.

Russians tend to make a great deal of their literary festivities—a tradition later to inspire the austere Chekhov's detestation of the frequent writers' 'jubilees', including his own, that he attended when he could not avoid them. As for the Pushkin celebrations of 1880, even the exuberant Dostoyevsky anticipated them with a sense of impending doom. Had he not already made a similar literary event the scene for the most powerful *skandal* in all his writings, the orgy of lectures and readings disrupted by his Nihilists in *Devils*?

That some similar fiasco threatened the Pushkin celebrations seemed evident from the frenzy of the preceding weeks and days. Preliminary chest-beatings and expressions of factional hostility seemed likely to develop into a pitched battle between the Europeanizing, Westernist clique led by Turgenev and the patriotic, Slavophile fancy of which Dostoyevsky, with some surprise, now found himself the head. Sensing the potentialities for drama, members of the public had paid up to fifty roubles apiece for the rental of windows overlooking the Strastnoy (now Pushkin) Square, where the draped statue stood. However, the unveiling ceremony passed without *skandal*, as did attendant religious services in the near-by Strastnoy Monastery, and even a session of literary readings at the University. This last occasion seemed to augur ill for the nationalist cause, since the Westernizing Turgenev received more applause than Dostoyevsky, who attributed this to the efforts of a claque of hired leftist students.[16]

All this was just a build-up to the final duel between the two prima donnas. The climax was to come when each delivered a lengthy solemn address at the Club of the Noblesse (later House of Unions) in Central Moscow, the same premises that were later to become the scene for proceedings infinitely more macabre, if only slightly more farcical— Stalin's great political show trials of the 1930s. There was, we conclude, something inimical to sobriety in the atmosphere of this historic building with its Hall of Columns.

On 7 June Turgenev's speech went off without incident, except that arch-patriots, Dostoyevsky included, felt that the Westernizing novelist, whom they considered anti-Russian, had displayed inadequate enthusiasm for his country's national poet: the level of gush had been considerable, yet seemed nowhere near adequate to so very special an occasion. Dostoyevsky was to speak on the following day, and spent the night in an agony of suspense. All that he had fought for, his Idea (the system of concepts promulgated in *The Diary of a Writer*), seemed to hang in the balance. He had nightmares in which Anna was unfaithful to him, and he feared disgracing both himself and his Idea by having an epileptic fit.[17] All seemed set, if not for a fiasco like that in *Devils*, at least for another Chinese vase incident—and with Dostoyevsky himself in the role of his Idiot.

In fact the occasion turned out triumphant beyond his rosiest expectations. To Anna, who remained at home at Staraya Russa with the two children during his three-week stay in Moscow, he described the scene as follows.

'The hall was packed. ... When I appeared thunderous clapping burst out, and for a long, long time they would not let me speak. I kept bowing and making signs ... but it was no use. There was ecstasy and enthusiasm, all due to the Karamazovs. ... I spoke loudly and fervently. (What a colossal triumph of our ideas over a quarter of

197

a century of errors!) But when at the end I held forth about the *world-wide unity* of people, the hall seemed to be having hysterics. When I'd finished—I can't convey to you the howl, the shriek of ecstasy. Strangers among the audience were crying, sobbing, embracing *and swearing to be better men, not to hate each other in future, but to love.* The meeting broke up and everyone rushed towards me on the platform.'[18]

Among those milling on the platform were ladies who held a large bouquet enhaloing Dostoyevsky's head, while tears, kisses, embraces and handkerchief-waving had broken out everywhere. There were shouts of 'Prophet' directed at the man who had now stolen the show from Turgenev, not to mention the long-eclipsed Pushkin. The old quarrel between Turgenev and Dostoyevsky was swept aside after Dostoyevsky had made a complimentary reference to his new friend's novel *A Nest of Gentlefolk* in his oration, whereupon Turgenev—supremely Karmazinov-like—had blown him a kiss across the hall. Now the two bearded sages were exchanging a tearful embrace. 'You are a genius, you are more than a genius': thus was Dostoyevsky hailed on all sides, and by former enemies, in an atmosphere suggesting that a new era of human brotherhood had dawned.

It had not. When journalists and critics of the left had time to collect their wits, they saw little to praise in Dostoyevsky's 'Pushkin Speech'. So thoroughly was he abused in the press that he felt as if he had committed forgery or swindled a bank.[19]

As for the contents of the speech, one might as well subject the Book of Revelation to logical analysis. Here is prophecy indeed, the most forceful statement of the Idea embodied in *The Diary of a Writer*. Pushkin is represented as the supreme embodiment of the Russian national genius. Two of his characters (Aleko in *The Gypsies* and Eugene, hero of *Eugene Onegin*) are ingeniously invoked as the type of the Russian 'Wanderer': embryonic socialists, who however errant, have a latent potentiality for wandering back to the truth. And Pushkin is praised as the prime incarnation of 'omnihumanity', the quality distinguishing the Russian *narod* and fitting it to preside over a new epoch of human brotherhood as the moral superior and teacher of Europe. These contentions, and much else in the speech, would surely have astonished the poet. Indeed, before Pushkin could have reconciled Dostoyevsky's words with his own character and achievements, he would have needed to mobilize more than a little of the special Russian skill now attributed to him in the speech: that of flexibly adapting himself to alien modes of thought. But surprised as Pushkin himself might have been, readers of *The Diary of a Writer*—and even of the 1861 *Series of Essays on Literature*—must have been less so. Dostoyevsky had said most of this many times before, but never with such verve.

The unveiling of the Pushkin monument
in Moscow, June 1880

Opposite Dostoyevsky in 1880
Below The study in Dostoyevsky's last
flat in St Petersburg, with the desk at
which he wrote *The Brothers Karamazov*
Bottom Dostoyevsky's coffin is borne to
the Aleksandr Nevsky Monastery, 31
January 1881

The Emperor Alexander II was
assassinated in St Petersburg on 1 March
1881

Rarely, perhaps, has a national inferiority complex been clothed in rhetoric so splendid as in the 'Pushkin Speech', a compelling yet deplorable document. It is a magnificent example of the orator's art, yet it degrades a great poet by harnessing him to rabid tribal sentiment such as Pushkin himself was admittedly known to express, but only exceptionally. The speech is, for good or ill, a key document in the great corpus of Russian Pushkinolatry: one of the country's most unfortunate cultural traditions, whereby foreigners are 'tactfully' informed that, not being Russian, they are by definition precluded from comprehending the Poet of Poets. The promoters of this view are, however, not generally to be found among the many Russians who know Pushkin's work well, as Dostoyevsky himself most certainly did. Still less are they usually to be found among those who have read Homer, Virgil, Dante and Shakespeare (to mention but a few relevant names) in their original tongues. That same humble skill lay outside Dostoyevsky's own range, though he could read French and German, and was well versed in other aspects of world literature. But how can anyone, towering genius or not, be taken seriously when assessing the significance of an individual major poet if so much of the world's major poetry is, to him, no more than a whole library of literally closed books?

These are mere rational considerations, however, and it must not be forgotten that we are dealing with a militant and aware anti-rationalist, a purveyor of revealed truth. Despite later hostile reactions from the left, many members of Dostoyevsky's audience remained under the spell of his inspired rhetoric. Soon afterwards readers rushed to buy a special edition of *The Diary of a Writer*, brought out to include the 'Pushkin Speech' and further thoughts by Dostoyevsky on the same subject. It was quickly sold out and went into a second edition.

He had become the man of the hour.

Exhausted by *The Brothers Karamazov*, Dostoyevsky planned to continue periodical publication of *The Diary of a Writer* from January 1881, as a preparation for the further long novels that he hoped to compose in due course. His epilepsy was now less troublesome and his affliction of the lungs, emphysema, seemed to have stabilized itself. To yet another aggravation, family squabbles, he was still vulnerable; as was shown on 26 January 1881, when his sister Vera Ivanova arrived to dispute the disposition of the long deceased Aunt Kumanina's estate. On the same day Dostoyevsky defied his doctor's advice by moving a heavy bookcase.

Suffering a series of severe lung haemorrhages, perhaps provoked by these irritations, he sensed that his end was near and asked for the ministrations of a priest. Meanwhile he, whose life and works had so thrived on the *skandal*, was not spared impropriety even as he lay dying. The ludicrous Pasha arrived on the scene, presumably hoping to derive some tangible benefit from his stepfather's imminent decease, and was arguing that a notary should be summoned to record the dying man's last wishes—a proposal which the attendant doctor opposed.

Anna Grigoryevna comforted her husband during his last hours, when he told her that he loved her and had never been unfaithful to her even in thought. He also sought consolation from the Gospel presented to him by the Decembrist ladies in 1850 on his arrival in Tobolsk as a chained convict.[20]

Fyodor Mikhaylovich died shortly before nine o'clock on the evening of 28 January 1881.

The next day saw the publication, by force of inertia, of the last issue of *The Diary of a Writer*. Meanwhile, as undertakers were touting for the widow's custom on the stairs, a high official of the Ministry of Internal Affairs arrived with an offer to pay the funeral expenses on behalf of the state. But the independent-minded Anna refused, even though she had little prospect of financial security in the future; all her husband had left her was five thousand roubles owed by *Russky vestnik* for *The Brothers Karamazov*. On 30 January, however, she agreed to accept a pension of two thousand roubles a year granted by the Emperor, a sum adequate to ensure her own and her two children's future. Still unaccustomed to her sudden bereavement, she pathetically ran into the room where poor Fedya's body lay to give him the good news, for she had temporarily forgotten that he had been mercifully released, at long last, from the tormenting world of roubles and copecks.

The funeral was celebrated on 31 January in a manner reflecting the rise in Dostoyevsky's popularity in his last years. Some thirty thousand souls turned out to see the coffin borne from his home to the Aleksandr Nevsky Monastery. There he lay in state, in the Chapel of the Holy Ghost, watched over by admirers who read the Psalter over him through the night. Arriving for the service on the following morning, Anna had difficulty in entering the building, so dense was the throng. The body was then conveyed to the Tikhvinsky Cemetery for burial after speeches had been made at the graveside by Vladimir Solovyov, Apollon Maykov and others.

Exactly a month later the Emperor Alexander II, whom Dostoyevsky had so revered, was done to death in the same city by a squad of bomb-throwing revolutionary assassins, and the event seemed to confirm the forebodings of the recently deceased Prophet who had comprehended both universal doom and universal brotherhood in his utterances.

Dostoyevsky had never enjoyed greater vogue within his own country than at the time of his death, a vogue that grew ever greater in the succeeding decades. Within forty years his novels had conquered the world. Both within and far beyond the enormous bounds of the Russian Empire they have been recognized as furnishing new insights into the human psyche and as revealing unsuspected depths of the human heart. Not least among the great novelist's admirers are those very 'Europeans' whom he had so loved, hated, despised and admired; those whom he had believed incapable of understanding Russia or her literature; peoples so alien to him, and yet so much his kin.

References

In order to avoid disfiguring the body of the text with an excess of figures it has often been necessary to consolidate them in groups at or near the end of the paragraph to which they apply. References are by authors' or editors' names, or by abbreviations, as listed in alphabetical order in the Index of Sources, pages 213–215.

1 *Boy and Youth* (pages 15–30)

1 Belchikov, 177–9.
2 Shchogolev, 97; *Works* (1926), 11 : 138.
3 Andrey Dostoyevsky, in Dvs, 1 : 57–8.
4 Carr, 11.
5 Miller, 6.
6 Andrey Dostoyevsky, in Dvs, 1 : 76–7.
7 Ibid., 82.
8 Ibid., 59.
9 Nechayeva (1939), 106–9.
10 Dostoyevsky, Andrey, 34.
11 *Works* (1926), 11 : 139; Dostoyevsky, Andrey, 94; L, 3 : 204.
12 L., 1 : 215, emphasis added.
13 L., 2 : 346, emphasis added.
14 L., 1 : 52.
15 L., 4 : 196.
16 Grossman (1965), 21.
17 Andrey Dostoyevsky, in Dvs, 1 : 68ff.
18 *Works* (1926), 11 : 189–91; Nechayeva (1939), 67.
19 Andrey Dostoyevsky, in Dvs, 1 : 84–5.
20 L., 2 : 178.
21 *Works* (1926), 11 : 169; Grossman (1965), 28.

2 *Cadet and Officer* (pages 31–46)

1 K. Trutovsky, in Dvs, 1 : 106.
2 A. Savelyev, ibid., 1 : 104; ibid., 1 : 405–6.
3 L., 1 : 49; 4 : 446.
4 D. Grigorovich, in Dvs, 1 : 123.
5 A. Savelyev, ibid., 1 : 99.

6 P. Semyonov-Tyan-Shansky, ibid., 1 : 210.
7 A. Savelyev, cited in Chulkov, 16.
8 L., 1 : 47, 59.
9 L., 1 : 57, 471.
10 *Works* (1926), 13 : 157.
11 Andrey Dostoyevsky, in Dvs, 1 : 88; Nechayeva (1939), 58.
12 Dostoyevsky, Aimée, 33.
13 Dostoyevsky, Andrey, 109–10.
14 Nechayeva (1939), 51, 56–9; Grossman (1965), 39–40; Arban, 164–5.
15 Fyodorov, passim.
16 Grossman (1935), 33.
17 L., 2 : 549, 551–2; S. Yanovsky, in Dvs, 1 : 157.
18 S. Freud, in Komarowitsch, xiii–xxxvi; and 'Freud', as indexed in Carr, and in Frank.
19 Frank, 87.
20 Arban, 228ff.
21 A. Riesenkampf, in Ln, 330.
22 Idem, in Dvs, 1 : 116–17.
23 L., 4 : 448–50.
24 L., 1 : 73.
25 Grossman (1935), 40.
26 Ibid., 38.
27 Belchikov, 60.
28 L., 1 : 71.

3 *Apprentice Author* (pages 47–59)

1 D. Grigorovich, in Dvs, 1 : 132–3.
2 *Works* (1926), 12 : 30–1.
3 Ibid., 29–32.
4 Ibid., 32.
5 V. Belinsky, in Belkin, 16.
6 N. Mikhaylovsky, ibid., 310, 332.
7 *Works* (1972), 1 : 467.
8 L., 1 : 80.
9 *Works* (1972), 1 : 471–2, 490; Ln, 1 : 87–8; V. Belinsky, in Belkin, 27, 32.
10 L., 1 : 84.
11 D. Grigorovich, in Dvs, 1 : 133; ibid., 1 : 399–400.
12 L., 1 : 103; D. Grigorovich, in Dvs, 1 : 134–5; A. Panayeva, ibid., 1 : 142–3.
13 S. Yanovsky, in Dvs, 1 : 155, 163.
14 Carr, 37–8; Frank, 390–1; L., 4 : 30; *Works* (1956), 10 : 565.
15 Grossman (1935), 48; Arban, 31; D. Grigorovich, in Dvs, 1 : 131–2.
16 L., 3 : 23.
17 Andrey Dostoyevsky, cited in Ln, 550; S. Freud, in Komarowitsch, xvi, xxi, xxv; Frank, 382ff.
18 L., 1 : 107, 113.

19 S. Yanovsky, in Dvs, 1 : 155, 166; A. Riesenkampf, in Ln, 325.
20 S. Freud, in Komarowitsch, xxiii; S. Yanovsky, in Dvs, 1 : 171; A. Riesenkampf, in Ln, 329.
21 L., 1 : 85, 131; Frank, 165.
22 L., 1 : 85; A. Panayeva, in Dvs, 1 : 140.
23 Mochulsky (1947), 83.
24 V. Belinsky, cited in Nechayeva (1972), 108–9.

4 *Political Criminal* (pages 60–70)

1 Frank, 220 ff.
2 Pipes, 293–4.
3 Belchikov, 177–9.
4 A. Palm, cited in Mochulsky (1947), 105; P. Semyonov-Tyan-Shansky, in Dvs, 1 : 211.
5 Grossman (1965), 103; Dvs, 1 : 410.
6 *Works* (1926), 11 : 8, 10, 134.
7 A. Milyukov, in Dvs, 1 : 186.
8 I. Debu, in Miller, 90–1.
9 Frank, 257.
10 S. Yanovsky, in Dvs, 1 : 172.
11 L., 1 : 165; Nechayeva (1972), 136.
12 L., 1 : 124–9.
13 L., 1 : 129–30.
14 A. Milyukov, in Dvs, 1 : 191.

5 *Convict and Exile* (pages 71–88)

1 L., 1 : 133.
2 L., 1 : 134.
3 Ibid.
4 I. Yastrzhembsky, cited in Nechayeva (1972), 148.
5 L., 1 : 135.
6 L., 1 : 136.
7 Ibid.
8 P. Martyanov, in Dvs, 1 : 240; *Works* (1972), 4 : 275.
9 L., 1 : 143.
10 *Works* (1972), 4 : 98.
11 A. Riesenkampf, cited in Dvs, 1 : 406.
12 *Works* (1956), 10 : 565.
13 L., 1 : 139.
14 L., 1 : 135–9; *Works* (1972), 4 : 280–1.
15 P. Martyanov, in Dvs, 1 : 237–40; Grossman (1935), 67.
16 L., 1 : 148.
17 L., 1 : 143.
18 A. Vrangel, in Dvs, 1 : 246–9.
19 Ibid.
20 *Works* (1972), 2 : 520ff.
21 A. Vrangel, in Dvs, 1 : 251.

22 Ibid., 1 : 251–4; L., 1 : 152.
23 L., 1 : 215, 537; 2 : 579.
24 L., 1 : 213.
25 L., 1 : 139, 145.
26 L., 3 : 85.
27 L., 1 : 246.
28 L., 1 : 165.
29 L., 2 : 291.
30 L., 1 : 142.

6   *Memoirist and Journalist* (pages 89–105)
1 L., 1 : 254.
2 L., 2 : 586.
3 *Works* (1956), 3 : 707.
4 L., 1 : 293.
5 L., 2 : 605.
6 N. Strakhov, in Dvs, 1 : 285–6.
7 Ibid., 1 : 270, 292.
8 *Works* (1926), 13 : 61.
9 N. Chernyshevsky, in Dvs, 1 : 319–20.
10 *Works* (1926), 11 : 24–5.
11 A. Herzen, cited in Nechayeva (1972), 213.
12 L., 1 : 310.
13 *Works* (1972), 5 : 51.
14 Suslova, 59.
15 N. Suslova, cited in Carr, 110; L., 1 : 403.
16 L., 1 : 326–31; Grossman (1935), 128.
17 *Works* (1972), 5 : 110, 113.
18 L., 1 : 398.
19 L., 1 : 400.
20 *Works* (1926), 11 : 22–30.
21 M. Brown, cited in Grossman (1935), 144.
22 See Dvs, 1 : 338.
23 S. Kovalevskaya, in Dvs, 1 : 348.

7   *Emerging Genius* (pages 106–126)
1 L., 2 : 225–6.
2 L., 1 : 411.
3 L., 1 : 418.
4 Suslova, 129.
5 P. Veynberg, cited in Grossman (1935), 158; *Works* (1972), 7 : 323.
6 Ibid., 7 : 332–4.
7 L., 1 : 353.
8 L., 1 : 430–1; *Works* (1972), 7 : 319, 326.
9 L., 1 : 437–8.
10 A. Dostoyevskaya, in Ln, 221–2.
11 Ibid., 222–5.

12 Ibid., 232–5.
13 Ibid., 234, 258; AGD (r), 32.
14 Cited in Hingley (1962), 84.
15 A. Dostoyevskaya, in Ln, 243; AGD (r), 27.
16 A. Dostoyevskaya, in Ln, 262.
17 AGD (r), 59, 66.
18 Ibid., 63.
19 *Works* (1972), 7 : 345–53.
20 D. Mackenzie Wallace, A. Nikitenko, cited in Hingley (1977), 241.
21 AGD (v), 122.
22 AGD (r), 79–81.
23 L., 2 : 262.
24 AGD (r), 109–14.

8   *Reluctant European* (pages 127–144)

1 L., 2 : 26.
2 L., 2 : 18–19.
3 AGD (d), 260.
4 L., 2 : 9, 29.
5 AGD (r), 132.
6 AGD (d), 223.
7 L., 2 : 30, emphasis added.
8 L., 2 : 32, emphasis added.
9 L., 2 : 30–2; AGD (d), 237–9.
10 I. Turgenev, cited in Zilbershteyn, 177–8.
11 L., 2 : 100–1; AGD (r), 126.
12 L., 2 : 130, 425.
13 L., 2 : 101.
14 AGD (d), 258, 354.
15 L., 2 : 44–5.
16 AGD (r), 143–4, 147–8; L., 2 : 117.
17 L., 2 : 128.
18 L., 2 : 71.
19 *Works* (1972), 9 : 390.
20 *Works* (1926), 13 : 44.
21 *Works* (1956), 6 : 714–18; *Works* (1972), 9 : 410–20.
22 L., 3 : 256.

9   *Scourge of Socialism* (pages 145–159)

1 L., 2 : 284.
2 L., 2 : 346–9.
3 L., 2 : 13, 256.
4 L., 2 : 255–6.
5 L., 2 : 283.
6 L., 2 : 294, 314.
7 L., 2 : 259, 262, 301.
8 L., 2 : 291.

9 I. Turgenev, cited in Magarshack, 250–1.
10 L., 2 : 291, 363–4.
11 E.g. Carr, 218.
12 L., 2 : 175, 244, 263–4, 474.
13 Wasiolek (1968), 16, emphasis added.
14 L., 3 : 21.
15 Mochulsky (1947), 376; Jones, 129.
16 *Works* (1956), 7 : 730ff.
17 AGD (v), 396; N. Strakhov, cited in Yarmolinsky, 299–300.

10   *Uneasy Compromiser* (pages 160–170)
1 AGD (r), 169–70.
2 Ibid., 170.
3 L., 3 : 67.
4 AGD (r), 214–20.
5 L., 3 : 88, 316–17.
6 L., 3 : 240.
7 L., 3 : 109, 124, 128.
8 Dostoyevsky, Aimée, 175–6.
9 AGD (r), 241–3.
10 L., 3 : 131, 143.
11 *Works* (1972), 17 : 345ff.; *Works* (1956), 8 : 642ff.

11   *Arbiter of Destiny* (pages 171–182)
1 AGD (r), 261–4.
2 See L., 2 : 231.
3 AGD (r), 266–7.
4 *Works* (1926), 12 : 460.
5 L., 3 : 206.
6 *Works* (1926) 11 : 508.
7 AGD (r), 282.
8 L., 2 : 284; *Works* (1926), 12 : 10.

12   *Man of the Hour* (pages 183–205)
1 *Works* (1972), 15 : 456; AGD (r), 291–4.
2 L., 4 : 6.
3 AGD (r), 311–13; S. Pavlova, cited ibid., 404.
4 L., 4 : 90; AGD (r), 317–20.
5 A. Suvorin, in Dvs, 2 : 328–9.
6 Grossman (1935), 278–9, 293.
7 L., 4 : 79.
8 *Works* (1972), 15 : 452–6.
9 L., 4 : 7.
10 L., 4 : 58.
11 L., 4 : 53–4.
12 *Works* (1972), 15 : 486.
13 L., 4 : 109–10.

14 *Works* (1972), 15 : 487ff.
15 Ibid., 511.
16 L., 4 : 169.
17 L., 4 : 167, 170.
18 L., 4 : 171.
19 L., 4 : 197.
20 AGD (r), 342–7.

Index of Sources

The following list of titles consists exclusively of works invoked in the References because they are cited in the text or otherwise used in evidence.

AGD (d) = Fülöp-Miller, René, and Dr Fr Eckstein, ed., *The Diary of Dostoyevsky's Wife*, tr. from the German by Madge Pemberton (London, 1928)

AGD (r) = Dostoevsky, Anna, *Reminiscences*, tr. and ed. Beatrice Stillman, introduction by Helen Muchnic (London, 1975)

AGD (v) = Dostoyevskaya, A. G., *Vospominaniya*, ed. with an introduction by S. V. Belova and V. A. Tunimanova (Moscow, 1971)

Arban, Dominique, *Les Années d'apprentissage de Fiodor Dostoïevski* (Paris, 1968)

Belchikov, N. F., *Dostoyevsky v protsesse petrashevtsev* (Moscow, 1971)

Belkin, A. A., ed., *F. M. Dostoyevsky v russkoy kritike: sbornik statey* (Moscow, 1956)

Carr, Edward Hallett, *Dostoevsky, 1821–1881: a New Biography*, with a preface by D. S. Mirsky (London, 1931)

Chulkov, Georgy, *Kak rabotal Dostoyevsky* (Moscow, 1939)

Dostoyevsky, Aimée, *Fyodor Dostoyevsky: a Study* (London, 1921)

Dostoyevsky, Andrey, *Vospominaniya Andreya Mikhaylovicha Dostoyevskogo*, ed. with introduction by A. A. Dostoyevsky (Leningrad, 1930)

Dvs = *F. M. Dostoyevsky v vospominaniyakh sovremennikov*, ed. V. V. Grigorenko and others, 2 vols (Moscow, 1964)

Frank, Joseph, *Dostoevsky: the Seeds of Revolt, 1821–1849* (Princeton, 1976)

Fyodorov, G., 'K biografii F. M. Dostoyevskogo: domysly i logika faktov', *Literaturnaya gazeta* (Moscow), No. 25, 18 June 1975, p. 7

Grossman, Leonid, *Zhizn i trudy F. M. Dostoyevskogo: biografiya v datakh i dokumentakh* (Moscow-Leningrad, 1935)

——, *Dostoyevsky* [a biography] (Moscow, 1965); the same, translated into English by Mary Mackler, as *Dostoevsky: a Biography* (London, 1974)

Hingley, Ronald, *The Undiscovered Dostoyevsky* (London, 1962, reprinted 1975)

——, *The Russian Mind* (New York, 1977)

Jones, Malcolm V., *Dostoyevsky: the Novel of Discord* (London, 1976)

Komarowitsch, W., ed., *F. M. Dostojewski: die Urgestalt der Brüder Karamasoff: Dostojewskis Quellen, Entwürfe und Fragmente, mit einer einleitenden Studie von Professor Dr Sigm. Freud* (Munich, 1928)

L = Dostoyevsky's letters in Russian: *F. M. Dostoyevsky: pisma*, ed., A. S. Dolinin, 4 vols (Moscow-Leningrad, 1928–59)

Ln = *Literaturnoye nasledstvo: F. M. Dostoyevsky, novyye materialy i issledovaniya*, ed. V. G. Bazanov and others (Moscow, 1973)

Magarshack, David, *Turgenev: a Life* (London, 1954)

Miller, Orest and Nikolay Strakhov, ed., *Biografiya, pisma i zametki iz zapisnoy knizhki s portretom F. M. Dostoyevskago i prilozheniyami* (St Petersburg, 1883)

Mochulsky, Konstantin, *Dostoyevsky: zhizn i tvorchestvo* (Paris, 1947); the same, translated into English with an introduction by Michael A. Minihan, as *Dostoyevsky: his Life and Work* (Princeton, 1967)

Nechayeva, V. S., *V semye i usadbe Dostoyevskikh (pisma M. A. i M. F. Dostoyevskikh)* (Moscow, 1939)

——, ed., *Fyodor Mikhaylovich Dostoyevsky v portretakh, illyustratsiyakh, dokumentakh* (Moscow, 1972)

Pipes, Richard, *Russia under the Old Regime* (London, 1974)

Shchogolev, P. Ye., ed., *Petrashevtsy v vospominaniyakh sovremennikov: sbornik materialov* (Moscow-Leningrad, 1926)

Suslova, A. P., *Gody blizosti s Dostoyevskim: dnevnik, povest, pisma*, ed., with an introduction by, A. S. Dolinin (Moscow, 1928)

Wasiolek, Edward, ed., with an introduction by, *The Notebooks for 'The Idiot': Fyodor Dostoevsky*, tr. by Katharine Strelsky (Chicago, 1967)

——, ed. with an introduction by, *The Notebooks for 'The Possessed': Fyodor Dostoevsky*, tr. by Victor Terras (Chicago, 1968)

Works (1926) = Dostoyevsky, F. M., *Polnoye sobraniye khudozhestvennykh proizvedeniy*, ed., B. Tomashevsky and K. Khalabayev, 13 vols (Moscow-Leningrad, 1926–30)

Works (1956) = Dostoyevsky, F. M., *Sobraniye sochineniy*, ed. L. P. Grossman and others, 10 vols (Moscow, 1956–8)

Works (1972) = Dostoyevsky, F. M., *Polnoye sobraniye sochineniy v tridsati tomakh*, 30 vols (Leningrad, from 1972; of this edition vols 1–17 have been published as the present book goes to press)

Yarmolinsky, Avrahm, *Dostoevsky: his Life and Art* (London, 1957)

Zilbershteyn, I. S., ed., *F. M. Dostoyevsky i I. S. Turgenev: perepiska*, with an introduction by N. F. Belchikov (Leningrad, 1928)

Index of Dostoyevsky's Works

Italicized page references indicate illustrations

General Index